The Holy Land in American Protestant Life 1800–1948

A Documentary History

Edited
with Commentary by

ROBERT T. HANDY

ARNO PRESS

A New York Times Company
New York, 1981

Ongoing research for the American-Holy Land
Project was made possible by a grant from
Harold and Elayne Bernstein and family.

Permission to use material from the *Bulletin* of American
Schools of Oriental Research 35 (1929), pages 18-21, was
granted by the American Schools of Oriental Research, Ann
Arbor, Michigan. (Document 5)

Permission to reprint pages 13-18 and 127-137 of William F.
Albright's *The Archaeology of Palestine and the Bible* was granted
by the *Bulletin* of American Schools of Oriental Research,
which itself reprinted the Albright material in 1974, based on
the original Fleming H. Revell Company publication, 1932.
(Document 6)

Permission to quote from *The Heart of the Levant*, pages 62-75,
by J. McKee Adams, was granted by the Foreign Mission Board
of the Southern Baptist Convention, Richmond, Virginia.
(Document 11)

Permission to use material from *Pastor Russell's Sermons: A
Choice Collection of His Most Important Discourses on All Phases of
Christian Doctrine and Practice* was granted by Watch Tower
Bible and Tract Society of Pennsylvania, Brooklyn, New York.
(Document 23)

Permission to reprint Henry A. Atkinson's " 'The Jewish
Problem' Is a Christian Problem," 3 (June 28, 1943), pages 3-4,
and Bayard Dodge's "Peace or War in Palestine," 8 (March 15,
1948), pages 27-30, was granted by *Christianity and Crisis*, New
York, New York. (Documents 27 and 28)

Library of Congress Cataloging in Publication Data
Main entry under title:
The Holy Land in American Protestant Life

Includes bibliographical references and index.
1. Protestants—United States-Attitudes—Addresses, essays, lectures. 2. Palestine—Addresses, essays, lectures. 3.
United States—Church history—19th century—Addresses,
essays, lectures. 4. United States—Church history—20th
century—Addresses, essays, lectures. I. Handy, Robert T.
BR525.H64   280'.4'0973   80-1052
ISBN 0-405-13466-5

Manufactured in the United States of America

To
ANITA M. and LOUIS J. PERLMAN
for their love of learning and
scholarship

Preface

It is often said that the Holy Land is, in varying ways, sacred to three faiths. As a church historian who has focused largely on North America, I early became intrigued by the way Protestant Christians in the United States have regarded the land of the Bible, the home of the central figure of their tradition. American Protestants have interpreted and used the imageries of Holy Land, Promised Land, and Zion in a variety of ways; many have journeyed to the Holy Land. Hence I welcomed the opportunity to work on an interfaith basis with scholars concerned with deepening our understanding of the complex relationships between America and the Holy Land. This volume of documents is one fruit of participation in the America-Holy Land Project.

A major concern of this documentary is to clarify the expressed attitudes of various types of American Protestants toward the Holy Land. Thus the contents emphasize published materials which had wide circulation and which helped to mold the opinions of major segments of the American public. I hope that this approach may encourage others to go further into important topics and areas that could be mentioned here only briefly.

Many persons—students, colleagues, editors, librarians, archivists, and scholars of various backgrounds and disciplines—have helped me in my efforts to interpret the importance of the Holy Land in American Protestant life, 1800-1948. I wish to extend special thanks to the project director, Dr. Moshe Davis, who over the years has given forceful leadership to the development of America-Holy Land studies, and who has helped to clarify the major categories of research: diplomatic policy, Christian devotion, Jewish attachment, and cultural aspects.[1] Though this volume centers in one of those categories, the material is not without significance for the others. I also thank those who have assisted me at various points in the research: Drs. W. Davidson Blanks, Robert H. Craig, the late Esther Feldblum, and Jonathan D. Sarna. I am grateful for the help of many others, too numerous to name, who have shared their knowledge and wisdom; sometimes a single brief conversation opened illuminating insights for which I will always be grateful.

Robert T. Handy

Union Theological Seminary, New York
April, 1981

---

[1]Moshe Davis, ed., *With Eyes Toward Zion: Scholars Colloquium on America-Holy Land Studies* (New York: Arno Press, 1977), esp. pp. xvii-xxii. See also the seventy-two-volume Arno Press collection, *America and the Holy Land*; a number of the passages selected for this volume can be found there. My studies were enriched by reading in early draft Vol. I of the America-Holy Land Studies, *Guide to America-Holy Land Studies: American Presence* (New York: Arno Press, 1980), ed. Nathan M. Kaganoff.

Contents

Preface   vii
Introduction   xi

I. THE BIBLE AND THE LAND

1. Edward Robinson: Explorer of the Land of the Bible   3
2. Robinson's Biblical Researches   25
3. The Land Illumines the Bible   37
4. A Minister on Pilgrimage Interprets the Bible   41
5. The American School of Oriental Research in Jerusalem   48
6. Albright and Palestinian Archaeology during the Mandate   52
7. Ancient Sodom in the Light of Modern Research   65

II. THE MISSIONARY VENTURE

8. American Protestant Missionary Pioneers in the Holy Land   75
9. An Indigenous Denomination's Mission to Jerusalem   83
10. A Cooperative Approach to Missionary Policy   90
11. An Evangelical Witness in the Heart of the Levant   98

III. PILGRIMS AND TRAVELERS

12. Tent Life in the Holy Land   107
13. A Church Historian's Travels in Bible Lands   112
14. A Preacher on Pilgrimage   122
15. Out-of-Doors in the Holy Land   131
16. Reflections of a Black Pastor   138

IV. AMERICAN PROTESTANT RESIDENTS IN THE HOLY LAND

17. Selah Merrill: Archaeologist and Consul   147
18. Edwin Wallace: Consul and Interpreter of the Holy City   154
19. The American Colony   164
20. "The Most Beautiful Y in the World"   173

V. RESTORATION: PRO AND CON

21. Prophetic Traditions   180
22. The Blackstone Memorial   194
23. Pastor Russell and Zionism   198
24. A Christian Assessment of Zionism, 1928   203
25. A Gentile's Survey of Zionism, 1929   213
26. A Pro-Arab View by a Biblical Scholar, 1938   220
27. A Christian Call to Open the Holy Land to Jewish Refugees   226
28. Prevailing Opinion in the Missionary Movement   230
29. The World Significance of a Jewish State   238
Epilog   245
Index   247

Introduction

Long before American Protestants in any significant numbers visited the Holy Land, it was familiar and fascinating to them because of their devotion to the Bible. Week after week the faithful heard sermons on biblical themes; many of these discourses went into detail on the history and geography of the Holy Land of ancient times. To be sure, the Protestantism of the colonial era was denominationally divided, and the diversity markedly increased during the period covered by this volume, 1800-1948. Yet there were certain unities in the midst of the plurality—unities which persisted largely because of the continuing dialogue with the Scriptures. Jerald C. Brauer once observed that two characteristics seem to mark American Protestantism: "One is a constant free experimentation and a search for a fuller manifestation of God's truth and will, and the other is a sustained effort to avoid going beyond the truth and light already known in the Bible and codified in certain basic beliefs and confessions."[1] The many diversities of Protestant life can be attributed largely to the free experimentation, while its coherences, which allow us to speak of Protestantism as an identifiable movement in religious history, have arisen largely out of its enduring biblicism. Its fascination with the Holy Land was continually revitalized by its devotion to the Bible.

In the colonial period of American life, biblical ways of thinking and speaking were pervasive in the culture. Carlos Baker has spoken of "the great synoptic metaphor which so stimulated the imaginations of the American colonists in the seventeenth and eighteenth centuries that they thought and spoke of themselves under the image of the Chosen People, undertaking a task of plantation as the crowning act of God's providential plan." Not only did they call America the Promised Land, but also, he adds, quoting Perry Miller, that "they grew to regard themselves as so like the Jews that every anecdote of tribal history seemed like a part of their own recollection."[2] The biblical images of Holy Land, Land of Promise, and Zion were not related primarily to the faraway land beside the Mediterranean to which travel was then rare indeed, but were generally transferred to their New World. The names of Zion and Jerusalem were often applied metaphorically to their new land and its churches. So the author of the first published history of Massachusetts, Edward Johnson, declared his high expectations for the new colony when he exclaimed, "this is the place where the Lord will create a new Heaven, and a new Earth in, new Churches, and a new Common-wealth together," adding that the faithful understood that they were called "to re-build the most glorious Edifice of Mount Sion in a Wildernesse."[3] The mood created by colonial leaders long persisted; centuries later an author could declare that "New England is also a holy land."[4] Meanwhile, others applied the name of Zion and of many other biblical places to their new villages and towns, thus transferring biblical terminology to their new land of promise.

As some of the early great expectations failed of fulfillment, however, Christian leaders tended to apply the imagery of Zion to their churches. So Jonathan Edwards, the leading theologian of colonial America, proclaimed in one of his sermons that "Zion, or the city of David of old, was a type of the church, and the church of God in the Scriptures is perhaps more frequently called by the name of Zion than by any other name."[5] This usage became common among Edwards's many followers and descendants; for example, Timothy Dwight, a grandson and an influential president of Yale as the eighteenth century closed and the nineteenth opened, explained that "under this name it is spoken of as *a Holy Hill*; as *loved by God*; as *the heritage of God*; as *the Zion of the Holy One of Israel*."[6] This transfer of Zion imagery to the church continued into the nineteenth and twentieth centuries in many quarters, despite the increasing knowledge of Palestine as reflected in this documentary. So the rigorous Presbyterian theologian Charles Hodge could write that "this usage is so pervading that the conviction produced by it on the minds of Christians is indelible. To them, Zion and Jerusalem are the Church and not the city made with hands."[7] Among Black people, the spirituals often made use of the imagery of the Promised Land. In his informative book, *The Gospel and the Land*, W. D. Davies has observed that:

> . . . in some Black spirituals—it is interesting to note—"the land," which Black Christians like other Christians had often treated as a symbol of the transcendental, was rehistoricized. "The land" was made to refer to Africa, Canada, and states north of the Mason-Dixon

line. Frederick Douglass wrote: "A keen observer might have detected in our repeated singing of

O Canaan, sweet Canaan,
I am bound for the land of Canaan,

something more than a hope of reaching heaven. We meant to reach the *North*, and the North was our Canaan."[8]

Such viewpoints as these could be extensively documented, but the focus of this book is on the Holy Land as it became known to Americans in the nineteenth and early twentieth centuries, though this background should not be forgotten.

In the nineteenth century it became increasingly possible for Americans to visit the lands of the Bible; as time went on the difficulties of travel slowly diminished. The primary motive for Protestant visitors to the Holy Land was to see the places where the events of the Bible took place; as one traveler put it, "a perfect knowledge of the Holy *Land* is needful to a perfect knowledge of the Holy *Scriptures*."[9] The centrality of the Bible continued to be heavily emphasized in nineteenth-century Protestantism; the rising popularlity of the Sunday school, whose classes were focused on the study of Scripture, was one guarantor of that. In many other ways the love of the Bible was inculcated—in revivals, conferences, conventions, and summer assemblies. The famous Chautauqua Assembly was once described as "no other than a gigantic Palestine class."[10] Hymns further riveted attention on the Bible and its setting; as late as 1950 Ralph McGill wrote, "I grew up knowing the old hymns in which Jordan's 'stormy banks,' Galilee, and 'Jerusalem the Golden' were sung mightily on the Sabbath and at Prayer meetings. As a boy I used to dream of some day seeing the golden domes of Jerusalem and the blue reaches of the Sea of Galilee."[11] Such dreams were more easily fulfilled in the twentieth century, but despite the difficulties, increasing numbers were drawn there throughout the nineteenth.

Those who did go often reported their findings in letters, speeches, articles, and books; some of the latter were widely read and went into many editions. There was a hunger to know more about the land of the Bible, the land where Jesus lived and the Church was founded. American Protestant attitudes toward the Holy Land in the nineteenth and twentieth centuries came into focus against the background of biblical knowledge as those who had been there described their experiences, feelings, and findings when their eyes fell on sacred sites and contemporary scenes—and as they interpreted what they saw. Selections from their influential writings, the primary content of this documentary, provide insights into the shaping of American Protestant views on the Holy Land that can be obtained in no other way. For the sake of convenience, those who went to the Holy Land for shorter or longer periods are treated in four parts of this book; admittedly there are some significant overlaps, for perhaps no classification scheme is fully adequate to human variety. A fifth part deals with the controversy over the restoration of Jews to the Holy Land, which cuts across the other categories.

In Part I, "The Bible and the Land," biblical scholars are the primary focus of attention. This disciplined and dedicated band has been highly influential in shaping Protestant attitudes toward the Holy Land of both past and present. From early Church times, Christians have desired to understand more fully both the Bible and the life and ministry of Jesus, and such understanding has implied the need to know more about the setting in which he did his work. As a contemporary biblical scholar has put it:

> The need to remember the Jesus of history entailed the need to remember the Jesus of a particular land. Jesus belonged not only to time, but to space; and the space and spaces which he occupied took on significance, so that the *realia* of Judaism continued as the *realia* in Christianity. History in the tradition demanded geography.[12]

The opportunity for sustained work in biblical geography and archaeology in the Holy Land did not materialize until the nineteenth century. Then one of the leading pioneers was an American, Edward Robinson, a minister and professor of biblical literature and the real founder of the scientific study of biblical geography. Raised in an atmosphere where the Bible was read regularly and devoutly, Robinson wrote, as he approached Jerusalem in 1838:

> From the earliest childhood I had read of and studied the localities of this sacred spot; now I beheld them with my own eyes; and they all seemed familiar to me, as if the realization of a former dream. I seemed to be again among cherished scenes of childhood, long unvisited, indeed, but distinctly recollected; and it was almost a painful interruption, when my companion (who had been here before) began to point out and name the various objects in view.[13]

Where Robinson led the way, others followed. In 1900 the American School of Oriental Research at Jerusalem was founded, and many biblical scholars took the opportunity to spend a semester or a year on a dig in the Holy Land. A forceful figure in the work of biblical archaeology was

William Foxwell Albright, a tireless worker and a prolific writer of articles and books describing what was being discovered. Convinced that such study made a contribution to intelligent piety, he wrote that "the uniqueness of the Bible, both as a masterpiece of literature and as a religious document, has not been lessened, and nothing tending to disturb the religious faith of Jew or Christian has been discovered."[14]

Not all those who wrote influential books on the Bible were biblical scholars in the strict sense, yet many were serious students of the Bible and helped to shape the attitudes of many American Protestants. Conspicuous among them was Harry Emerson Fosdick, the founding minister of New York's Riverside Church. Author of several important books on the Bible, he explained that "after years of studying the Bible I found the Book vivified and illumined by studying the country where it grew and where its major scenes were set."[15] For him and for many others, the Protestant interest in the Holy Land has its roots in the traditional centrality of the Bible in faith and worship, and the desire to know the book as fully as possible.

Part II, "The Missionary Venture," concerns another important group that influenced Protestant attitudes toward the Holy Land, the missionaries. A great enthusiasm for foreign missions swept over Christendom in the early nineteenth century; there was confident hope in many quarters that the world would be won to Christ. A series of missionary societies were founded, and their agents and representatives set to work in every region of the globe. Soon these Americans "were a primary force in helping Christianity become the first and only religion with a widely dispersed, intercontinental constituency."[16] The missionaries went out with a sense of the superiority of their faith and their Western civilization.

In many places they were considerably more successful than they were in the Holy Land. By 1818 the American Board of Commissioners for Foreign Missions launched a mission there, to help both in the reformation of the Oriental churches and in the conversion of Moslems. The missionaries encountered a troubled and resistant Palestine, however. Their work in Syria and Lebanon went better, so that in 1844 the Jerusalem station was closed. Missionaries from other denominations came to carry on the enterprise in the Holy City on a continuing basis; their work in education was especially appreciated by the natives, but no Christian group was conspicuously successful in gathering converts.

In helping to shape the American Protestant mind in its understanding of the Holy Land, however, the missionaries played a key role. In 1859, for example, William A. Thomson, who for a quarter-century served the American Board in Syria and Palestine, wrote a work entitled *The Land and the Book*, said to be "the most popular book ever written by an American missionary, and one of the best."[17] The two-volume study appeared in many editions and sold more than 200,000 copies, evidently more than any other American book of its kind except Harriet Beecher Stowe's *Uncle Tom's Cabin*. Thomson envisioned the Holy Land as:

> [O]ne vast tablet whereupon God's messages to men have been drawn, and graven deep in living characters by the Great Publisher of glad tidings, to be seen and read of all to the end of time. The Land and the Book—with reverence be it said—constitute the ENTIRE and ALL-PERFECT TEXT, and should be studied together.[18]

Writing of the nineteenth century, the "Great Century" of Christian missions, Kenneth Scott Latourette, author of a massive seven-volume work, *A History of the Expansion of Christianity*, explained that "the contacts of Americans with the Near East had been predominantly through Protestant Missions."[19] The view that many Protestants glimpsed of the Holy Land was often refracted through missionary eyes throughout most of the period discussed in this book.

Part III, "Pilgrims and Travelers," is by far the largest of the four categories in terms of the number of people considered. Multitudes of pilgrims of the three faiths have been journeying to the Holy Land for centuries. Among Christians, Protestants are less given to pilgrimage in any formal sense, but some who went did clearly think of themselves as pilgrims, renewing their piety in the land of the Bible and of their Savior. Examples are William C. Prime, a devout layman who journeyed there in the mid-nineteenth century and wrote *Tent Life in the Holy Land*, and T. De Witt Talmage, a prominent pastor of the latter part of the century who led a group of pilgrims there and then characteristically delivered a series of sermons, later published, on his experiences.

Others who went thought of themselves primarily as travelers and observers, but sometimes they did become pilgrims in a genuine sense while they were there. An illustration is Henry Van Dyke, a Presbyterian minister who long served as professor at Princeton University and was a prolific author. As a youth he dreamed of going to Palestine, but later on, he found himself hesitant to go, lest the journey prove disenchanting and his religious beliefs be rudely shaken; he lived in a time when historical and critical study of the Bible seemed to many to be a threat to piety. Then, after his faith had been strengthened during illness, a friend offered the trip in exchange for impressions of travel for a magazine. So he went as a writer, but there was a pilgrim lurking in him. He expressed a central theme in the Protestant pilgrimage motif—the desire to be in the land where Jesus lived, to walk in his footsteps, to see what he might have seen. The faith of Protestantism is both bibliocentric and Christocentric. In listing his reasons for going to the Holy Land, he reported that it was "most of all because I greatly desired to live for a little while in the country of Jesus, hoping to learn more of the meaning of His life in the land where it was spent, and lost, and forever saved."[20] So he became a pilgrim too, and reflected that stance in his book, *Out-of-Doors in the Holy Land*.

W. D. Davies has suggested the religious premises on which Christian pilgrimages are based in explaining that "the New Testament finds holy space wherever Christ is or has been: it personalizes 'holy space' in Christ, who, as a figure of History, is rooted in the land; he cleansed the Temple and died in Jerusalem, and lent his glory to these and to the places where he was, but, as Living Lord, he is also free to move wherever he wills."[21]

Many of those who went as pilgrims—or who went for other reasons but in some sense became pilgrims—were really seeking the Holy Land of the first century, and hence have not been particularly concerned with the land as it has become and often deplored modernization. A Methodist minister, Frank McCoy Field, writing at the very end of the period considered in this book, explained:

> We must take note of changes which have taken place since his [Christ's] day, but we can be thankful that, until about the time of the Second World War, Palestine has been a land of few changes. . . .
> But for the most part, as Van Dyke so aptly showed in *Out-of-Doors in the Holy Land*, it is the land itself and the outdoor features which have changed but little in nineteen hundred years that bring us our greatest satisfaction in inspiration and instruction. They represent the land which Jesus knew.[22]

The pilgrims characteristically sought the Holy Land of the past—of the Bible and their Lord.

Many others who came thought of themselves not as pilgrims, however, but as travelers, observers, or workers with particular projects or assignments to fulfil. This is not to say that they were devoid of religious feeling. Many of them wrote articles and books, which often enjoyed a wide circulation back home. Some of these travelers were on serious business, such as naval Lieutenant W. F. Lynch, who commanded the famous

expedition to explore the Jordan Valley and the Dead Sea in 1847–48. His
account of that historic trip is generally very descriptive and matter-of-
fact; only rarely does his personal piety peek through. Rare indeed are such
passages as this in his 500-page report:

> We were in a most dreary country; calcined hills and barren
> valleys, furrowed by torrent beds, all without a tree or shrub, or sign
> of vegetation. The stillness of death reigned on one side; the sea of
> death, calm and curtained in mist, lay upon the other; and yet this is
> the most interesting country in the world. This is the wilderness of
> Judea; near this, God conversed with Abraham; and here, came John
> the Baptist, preaching the glad tidings of salvation. These verdureless
> hills and arid valleys have echoed the words of the Great Precursor;
> and at the head of the next ravine lies Bethlehem, the birth-place of
> the meek Redeemer,—in full sight of the Holy City, the theatre of the
> most wondrous events recorded on the page of history,—where that
> self-sacrifice was offered, which became thenceforth the seal of a
> perpetual covenant between God and Man![23]

Another traveler to the Holy Land came for quite a different reason—
the church historian Philip Schaff, seeking health and solace after a
domestic crisis. His book, *Through Bible Lands*, is much like many other
travel accounts, except that he showed a much more sympathetic interest
toward the permanent residents of the Holy Land than did many others
who journeyed through, notebook in hand. In his observations in 1877,
Schaff noted how the Jews "look forward to the restoration of their race
and country. Their number in Jerusalem is growing rapidly and amount
fully to one third of the whole population." Aware of the philanthropies of
Baron Rothschild and Sir Moses Montefiore, Schaff thought that "they
ought to buy Palestine and administer it on principles of civil and religious
liberty." The distinguished scholar sympathetically observed the prayers at
the Western Wall of the Temple, interpreting the scene from his
Protestant perspective in saying, "The scene at the Wailing Place was to
me touching and pregnant with meaning. God has no doubt reserved this
remarkable people, which like the burning bush is never consumed, for
some great purpose before the final coming of our Lord."[24]

Many travelers to the Holy Land have been retired ministers for whom
grateful congregations have on occasion made such trips possible. When
the distinguished pastor emeritus of Harlem's Abyssinian Baptist Church,
Adam Clayton Powell, Sr., toured the land in the late 1930s he understood
his task, as he reported it in a series of sermons later published, to be that of
opposing the resurgent tide of anti-Semitism of his time.

Part IV, "American Protestant Residents in the Holy Land," includes the work of both diplomats and colonists. Americans sensitized to church-state tensions by twentieth-century debates may be surprised to find that a number of prominent American diplomatic officials in Palestine in the late nineteenth and early twentieth centuries were Protestant ministers or former ministers who made little effort to be religiously neutral. The Reverends Selah Merrill, Frank S. DeHass, and Edwin S. Wallace all served terms as consul in Jerusalem; all wrote at least one tome growing out of their years in the Holy Land. DeHass, for example, stated his reason for going with surprising frankness: "The author's object in accepting an appointment under the United States Government was not the honor or emoluments of office," he wrote, "but a desire to visit the lands of the Bible, that he might see for himself how far the manners, customs, and traditions of the people and topography of those countries agreed with the inspired word."[25] Selah Merrill had first come to the Holy Land as an archaeologist; he continued his investigations during his three terms as consul and produced several important volumes on his archaeological findings. Edwin Wallace, consul in Jerusalem from 1893 to 1898, produced an interpretive work on Jerusalem. Another Protestant minister, Otis A. Glazebrook, a friend of President Wilson, was consul at Jerusalem in 1914, at the beginning of World War I; he played a role in Palestinian affairs at a critical time in 1919. Such persons were in a position not only to influence the American public, but also to shape State Department views on the Middle East.

Another group of American Protestant residents in the Holy Land came to plant what they hoped would be permanent colonies, few of which measured up to the hopes of the founders. For example, the Mount Hope Colony was founded in Jaffa in 1853 by Clorinda Minor and a group of American Millerites who expected the imminent return of Christ. The colony did not long survive, for in 1866 at the same location a group of families primarily from Maine settled under the leadership of George Jones Adams, president of the Church of the Messiah Emigration Association.[26] The colony was soon much reduced in size, but a remnant survived into the period of World War I.

Much better known is the American Colony of Jerusalem, founded in 1881 by Horatio and Anna Spafford, who were seeking comfort in the Holy Land after the tragic loss of four daughters in an accident at sea. The colony grew to include about 150 residents, who engaged in ministries of welfare, teaching, and nursing. A sharp dispute arose between the colony and several of the American consuls; it was finally resolved by the intervention of an American journalist. During World War I the colony was providing meals for some 6,000 persons daily. In the 1920s Harry Emerson Fosdick served as president of a New York committee for the colony, and Lowell Thomas called attention to its work.

Another group of residents have been involved in business and philanthropic enterprises; conspicuous among the latter are those who were active in leading the Jerusalem YMCA. Organized originally under British auspices, the Y came under predominant American influence after World War I. An impressive new building, often called "the most beautiful Y in the world," was dedicated in 1933.

Part V, "Restoration: Pro and Con," deals with a tension that emerged sharply within Protestantism in the twentieth century, though its roots run deep into history. The first four parts consider various groups of Americans abroad who were influential in shaping attitudes toward the Holy Land across a century and a half of history. The deep and continuing interest that many Protestants have in the Holy Land was greatly stimulated by those who had been there. When differences of opinion arose within these groupings, they were reflected in the larger Protestant public. In seeking to understand the attitude of American Protestants toward the restoration of the Jews to Palestine and later toward the emergence of Israel as an independent state, it is important to see how varying attitudes toward the Bible shaped opinion. For some, restoration was a matter of biblical prophecy—an attitude was reflected in various writings throughout the period 1800-1948, particularly in the work of William E. Blackstone, author of the famous Blackstone Memorial of 1891. Some who adhered to conservative modes of interpreting the Bible were strongly pro-Zionist, such as Charles Taze Russell, founder of the movement that became known as Jehovah's Witnesses. A number of prominent fundamentalist leaders in the older denominations shared somewhat similar attitudes, however. For example, the pastor of the First Baptist Church in New York City, I. M. Haldeman, emphasized in 1914 the return of the Jews to the Holy Land, saying:

> The promises of this restoration form almost the staple of the prophetic utterances. The Word of God is crowded with them. In every form of statement, typical, figurative, poetic, symbolic, open and didactic, does the living God proclaim, by sworn oath, by solemn pledge, upon the stake of his own integrity, that his people shall yet dwell in the land of their inheritance.[27]

With many others who were committed to some version of

premillennialism—that Christ would soon appear to usher in the millennium—Haldeman believed that at the end the restored Jews would be converted to Christianity, but others, like Blackstone, who espoused the dispensationalist millenarian view, drew a distinction between Kingdom and Church. According to their teaching, as C. Norman Kraus has put it, "the millennial Kingdom is a fulfillment of Jewish aspirations to national political sovereignty under the re-established throne of David, and . . . it has no organic relation to the Church."[28] Such dispensationalists tended to be Christian Zionists and welcomed the independence of the State of Israel as partial fulfillment of prophecy.[29]

Those who had accepted historical and critical approaches to the Scriptures often interpreted the ancient prophecies in the context of the times in which they were written, not as oracles for later centuries. Though they were by no means of one mind on the issues of restorationism and Zionism, many of the biblical scholars who came to the Holy Land for archaeological study in the first half of the present century made their first contacts in Palestine under Arab guidance, and their perspectives were in part set by that fact. Many of them found the period of the League of Nations mandate to their liking. When G. Ernest Wright described some of the major achievements in biblical archaeology between the world wars, he noted that "it all took place at the best of all possible periods from the archaeologist's point of view—the time of mandates, when the countries in question welcomed western work and control was maintained by western directed departments of antiquities."[30] Hence some biblical scholars sharply opposed the advance of Zionism.

So did many missionaries, though they too were not all of one mind. The prevailing tendency was noted by Frank E. Manuel in these words:

> A group whose strength and subtlety have sometimes been ignored were the Protestant missionaries. They had built American universities and had become a dominant civilizing agent in the Near East. Apprehensive that the penetration of Palestine by a Jewish state would introduce into the Near East an element to compete with their own cultural concepts, they were vigorous antagonists to Zionism.[31]

There were, however, some influential missionary figures on the other side.[32]

Among some of the more liberally inclined Christians, sentiment for restoration and the emergence of a Jewish state was influenced by the struggle against anti-Semitism and by humanitarian considerations in the face of growing numbers of Jewish refugees, especially in the 1930s and

xxii   The Holy Land in American Protestant Life

1940s. After the Balfour Declaration of 1917, an expression of this position
was penned by Adolph A. Berle in his *The World Significance of a Jewish State*.
Other liberals tried to find a middle position in the face of rising tension;
Harry Emerson Fosdick, in his assessment of the situation in 1927, favored
the position of Zionist moderates; John Haynes Holmes was less qualified
in his advocacy of Zionism. The liberal element was strong in an agency
founded in 1942, the Christian Council on Palestine, although a few
conservative figures were also involved. The council was chaired by
Henry A. Atkinson, general secretary of the Church Peace Union, and had
the active support of a number of prominent Protestant leaders. This
council merged in 1946 with the more politically focused, lay person-
dominated American Palestine Committee, founded in 1941, to form the
American Christian Palestine Committee. In its publicity, the linkage of
opposition to anti-Semitism and concern with refugees with sympathy
toward the independence of Israel was evident; for example, "The tragic
history of the last few years should have gone far to demonstrate the
validity of the Zionist conviction that the most fundamental cure for anti-
Semitism is the normalization of the status of the Jews."[33] Such normalization, it was affirmed, could be best achieved by establishing a national
homeland for the Jews in the Holy Land.

Christians from widely divergent backgrounds thus participated in what
Samuel Halperin has described as a buildup of support for a Jewish
Palestine in the 1940s. He reported as the salient finding of his work, *The
Political World of American Zionism*, "the fact of widespread and influential
Christian support for the Zionist cause," and added as a supplementary
conclusion, "that expressions of Christian Zionist sentiment were both
genuine and indigenous to the American culture."[34] But many sharply
disagreed; after 1948 the tension was to increase further.[35]

American Protestant attitudes toward the Holy Land changed and
developed in many patterns from the colonial period to 1948, especially
through the influence of those who took the opportunity to travel there
and then reported what they found to their constituents back home. The
selections that follow, drawn from a wide range of materials, open
windows of insight on a place of great interest and attraction not only to
American Protestants, but to all who share an interest in the Holy Land.

Notes

1. Jerald C. Brauer, *Protestantism in America: A Narrative History* (Philadelphia: Westminster Press, 1953), p. 7.

2. Carlos Baker, "The Place of the Bible in American Fiction," in James Ward Smith & A. Leland Jamison, eds., *Religious Perspectives in American Culture* (Princeton: Princeton University Press, 1961), p. 245. The Miller quotation is from *American Heritage* 7 (December 1955): 60.

3. J. Franklin Jameson, ed., *Johnson's Wonder-Working Providence* (New York: Charles Scribner's Sons, 1872), pp. 25, 52.

4. Howard A. Bridgman, *New England in the Life of the World* (Boston: Pilgrim Press, 1920), pp. 4-5.

5. Jonathan Edwards, Sermon XXX, "The Fearfulness which will hereafter Surprise Sinners in Zion, Represented and Improved," in *The Works of President Edwards* (New York: Leavitt, Trow & Co., 1849), IV, 489.

6. Timothy Dwight, *Theology Explained and Defended, In a Series of Sermons*, IV (New York: Harper & Bros., 1851-52), p. 219.

7. Charles Hodge, *Systematic Theology*, III (New York: Scribner, Armstrong, & Co., 1874), p. 809.

8. W. D. Davies, *The Gospel and the Land* (Berkeley: University of California Press, 1974), p. 116, fn. 108.

9. Robert Morris, *Freemasonry in the Holy Land* (New York: Masonic Publishing Co., 1872; reprinted by Arno Press, 1977), p. 14.

10. Leon Vincent, *John Heyl Vincent: A Biographical Sketch* (New York: Macmillan Co., 1925), p. 91.

11. Ralph McGill, *Israel Revisited* (Atlanta: Tupper & Love, 1950), p. 2.

12. Davies, *The Gospel and the Land*, p. 366.

13. Edward Robinson, *Biblical Researches in Palestine . . .* , 3 vols. (Boston: Crocker & Brewster, 1841; reprinted by Arno Press, 1977), I: 326.

14. William Foxwell Albright, *The Archaeology of Palestine and the Bible* (New York: Fleming H. Revell Co., 1932), pp. 127-28.

15. Harry Emerson Fosdick, *A Pilgrimage to Palestine* (New York: Macmillan Co., 1927; reprinted by Arno Press, 1977), p. vii.

16. Joseph L. Grabill, *Protestant Diplomacy and the Near East: Missionary Influence on American Policy, 1810-1927* (Minneapolis: University of Minnesota Press, 1971), p. 6.

17. David H. Finnie, *Pioneers East: The Early American Experience in the Middle East* (Cambridge: Harvard University Press, 1967), p. 187.

18. William A. Thomson, *The Land and the Book: or, Biblical Illustrations*

Drawn from the Manners and Customs, the Scenes and Scenery of the Holy Land, 2 vols. (New York: Harper & Bros., 1859), II: xv.

19. Kenneth Scott Latourette, *Advance Through Storm . . .* , vol. 7 of *A History of the Expansion of Christianity* (New York: Harper & Bros., 1945), p. 262.

20. Henry Van Dyke, *Out-of-Doors in the Holy Land: Impressions of Travel in Body and Spirit* (New York: Charles Scribner's Sons, 1908; reprinted by Arno Press, 1977), p. x.

21. Davies, *The Gospel and the Land*, p. 367.

22. Frank McCoy Field, *Where Jesus Walked: Through the Holy Land with the Master* (New York: Exposition Press, 1951; reprinted by Arno Press, 1977), pp. 16, 21.

23. W. F. Lynch, *Narrative of the United States' Expendition to the River Jordan and the Dead Sea* (Philadelphia: Lea & Blanchard, 1849; reprinted by Arno Press, 1977), p. 383.

24. Phillip Schaff, *Through Bible Lands: Notes on Travel in Egypt, the Desert, and Palestine* (New York: American Tract Society, 1878; reprinted by Arno Press, 1977), pp. 249, 250, 252.

25. Frank S. DeHass, *Buried Cities Recovered* (Philadelphia: Bradley & Co., 1885; reprinted by Arno Press, 1977), p. 9.

26. Moshe Davis, ed., *Guide for America-Holy Land Studies* (Jerusalem: Institute of Contemporary Jewry, 1973), pp. 37, 45–46.

27. I. M. Haldeman, *The Signs of the Times*, 5th ed. (New York: Charles C. Cook, 1914), pp. 441–42.

28. C. Norman Kraus, *Dispensationalism in America: Its Rise and Development* (Richmond: John Knox Press, 1958), p. 24; see also pp. 53, 85, 105.

29. See Yona Malachy, *American Fundamentalism and Israel: The Relation of Fundamentalist Churches to Zionism and the State of Israel* (Jerusalem: Institute of Contemporary Jewry, 1978), esp. Part IV.

30. G. Ernest Wright, "The Phenomenon of American Archaeology in the Near East," in J. A. Sanders, ed., *Near Eastern Archaeology in the Twentieth Century: Essays in Honor of Nelson Glueck* (Garden City: Doubleday & Co., 1970), p. 18.

31. Frank E. Manuel, *The Realities of American-Palestine Relations* (Washington: Public Affairs Press, 1949), p. 3.

32. Carl Hermann Voss, *Answers on the Palestine Question* (New York: American Christian Palestine Committee, 1948), p. 37. See also his essay, "The American Christian Palestine Committee," in *Essays in American Zionism, 1917–1948* (The Herzl Year Book, vol. 8; New York, 1978), pp. 242–62.

33. Voss, *Answers on the Palestine Question*, p. 33.

34. Samuel Halperin, *The Political World of American Zionism* (Detroit: Wayne State University Press, 1961), p. 187.

35. See Hertzel Fishman, *American Protestantism and a Jewish State* (Detroit: Wayne State University Press, 1973).

The Holy Land
in American Protestant Life
1800-1948

I

The Bible and the Land

1. Edward Robinson: Explorer of the Land of the Bible

The centrality of the Bible among American Protestants has long been a key to their fascination with the Holy Land, seen as the stage on which the events described in the biblical books took place. Devotion to the Bible and an attraction to the land where it all happened were richly displayed in the career of Edward Robinson (1794-1863), an American professor of biblical literature. His researches and writings made an internationally recognized contribution to the study of biblical geography and archaeology.

When Frederick Jones Bliss (1859-1937) delivered the Ely Lectures for 1903 at Union Theological Seminary in New York on the theme of the development of exploration in Palestine, he devoted an entire lecture to Robinson, describing his career and contributions. An American born in Syria in a missionary family, Bliss graduated from Amherst College and Union Seminary and then devoted himself to archaeological work in Syria and Palestine.

Robinson was such a major figure in modern biblical scholarship and was so important in deepening American interest in the Holy Land that attention to him and his work comes fittingly early in this volume.

Source: Frederick Jones Bliss, *The Development of Palestine Exploration: Being the Ely Lectures for 1903* (New York: Charles Scribner's Sons, 1906; reprinted by Arno Press, 1977), pp. 184-206, 208-23. For more on Robinson, consult Henry B. Smith and Roswell D. Hitchcock, *The Life, Writings and Character of Edward Robinson* (New York: A. D. F. Randolph, 1863; reprinted by Arno Press, 1977).

In taking up the work of Robinson, it is important for us to realize what stage we have reached in the development of Palestine Exploration. He stands at the focal point where all the various lines converge. There is hardly a traveller or author considered in the previous lectures that he does not quote, there are few places mentioned—situated to the west of Jordan—that he does not visit, there is hardly a subject treated that he does not amplify or at least touch upon. Finding numberless threads twisted and knotted, he smooths them out, adds new strands of his own, and weaves all into a symmetrical pattern.

This is the place, then, swiftly to recapitulate the story which, with some detail, we have been considering. Like all histories of development, it shows periods of stagnation as well as of positive retrogression. In short, it mirrors in a series of images the Spirit of the Ages. We have seen that to the early Egyptians and Mesopotamians Syria and Palestine had little interest beyond the chance they gave for conquest or for trade. We have seen that in the day of Hebrew supremacy the Holy Land was of small account to contemporary Greeks, whose chief historian (Herodotus) refers to it only incidentally. We have traced the wider diffusion of correct knowledge following the Eastern campaigns of Alexander the Great. In the first century before and the two centuries after the birth of Christ we have found the geography of Syria and Palestine treated by Greeks and Romans with the best science of their day. Strabo, Pliny, and Claudius Ptolemy furnished broad outlines filled in with details of more or less accuracy. In the Onomasticon of Eusebius and Jerome, who were domesticated in the Holy Land and were the first to recognize a true Biblical geography, our subject reaches a lofty point not again attained for many centuries. For from the Bordeaux Pilgrim, early in the fourth century, to the Monk Bernard, late in the ninth, Western travellers to Palestine were impelled by no other motive than worship. The pre-Crusading pilgrims cared more for the marvels associated with a place than for the way leading to it, or for a strict proof of its authenticity. Purblind children of the Dark Ages, they knew how to pray fervently; see clearly they could not. Their spiritual descendants have never ceased from the Holy Land. Year by year from the steppes of Russia countless hordes of them flock thither.

Not much improvement is found during the century of Latin Kings. Fetellus, indeed, collects a large quantity of place-names, but his attempts to locate these are indefinite. Theoderich shows the dawning of a true sense of topography in his little picture of Judea and his brief description of the environs of Jerusalem. William of Tyre makes a creditable though somewhat jejune attempt to view the land as a whole, giving divisions and boundaries. But we applaud these efforts much as we would the superiority shown over their fellows by clever High-school boys. Carrying on the comparison to the thirteenth century, during which the Franks still had a foothold in the land, we note that Jacques de Vitry deserves honorable mention for his description of the various Christian sects; and Burchard for a more systematic arrangement of geographical facts, for his improvement upon Theoderich's Jerusalem topography, and for his tolerant spirit in dealing with Moslems and native Christians, better understood by him than by Jacques de Vitry. After the final expulsion of the Franks, we find, during the fourteenth and fifteenth centuries, on which was breaking the dawn of the Modern World, continued advance along the same lines. Marino Sanuto's vast work repeats indeed the false identifications of Burchard and his predecessors, but he exhibits research in other quarters. The alleged Mandeville shows a charity born of his world-wide travels. Ludolph von Suchem brightens his tale of the oft-trodden routes by picturesque anecdotes and a lively style. Bertrandon de la Brocquière anticipates a modern note in strongly accentuating his personal adventures. The high-school scholars of the mediaeval period are approaching their day of graduation.

In striking contrast to the Western visitors are the Moslem geographers from the middle of the ninth to the close of the fifteenth centuries. Mukaddasi (A.D. 985) is far in advance of Theoderich, who wrote about two centuries later, though each described the land as held by his own race. In comparison with Yakût's magnificent Geographical Dictionary, written in 1225, the History of his contemporary, Jacques de Vitry, is indeed paltry stuff. The justification for our having in a previous lecture passed over the Moslem authors so cursorily lies in our conception of Exploration which assumes that explorers are alien to the land that they describe. Such indeed were the Crusaders even after their firm establishment. Such were hardly even the Persian travellers, any more than is the American an alien who visits England.

It has been shown, I think, that Felix Fabri (1483) was the first typical modern explorer, as far, at least, as his manner of treating his material is concerned. After him we have traced a gradual widening of the area of Exploration; not geographically, but in the sense of its including more subjects. The hitherto almost neglected department of archaeology begins to attract Cotovicus at the end of the sixteenth century. Toward the close of the seventeeth century it comes fairly to the front in the works of De la Roque and Maundrell. By the time of Robinson it had become distinctly specialized in splendidly illustrated monographs on Petra and Baalbec. The natural history of the country is brought into prominence by Du Mans in the middle of the sixteenth century. He is closely followed by Rauwolf, the pioneer scientific botanist of the Holy Land. At the beginning of the eighteenth century Shaw gives an admirable and popular account of its various physical aspects. A few years later we find Hasselquist, the pupil of Linnaeus, making collections in Natural History. In Geology we have the judicious observations of Rüssegger, a contemporary of Robinson himself.

We have seen that in geography, and especially in the art of Scriptural Identification, the progress in Western Palestine was not commensurate with that along other lines. Notwithstanding Pococke's attempt to break with the false Crusading traditions, these continued, in most cases, to hold sway, even over subsequent travellers. In Eastern Palestine, too, exploration cannot properly be said to have progressed: before the researches of the indefatigable Seetzen it can hardly be said even to have begun. Hence

Seetzen and Burckhardt, with the companions Irby and Mangles, all veritable pioneers, stand out as brilliant exceptions in the matter of geographical advance, so slight in the case of other travellers before Robinson. We have noted that in the early part of the nineteenth century emphasis began to be laid upon another feature, the importance of which is ignored or practically denied by many scientific explorers. Châteaubriand and Lamartine will long be remembered for their word-paintings of the Holy Land, rich in local coloring.

Robinson, then, found the main highways of Western Palestine well trodden, but the by-paths little known.[1] False identifications of Sacred sites, stereotyped centuries before, still persisted in ignoring the correct nomenclature abundantly preserved among the peasants of the land. To explore the obscure as well as to re-examine the known sites, to determine the correct Biblical topography, uninfluenced by ecclesiastical tradition, such was the task to which he set himself.

"The time had come," to quote Dr. Roswell D. Hitchcock, for eight years Dr. Robinson's colleague in the Union Theological Seminary, "the time had come for a scholar equal to Reland (whose work was not based on personal investigation of the Holy Land) in acuteness and breadth of judgment, to enter this tempting field with thermometer, telescope, compass, and measuring-tape, but, above all, sharp-eyed and sufficiently sceptical, and then make report of what he had seen and measured. Such a man was our late associate, raised up, endowed, and trained for this very purpose; so keen of vision that nothing escaped his notice; so sound and solid of judgment that no mere fancy could sway him; so learned that nothing of any moment pertaining to his work was unknown to him; and yet, withal so ardent in his religious affections as to pursue his task like a new crusader. There never was a man better suited to his calling."

For a justification of this unqualified praise of Robinson's critical faculty, as well as of his attainments, we shall presently consider his Biblical Researches; for a justification of the statement that he was "raised

---

[1] One concrete example will suffice to illustrate the indefinite nature of knowledge regarding Palestine before the time of Robinson. Not till a year before his visit was one of the most salient features of the land suspected—namely, the deep depression of the Jordan Valley and of the Dead Sea below the level of the Mediterranean. No one seems to have thought it necessary to explain the extraordinary variations from the rest of Palestine in its flora and fauna. In 1837 More and Beke noticed the depression by means of the boiling point of water, estimating it to be about 500 feet. Russegger and Bertou in 1838 made the depression to amount to more than 1,300 Paris feet. Before Robinson's second visit the true depression—about 1,300 English feet—was scientifically ascertained by Lieut. Lynch.

up, endowed, and trained for this very purpose," we may first turn to the story of his life as told by Dr. Hitchcock.[2]

Edward Robinson was born of a sturdy New England stock, on April 10, 1794, at Southington, Conn. His father, like most of the Congregationalist ministers of his time, supplemented his slender stipend by business. Edward found, thus, in his farm-home, the intellectual and the practical closely linked. Without detriment to preaching and pastoral duties, his father looked after herds of oxen, hives of bees, saw-mill, and grist-mill. The lad was not strong enough to help his father in the more laborious work of the farm, but he became an expert weaver, and invented many contrivances for facilitating manual labor. At the age of sixteen he was placed by his father, who had no idea of sending him to college, as apprentice in a store, with especial charge of the drug department. Previously to this time he had passed through the common schools, had received private instruction from a neighboring clergyman, and had actually taught school himself. A passion for learning, thus fostered, caused him to rebel against a commercial career, and after two years in the store he got his father's permission to enter the first Freshman class at Hamilton College.

In this new institution, situated at Clinton, N.Y., "on the verge of the wilderness and almost within sight of the wigwams of the Oneidas," Robinson had a foretaste of the great Eastern solitudes through which he was destined to pass in later years. Toward these solitudes his thoughts were turned very early and turned continuously. The love of Palestine had fired the dreams of his boyhood; and, to quote from a sentence in the Introductory Section to his Researches "the journey had been the object of my ardent wishes and had entered into my plans of life for more than fifteen years." But his specializing interest in Biblical Studies did not show itself at once. After graduation, he first entered a law office, and later became tutor at Hamilton in Greek and Mathematics. His marriage, in 1818, with Miss Eliza Kirkland, who had inherited a large farm from her father, again brought into his life the daily union of business and study, the best possible preparation for an explorer, the range of whose notes must often bear a close relation to the management of the commissariat. For four years Mr. Robinson divided his time between editing a part of the

[2] The Life, Writings, and Character of Edward Robinson, D.D. L.L.D., read before the New York Historical Society by Henry B. Smith, D.D., and Roswell D. Hitchcock, D.D. New York: A. D. F. Randolph, 1863.

Iliad and superintendence of the farm. This was left to him by his wife, who died within a year of their marriage.

In 1821 he moved to Andover, Mass., for the purpose of publishing his book. Here, under the influence of Professor Moses Stuart, the Hebraist, his studies took a new turn, pointing more directly to the work by which he is most widely known. Within two years he was appointed Instructor of Hebrew in the Theological Seminary. At about this time he was licensed to preach, but he was not regularly ordained till he went to New York as professor at Union. Resigning his tutorship after three years' occupancy, he sailed for Europe, where his studies brought him into close personal contact with such men as Gesenius, Tholuck, and Neander. At Halle he married Therese Albertine Luise, daughter of a professor in the University, and herself a writer of distinction. Shortly after his return from Europe he was appointed Professor Extraordinary of Sacred Literature at Andover, without salary. While occupying the chair—which he was obliged to resign in 1833 on account of ill-health—he founded the Biblical Repository, which, under his editorship, to quote Dr. Hitchcock, "had almost oracular authority on both sides of the Atlantic." Relieved of his professorial duties, he passed in Boston four years of uninterrupted study, the chief results of which were his equally famous translation of Gesenius's Hebrew Lexicon and his own Greek and English Lexicon of the New Testament. A call to the professorship of Biblical Literature in the Union Theological Seminary was accepted under one condition: he desired before entering on his duties to carry out his intention of exploring the Holy Land. The trustees of the Seminary, thus early in its career, established that tradition of encouragement to critical research still characteristic of the institution, by acceding to his request. Fifteen years later, of their own initiative, they voted him a second leave of absence for a second exploration of Palestine, which they well knew he desired to make as a supplement to his earlier researches. In the autumn of 1852 Dr. Robinson was again in his professor's chair, which he continued to occupy, with an interruption due to an operation for cataract, till very near his death, which occurred on January 27, 1863, in his sixty-ninth year. . . .

On April 12, 1838, Dr. Robinson entered the borders of Palestine at Beersheba, with his companion, Dr. Eli Smith, for many years a missionary in Syria. Exactly one month before, the travellers had set out from Cairo for their land journey to Sinai. Proceeding from the Holy Mount to Akabah, they had entered what Robinson calls a "terra incognita" to geographers, the few travellers who had crossed it in various directions having left no adequate report. The day before striking Palestine proper, our explorer had recovered the site of the ancient Elusa, lost for more than eleven centuries. This unexpected recovery was prophetic of what lay in store beyond the border-line. Robinson was destined to reconstruct the map of Palestine; again to quote Dr. Hitchcock: "He found it afloat like an island in the sea, almost like a cloud in the sky of fable, and left it a part of Asia." But how little he realized his destiny may be told in his own words: "I entered upon my journey without the slightest anticipation of the results to which we were providentially led. My first motives had been simply the gratification of personal feelings. . . . I had long meditated the preparation of a work on Biblical geography, and wished to satisfy myself by personal observation as to points on which I could find no information in the books of travellers. This, indeed, grew to be the main object of our journey, the nucleus around which all our inquiries and observations clustered. But I never thought of adding anything to the former stock of knowledge on these subjects; I never dreamed of anything like discoveries in this field. Palestine had for centuries been visited by many travellers; and I knew that Schubert had just preceded us to explore the country in its physical aspects, its botany and geology; and we could hope to add nothing to what he and others had observed."[3]

These modest anticipations led to a modest scientific equipment. For instruments the travellers had only the ordinary surveyor's and two pocket-compasses, a thermometer, telescope, and measuring-tapes. For books they had their Bibles, both in English and in the original tongues; the works on Palestine of Reland and Raumer, the travels of Burckhardt and Laborde, and a compilation called the "Modern Traveller." On their second journey these were supplemented by Ritter's great work, partly still in proof-sheets. For maps they took that of Berghaus, the best up to date, but proving of little service in the parts of the country visited, and Laborde's map of Sinai and Arabia Petraea. . . .

For the economical nature of his journeys, Robinson was greatly indebted to his companion, who was practically a domesticated native of the land. This debt he fully acknowledges. When detailing the plans which had been made for the joint journey as early as 1832, Robinson says: "I count myself fortunate in having been thus early assured of the company of one who, by his familiar and accurate knowledge of the Arabic language,

---

[3] Researches, vol. i, p. 32. All references are to the 1856 edition of his Biblical Researches in three volumes, which include the later researches.

by his acquaintance with the people of Syria, and by the experience gained in former extensive journeys, was so well qualified to alleviate the difficulties and overcome the obstacles which usually accompany Oriental travel. Indeed, to these qualifications of my companion, combined with his taste for geographical and historical researches, and his tact in eliciting and sifting the information to be obtained from an Arab population, are mainly to be ascribed the more important and interesting results of the journey. For I am well aware that, had I been obliged to travel with an ordinary uneducated interpreter, I should have naturally undertaken much less than we together have actually accomplished, while many points of interest would have been overlooked, and many inquiries would have remained without satisfactory answers."[4]

Robinson, as we have seen, entered Palestine from the south on April 12, 1838. Two months and a half later, on June 26th, he rode into Beyrout, and his first journey was over. In our brief review of his work we shall be obliged to consider his two journeys together. And, in fact, the second links on to the first in a remarkable manner. In preparing his first Biblical Researches and in considering the criticisms made upon these, our traveller recognized not only that certain portions of the Holy Land demanded from him a fuller examination, but also that certain points on which doubt had been expressed should be investigated anew. "Questions," he says, "not infrequently arose which personal inquiry on the spot might have solved in half an hour, but to which no amount of reading or investigation at a distance would ever afford an answer, inasmuch as they had never been brought before the mind of any traveller."[5] The chief *lacunae* occurring in the earlier visit were Galilee and the regions east and west of the great northern road leading from Jerusalem to Shechem. Accordingly, Monday, April 5, 1852, found Dr. Robinson with Dr. Smith riding southward from Beyrout on the very road along which they had travelled together northward just about fourteen years before. How firm was the link binding the two journeys together, let us hear in Dr. Robinson's own words. After speaking of pitching their first camp at Neby Yûnis, he says: "Here we were once more in our own tent, not the same, indeed, as formerly, yet so like it as hardly to be distinguished; the furniture and all our travelling equipments were similar; several articles were the very same; and our places in the tent were as of old. It was as if we were continuing a journey of yesterday, and the intervening *fourteen* years

[4]Researches, i, pp. 1 and 2.
[5]III, p. i.

seemed to vanish away. And when we reverted to the reality we could not but gratefully acknowledge the mercy of God in preserving our lives and permitting us once more after so long an interval to prosecute *together* the researches which we had together begun. We could not but regard it as a high and certainly an *unusual* privilege thus, after fourteen long years, again to take up the thread of our investigations at the very point where they had been broken off."[6] Dr. Smith, who had been our explorer's companion during the entire first journey, accompanied him on the second as far as Jerusalem and thence northward to the foot of Hermon. But with the departure of Dr. Smith for Sidon, Robinson's good fortune in having a missionary guide did not leave him. Dr. Thomson, described by Renan as "the man who has traversed Syria the most extensively,"[7] accompanied him to Banias and back to Hasbêya, and thence to within a day's journey of Damascus. Here he was joined by Dr. Robson of the Damascus Mission, who travelled with him to Baalbec, then around the northern end of Lebanon to the Cedars, and so to Beyrout, which was reached on June 19th.

Collating the two journeys, we find that Dr. Robinson was travelling in Syria and Palestine only five months. The maximum period of his investigations, including his tour from Cairo to Beersheba and delays in Beyrout, before and after his travels, covered, in all, about seven months.[8] But from his brief opportunities what a wealth of knowledge did he gather! How great an extent of ground did he cover! Tracing in ink his routes on the map of Judea we make a close net-work of crossing lines.[9] Less close are the lines in Samaria, Galilee, the Lebanon, and Syria proper, yet even here the ramification is remarkable. But the map shows blank stretches. Between Gaza and Tyre, a distance of over 140 miles, the sea-coast is blackened only by a dot at Acre. Thus, the Philistine towns of Ascalon and Ashdod were unvisited, Caesarea and Carmel were unexplored, the ladder of Tyre was not crossed. Eastern Palestine, again, was practically untouched. The Jordan was crossed only when our explorer made his brief raid which resulted in the recovery of the ancient Pella and

[6] III, pp. 34–35.
[7] Mission de Phenicie, p. 883.
[8] Note that the shorter period includes his two stays in Jerusalem, and that he profited by a delay in Beyrout to make excursions in the Lebanon.
[9] Our author tells us (i, p. 434) that they avoided passing for any distance over the same ground twice in their many excursions from Jerusalem, except the short interval between Jerusalem and Bethlehem.

farther north where he examined its main sources. Local disturbances prevented his penetrating the Haurân, and impending illness forced him to give up a proposed trip to Hums and Antioch in Northern Syria. Thankful as we are for what he has given us, we cannot help regretting that circumstances prevented this wonderful man from reporting on every nook and cranny of the Holy Land he loved.

Following his journeys, we are struck with the leisurely rapidity with which they were made. He never wasted any time; he never was in a hurry. It may be added that he seldom got excited. Canon Tristram, who certainly does not himself lack the art of expressing enthusiasm, notes that the wild scenery about the Natural Bridge, over the Litany, is called "magnificent even by the impassive Dr. Robinson." And yet it must not be hastily assumed that he was not moved by very deep feeling. His search for the long-lost Eleutheropolis, the ancient Beto Gabra, appeared to be rewarded by a visit to Beit Jibrîn, whose remains were found to accord well with the historical notices of the Greek city. One piece of evidence, however, remained to be tested. The Onomasticon states that a village called Yedhna lay six miles from Eleutheropolis. Robinson, hearing that a village by the name of Idhna was in the hills to the east, mounted, at 6 A.M., in quest of the missing clew. "I know not when I have felt more the excitement of suspense," he writes, "than while travelling this short distance. A question of some historical importance was depending on the circumstance whether we reached Idhna at eight o'clock. If so, our researches for the long-lost Eleutheropolis would be crowned with success; if not, we were again afloat and certain of no thing. . . . At 7:50 we came to the head of the valley. . . . It now wanted ten minutes to eight o'clock, and as yet nothing was to be seen of Idhna. But as we reached the top of the ascent, the village lay before us, somewhat lower down on the other side, and precisely at eight o'clock we entered the place and dismounted at the house of the Sheikh. We thus proved Idhna to be just two hours, or six Roman miles, from Beit Jibrîn, which is the specified distance of Yedhna from Eleutheropolis."[10] Not a picturesque adjective here, but is not the little narrative tense with the excitement of the rider?

Before reviewing the contents of the Biblical Researches, which embody the results of Robinson's travels, it may be well to note the form which these took. This was a matter of some weighty consideration to the author himself. The material existed in the journals of Drs. Robinson and

[10]II, pp. 56, 57.

Smith, compiled every evening from notes taken during the day. Through a friend of Dr. Robson, companion to Dr. Robinson in his northern tour, I have learned that no amount of fatigue prevented the explorer from writing up his journal in his tent, sometimes as late as eleven at night. The value to an explorer of such systematic habits cannot be over-emphasized. The yielding to a headache by one traveller at some inaccessible spot may lay the necessity of a long journey upon another. Robinson himself points out, with kindly humor, that some discrepancies between Burckhardt's recorded observations and his own were probably to be explained by the latter's confession that he had not taken notes for two days. Smith's journals were never seen by Robinson till the first journey was over, and the recognition of the almost entire coincidence of the two records brought both surprise and satisfaction. How best to present to the world these joint observations was another question. Yielding to the advice of his friends, Robinson abandoned his original plan of embodying in his memoir only the results of his exploration, without reference to personal incidents. Hasty judgment might convict him of turning away from the more scientific treatment. But I think that his careful students come to feel that he rightly gave weight to the consideration that the narrative form would best help the reader to follow "the manner in which the promised land unfolded itself to our eyes and the process by which we were led to the conclusions and opinions advanced in this work."[11] Thus admirably did he foreshadow the historic method which to-day—to give one example— places the History of Doctrine above Dogmatics.

We are bound to admit, however, that Robinson yielded to some of the temptations to which the editor of his own journals is subjected. As a rule, the personal incidents are instructive, often illustrating folk-lore, as when he details his entertainment by the governor of Akabah,[12] or describes the children of his Arab cameleer,[13] but such passages as that taken up with the midnight barking of a dog causing alarmed anticipation, which came to nothing, are of no relevance.[14] Generally speaking, however, Robinson's style is condensed and full of meat. Apart from the rich historical discussions, a most important feature in dealing with a given site is a rapid review showing how far and in what period it had hitherto been known to

[11]Preface, p. vii.
[12]I, p. 164.
[13]I, p. 149.
[14]I, p. 183.

visitors. "He used freely," says Dr. Hitchcock, "whatever lay open to be freely used. But he took the learning of others, whether dead or living, not for a Jacob's pillow to sleep on, but for a Jacob's ladder to climb by." By a somewhat laborious process of collating his three volumes, I might, relying upon no other source, have sketched the development of Palestine Exploration, with a general description of the routes taken by the chief travellers, from the Bordeaux Pilgrim to the great author himself!

In contrast to the squabbling for priority which soils the pages of so many explorers, Robinson's determination to give every traveller or geographer his due is at once refreshing and edifying.[15] His achievement, however, in this line is not always commensurate with his spirit. Even this Homer nods. Ziph, he says,[16] is mentioned by no writer since Jerome, yet I find the name in Fetellus, Burchard, and Marino Sanuto, authors often quoted by him. Ekron he declares[17] to have been entirely overlooked by all Frank travellers since the time of the Crusades, yet Sandys[18] mentioned it when in 1611 he travelled from Gaza to Jerusalem, and Shaw (1722)[19] gives it as an illustration of the survival of an old name, placing it correctly on his map. Both Sandys and Shaw are given the star of praise in Robinson's bibliography. But I refrain from giving further examples. Having discovered spots on the sun, their exact number we do not need to count. After all, they are invisible to the naked eye.

The manuscript of the "Researches" describing the first journey, prepared in Berlin, was completed in August, 1840. The simultaneous publication in English and German aroused unbounded enthusiasm in scientific quarters, while it provoked hostile criticism on the part of the traditionalists whom Robinson had antagonized with such severity. Friend and foe, however, recognized in it an epoch-making work. It obtained for him the gold medal of the Royal Geographical Society of London. The great geographer Ritter called it "a classic in its own field—a production which has already set the geography of the Holy Land on a more fixed basis than it ever had before, and which will ensure its continued

[15] Note his quaint remarks on the identification of Khurbet Fahil with Pella, which had struck him in reading the works of Irby and Mangles, and which "was entertained by Kiepert, who likewise used the volume in making out the maps for my work. By which one the suggestion was first made to the other it may now be difficult to determine." (III, p. 323.)
[16] I, p. 492.
[17] II, p. 228.
[18] Sandys's Travailes, p. 118.
[19] Shaw, vol. ii, p. 43.

advance."[20] Olshausen's prophecy that "the admirable principles of investigation which are unfolded in Robinson's work will serve as a beacon for all future explorers," was fulfilled by the Officers of the Palestine Exploration Fund. Speaking in Manchester in 1875 of the Fund's Survey, Conder, the worthy successor of Robinson, declared: "The results of his travels formed the groundwork of modern research, and showed how much could be done toward recovering the ancient topography. He proved that the old nomenclature clings to Palestine in an extraordinary manner and that in the memory of the peasant population the true sites have been preserved undiscovered by the Frank invaders. . . . It is in his steps that we have trod. With greater advantages, more time and more money, we have been able to more than double the number of his discoveries, but the cases in which we have found him wrong are few and far between."[21] . . .

Having acknowledged Robinson's limitations in the field of archaeology, we hasten to add that he made many important contributions to this science. Though the fragment of an arch, projecting from the west wall of the Haram enclosure at Jerusalem, was noticed by Catherwood in 1833, its identification with the bridge which, according to Josephus, connected the Temple with Mt. Zion, was made by our explorer, and appropriately bears the name of Robinson's Arch to this day. He was the first to call proper attention to the remains of a large city which once had been built at Petra, covering an area not much less than two miles in circumference.[22] His predecessors here had almost entirely confined their observations to the unique rock-dwellings. He, too, was the first traveller to report on the dark windings of the Tunnel leading for over 1,700 feet from the Virgin's Fountain to the Pool of Siloam; and the careful measurements he took agree very closely with those of Sir Charles Warren, thirty years later.[23] Important discoveries were made in Galilee. By comparing several ancient structures, showing a peculiar architecture, with the remains of a building which had been previously recognized as a Jewish synagogue, Robinson proved that all these buildings fell under the same category. He was thus the first to recognize a synagogue at Tell Hûm, one of the claimants for the

---

[20] See Gage's translation, vol. ii, p. 70.
[21] Q. S., 1876, pp. 34 ff. We may add that Renan in his Mission de Phénicie (p. 785) refers to the "vast and conscientious work of Robinson."
[22] II, p. 136.
[23] I, p. 338; cf. Recovery of Jerusalem, p. 239.

site of Capernaum.[24] He also made an especial examination of the temples in the vicinity of Mt. Hermon, between Hermon and Damascus, and in the Anti-Lebanon, in many cases giving elaborate measurements.

We have now come to the chief objects of Robinson's Researches, the physical geography of the Holy Land and the identification of Biblical sites. Here he placed his main stress. His geographical investigations often led him to take new routes in order to fill in *lacunae* in former descriptions. His search for lost sites led to his exploring many a small place unnoticed before. For the work of identification elaborate preparation was made. Convinced of the worthlessness of ecclesiastical tradition, convinced that in the modern names the ancient nomenclature lay in fossil form, Drs. Robinson and Smith avoided as far as possible all contact with the convents and the authority of the monks, resolving to apply for information solely to the native population. While visiting the chief centres, as Jerusalem or Gaza, they collected lists of the names of the modern villages and of the ruins of the surrounding districts from the inhabitants or from wandering Bedawin.[25] In searching for a given site they never defeated their object by asking a direct question, to which the amiable Syrian usually gives the answer best calculated to please, but they employed a method of cross-examination worthy of a lawyer. Thus equipped, both by method and preparation, they were able sometimes in one brief visit greatly to enrich the subject of Biblical identification. From the top of the hill of Maîn, east of Hebron, they could distinguish eight villages and ruins bearing the Arabic equivalents of the names of eight towns of Judah. Thus, in one sweep of the eye, our travellers added to the list of recognized Biblical sites the names of Ziph, Anab, Jattir, Maon, Eshtemoa, Juttah, and Shocoh in the Mountains.[26] Some of these had not been mentioned since the time of Jerome; others occur in Seetzen's map, but with no attempt at identification. In Kurmul alone had modern travellers previous to Robinson

---

[24] III, p. 346. Robinson missed the ruins at Kasyûu (a site declared afterward by Renan to be of prime importance for Jewish remains), but on reading later the notes of Porter, he suggests that the ruins there described may be those of a synagogue (iii, p. 363). On the other hand, in the large edifice at Kadesh Naphtali, declared by Robinson to be a synagogue, Renan sees a heathen temple (iii, p. 368); cf. Renan's Mission de Phénicie, pp. 684–5 and 762 ff.

[25] I, p. 256. Robinson acknowledges that this method had been successfully employed by Seetzen and Burckhardt in Eastern Palestine, but states that up to his time no one had followed this example in Western Palestine.

[26] I, p. 494.

recognized an ancient site—the Carmel of Judah.[27] In a two days' excursion, north and northeast of Jerusalem, our travellers placed on a firm basis the identification of Anathoth, Geba, Michmash, and Bethel.[28] Among scores of other additions made by Robinson to the modern science of Biblical Identification are the interesting sites of Shiloh, Beth-Shemesh, Mareshah, and the Vale of Elah.[29] He, too, was the first in our day carefully to work out the identification of Megiddo with Lejjûn and of Jezreel with Zera'în.[30] Nor was this work of his confined to Biblical sites. His eager search for Eleutheropolis indicates how keen was his scent for Greek and Roman places not mentioned in the Scriptures. Even out-of-the-way Crusading remains interested him. Tristram, visiting the almost inaccessible Kula'at Kurein, southeast of Tyre, in 1863, draws a plan of the castle and says: "It is strange that history affords not the slightest clew to the origin and builders of the fortress."[31] Thomson, to whose description he refers, gives the good Canon no help. And yet our Robinson, passing in the vicinity of the Castle eleven years before casually but correctly remarks that it is the Montfort of the Crusaders.[32]

The judicious temper of mind controlling his observations is well illustrated by his comparison of the impressions gathered by viewing the district around the Waters of Merom from the high mountains to the west, with those resulting from examination at shorter range: "The whole plain of the Huleh was before us. . . . We thought we could here trace clearly the various streams flowing through the plain and distinguish accurately their points of juncture. These I carefully noted, but the subsequent result taught me a lesson in respect to judgments formed under such circumstances; I mean when looking down from a lofty point of view upon an extensive tract of country below. A few days afterward when I came to traverse the Huleh, and follow the streams to their junction, most of my

[27] All these identifications, except that of Anab, are adopted in Armstong's Names and Places.
[28] I, pp. 436 ff.
[29] In the indexes of Ancient Geographical Names (at the end of vols. ii and iii, respectively) Robinson marks by an asterisk: "Ancient places now first visited or identified." Collating the two indexes, we find over 160 thus marked. These, however, include some places not mentioned in Sacred history.
[30] Lejjûn is the Roman Legio; the ancient site of Megiddo was doubtless at the neighboring Tell-el-Mntasellim, where Dr. Robinson, with his usual non-comprehension of mounds, found no traces of a city. But he was on the right track.
[31] The Land of Israel, p. 80.
[32] III, p. 66.

notes proved to be entirely wrong."[33] Such a reporter himself furnishes the criterion by which his observations may be judged.

As a final illustration of his candor, of his rejecting the explorer's temptation to make an identification at any price, we may cite his discovery of the ruins of er-Ruheibeh, covering a level tract of eight or ten acres, a day's ride southwest of Beersheba. "These ruins," he says, "have apparently been seen by no former traveller and it was only by accident that we stumbled upon them. The place must anciently have been of some note and importance; but what city could it have been? This is a question which, after long inquiry, and with the best aid from the light of European science, I am as yet unable to answer."[34] A less conscientious explorer would have made the identification with Rehoboth, one of Isaac's wells in the vicinity of Beersheba, but the apparent absence of a well, together with other reasons, led him to reject this. It was left to a later traveller to discover wells here, and this identification finds a tentative place in Armstrong's "Names and Places."

We have noticed the scepticism regarding ecclesiastical tradition controlling Robinson's researches; a scepticism not negative but brilliantly positive; a scepticism not barren but productive of a rich harvest; destruction followed, when possible, by reconstruction. But he had the defect of his quality. His methods of destruction are sometimes open to criticism. Hearty recognition we have already given to his admirable fusion of accurate observation, clear judgment, and downright common-sense; we are bound now to take count of his lapses from a calm and scientific temper.[35] Spots held in peculiar veneration by the Roman Catholic and Eastern clergy seem to have been thereby rendered obnoxious to him, and were visited with obvious reluctance. Thus, the day after his first arrival in Jerusalem, in 1838, he witnessed part of the Easter ceremonies in the Church of the Holy Sepulchre, "but," he says, "to be in the ancient City of the Most High and to see these venerated places and the very name of our Holy Religion profaned by lying and idle mummeries, while the proud Mussulmen looked on with haughty scorn—all this excited in my mind a feeling too painful to be borne, and I never visited

---

[33] III, p. 370.
[34] I, p. 197.
[35] Note the too sweeping character of his famous dictum: "That all ecclesiastical tradition respecting ancient places in and around Jerusalem and throughout Palestine IS OF NO VALUE, except so far as it is supported by circumstances known from the Scriptures, or from other contemporary testimony." (Vol. iii, p. 263.)

the place again."[36] Here speaks the Puritan, not the Explorer. Robinson's personal attitude toward ritual was his own affair, but to have let this stand in the way of his thorough examination of one of the most interesting buildings in the world was not worthy of one who crawled on hands and knees through the windings of the Siloam Tunnel. In 1838 he did not know that he was to revisit Palestine, hence this brief glimpse of the Holy Sepulchre was intended to be final. In 1852 he did so far overcome his prejudices as to enter the Church, "mainly," he acknowledges, "in order to look at the Tomb of Joseph and Nicodemus, so called."[37] Judging Robinson by the great mass of his work, we would expect him to be fair in every historical discussion. But judging Robinson by his biased attitude in visiting the Holy Sepulchre, we should be prepared to find that his usual impartiality is somewhat relaxed; that his usual clear judgment is some-what obscured in dealing with its alleged discovery as recounted by Eusebius. On strict examination his exegesis is not found to be fully warranted. His conclusions, though partially legitimate, appear to me to be somewhat too sweeping and their explanation somewhat *ex parte*. In view of the authority that may be justly attached to Robinson's conclusions in the vast majority of cases, we should dwell for a moment on the exceptional case, especially as it involves his *cause célèbre*, which made his book the subject of fierce controversy. Here he is both lawyer and jury. My complaint is not against the verdict of the jury, but against the special pleading of the lawyer.

Any discussion of Eusebius's account is complicated by the apparently contradictory elements which it contains. Certain passages appear on first reading to favor the view that the alleged discovery of the Holy Sepulchre by Constantine's agents was based on previous information; others appear to involve the idea that it was held to be the result of miraculous intimation or intervention. Now we may assume that under Eusebius's rhetoric there was a meaning perfectly clear to himself. Holding no brief for or against the traditional site, I believe that a harmony may be found in the passages, without doing violence to any of these.[38] Briefly but

[36] I, p. 224.
[37] III, p. 180.
[38] I do not propose here to discuss the site of the Holy Sepulchre, nor the various accounts of its alleged discovery, nor even Robinson's topographical arguments against the traditional site. The scope of this sketch does not include such matters. My aim is merely to illustrate a certain bias in Robinson by showing how he deals with Eusebius's narrative. The whole subject of "Golgotha and the Holy Sepulchre" has been critically treated by Sir Charles Wilson in a series of papers in the Q. S. of the P. E. F. (Jan., 1902-Jan., 1904, inclusive), soon to be published in book form.

essentially his account is as follows: At some time previous to Constantine, the place of the Saviour's resurrection in Jerusalem had been purposely consigned to darkness and oblivion by ungodly men, who, after covering it up with earth, had erected on the site a shrine to Aphrodite. The Emperor, being inspired by the Divine Spirit, "could not bear to see the place concealed by the artifices of adversaries," but, calling upon God to help him, gave orders that the place should be purified. The shrine was destroyed, the mound was removed layer by layer, until at last, "contrary to all hope," the sepulchral cave was brought to light. Thereupon the Emperor commanded the erection of a house of prayer on the site, "not having hit upon the project without the aid of God, but having been impelled to it by the Spirit of the Saviour himself." "This project he had had for some time in mind and had foreseen as if by superior intelligence what was going to happen." To Macarius, Bishop of Jerusalem, he wrote as follows: "No power of language appears worthy to describe the present wonder. For that the token of that most holy Passion, long ago buried underground, should have remained unknown for so many cycles of years until it should shine forth to his servants, . . . truly transcends all marvel."[39]

Now, Robinson seems to have overlooked the fact that this account appears distinctly to assume that before Constantine gave orders for the destruction of the shrine of Venus, he believed that the Holy Sepulchre lay concealed somewhere beneath it.[40] On the other hand, he makes wrong application of the passages indicating that Constantine was moved by Divine Intimation. "What, then," he says, "after all, is the amount of testimony relative to an idol erected over the place of the resurrection and serving to mark the spot? It is simply that writers (*i.e.*, Eusebius and later historians) *ex post facto* have mentioned such an idol as standing, not over the Sepulchre known of old as being that of Christ, *but over the spot fixed*

---

[39]Our Summary is condensed from Dr. Bernard's translation of Chaps. 26–30 of Eusebius's Life of Constantine, P. P. T., vol. i. We cannot here enter into a discussion of the ambiguous passage quoted from the letter to Macarius, which may or may not refer to the Invention of the Cross, otherwise unnoticed by Eusebius. Robinson says (iii, 257, note 2), "It makes no difference to the argument which way it is understood," holding that the language is too strong to apply merely to the removal of obstructions from a well-known spot. To us the passage would appear to be natural if referring to the discovery of the Cross, highly rhetorical if applied to the recovery of the cave; but highly rhetorical is just what Eusebius is throughout the whole discussion.

[40]But see note 1 on page 218.

upon by Constantine as that Sepulchre." "Their testimony proves conclusively
that an idol stood upon that spot, but it has no bearing to show that the spot
was the true sepulchre."[41] "Indeed, the whole tenor of the language both
of Eusebius and Constantine goes to show that the discovery of the Holy
Sepulchre was held to be the result not of a previous knowledge derived
from tradition, but of a supernatural interposition and revelation."[42] "The
alleged discovery of them (Calvary and the Tomb) by the aged and
credulous Helena, like her discovery of the cross, may not have been
improbably the work of pious fraud. It would, perhaps, not be doing
injustice to the Bishop Macarius and his clergy if we regard the whole as a
well-laid and successful plan for restoring to Jerusalem its former consideration, and elevating the See to a higher degree of influence and
dignity."[43]

Here, for a moment, we must part company with Robinson. Eusebius,
indeed, in ascribing motives to the builders of the shrine of Aphrodite,
appears to be employing *ex post facto* reasoning. His narrative has no
scientific bearing to show that the spot enshrined the true Sepulchre of
Christ. It does not prove that Constantine was acting on correct information. But it does imply that Eusebius believed that the Emperor was acting
upon some sort of information.[44] The phrases showing that Constantine
was moved by Divine Intimation, held by Robinson to indicate that the
discovery was regarded as the result of a supernatural interposition and
revelation, apply strictly only to the work of purification and construction.
Later writers, indeed, represent the search as having been guided by such
influences, but had there been no question of tradition or no tradition,
these phrases of Eusebius would not necessarily have been held to mean
other than that Constantine was moved to a good work by Divine
Providence. Dr. Robinson might have said the same of his own researches!

Eusebius's affirmation that the discovery was held to have been "beyond
all hope," Robinson would find inappropriate if applied to a spot "defi-
nitely known and marked by long tradition." Well, so it would be. But
our exegesis of Eusebius's narrative necessarily involves no more than
the existence of some sort of a tradition. That it was not generally known,
at least not generally credited, is suggested by the statement ascribing

[41] I, p. 413; cf. iii, pp. 257 ff. The italics are Robinson's.
[42] I, p. 414.
[43] I, p. 418.
[44] Possibly Robinson might have conceded this point, holding, however, that said information
was fabricated by the clergy.

Constantine's foresight as to what was going to happen to "superior intelligence." That it was not even known to Eusebius ten years previous to the alleged recovery is suggested by his silence regarding it when, in 315, he mentioned another tradition placing the site of the Ascension on the Mount of Olives, whither pilgrims flocked to worship from all parts of the earth.[45] Eusebius does not refer to Helena's agency in the matter, but later writers represent her excavations as being the result of "diligent inquiry." As an excavator I can enter into the feelings of those who, having staked their hopes upon a given site, hopes based either upon diligent inquiry or upon some dubious historical indication, labor day after day in removing layer after layer of *débris* without striking the desired object, and then, when at last this appears to be found, exclaim: "This certainly was beyond all hope!"

Some sort of tradition, then, I think may be legitimately inferred from Eusebius's account. The value of such a tradition, however, is quite another matter. Against its authority, supposing it to have existed, Dr. Robinson argues clearly and, it seems to me, decisively from analogy with a tradition of "precisely the same character and import," which is known to have been believed ten years before the journey of Helena, namely, the tradition respecting the place of the Ascension, to which we have just referred. This actual tradition, says Robinson, though its claims to credibility can be supported by all the arguments used in favor of the supposed tradition respecting the Holy Sepulchre, is itself unquestionably false, since it is contradicted by the express declaration of Luke, who states that Jesus led out His disciples as far as Bethany, and while He blessed them He was parted from them and carried up into Heaven.[46]

Have we not, after all, come back very close to Robinson? Is there much difference between an obscure and discredited tradition, such as we postulate, and his view of no tradition? Little difference as affecting the genuineness of the site, but great difference as affecting the reputation of the good Bishop Macarius. The phrase "pious fraud" separates us still.[47]

---

[45] Eusebius, Demonstr. Evang., 7, 4.
[46] I, p. 416.
[47] There remains, of course, the matter of the "Invention of the Cross." But whether Macarius had any cognizance of this is not proven, as the first explicit reference to it is by Bishop Cyril, who at the time of Helena's journey was only eleven years old. Even granting that this closely followed on to the discovery of the alleged Holy Sepulchre, we must also grant that from the sudden realization of expectations which had been described as "beyond all hope" a credulous age might easily have evolved a belief which would differ essentially because morally from the "well-laid and successful plan" of a "pious fraud."

Take it back, Dr. Robinson! The finely written manuscript of your Researches, brought out from the Archives of the Union Theological Seminary, lies open before me, at the very page containing your accusation. I seem to hear your voice speaking to me, as it spoke to students of this school years and years ago. Bid me tell your students, born since you were translated, that the accusation is withdrawn, and that you have made your peace with Macarius.

We cannot leave the journeyings of our Union professor without instancing his powers of endurance, his admirable pluck, and his just as admirable prudence. On the day when he first entered Jerusalem at 6 P.M., he had left Dhoheriyeh at quarter past two in the monring, he had taken a ramble through the streets of Hebron, and he had been on a camel for nearly sixteen hours. And yet at nine o'clock the next day he was in the Church of the Holy Sepulchre, witnessing the Easter ceremonies. No wonder that after the tense strain of three and a half months he was taken, at the close of the first journey, with an illness that almost cost him his life at Vienna. No wonder that an impending illness cut short his exploration of Northern Syria in 1852. The intense strain was not only one of fatigue, but of excitement, if not of actual danger. From the matter-of-fact narrative of Dr. Robinson we can reconstruct for ourselves a series of pictures of his Petra adventures. We can see him quietly strolling about, taking notes on the monuments, while Dr. Smith is dealing with the demands of the local Sheikh for tribute money, accentuated by the firing of guns and the drawing of swords. We can see the travellers riding off, not a para the poorer, though they know that now the ascent of Mt. Hor must be given up. We can see the aged Sheikh following them, declaring that their good-will is better than money, and begging them to make the ascent on any terms they please. And finally we can see them continuing tranquilly on their journey back to Jerusalem, having lost the view from Mt. Hor, but having decided, once out of the old man's clutches, not to place themselves in his power again.

Robinson, as has been frequently intimated, regarded his researches in Palestine merely as preparatory to a systematic work on the Physical and Historical Geography of the Holy Land. This he actually began after his first journey, following a scheme abandoned later, when his second journey had furnished him with new data. His new plan was to cover the ground in two volumes: Vol. I., The Central Region—Palestine with Lebanon and Sinai. Vol. II., Outlying Countries. Vol. I. certainly and Vol. II. probably were to have been divided into three parts—Physical Geography, Historical Geography and Topographical Geography. Realizing the vast scope of this scheme, he felt that others might have to carry it out to completion, but volume first he hoped to finish. "But," writes his wife in the preface to the posthumous publication, "it was otherwise decreed above; and a comparatively small portion—thorough and complete in itself, however, without a missing note, without the omission of a single word to be subsequently inserted—is all that is left to the world from the hand of the earnest, faithful investigator."[48] The portion written and published was only the first division—Physical Geography—of Vol. I., and this only so far as it applied to Palestine proper. Even this part was not completed, as chapters relating to the Flora and Fauna are missing. As an appendix there is inserted an Essay called "The Physical Geography of Syria Proper," which formed the commencement of his work on Biblical Geography according to the original plan.

Referring to this uncompleted work in his speech before the New York Historical Society, February 3, 1863, Dr. Hitchcock said: "There lives no man to finish it; and when one shall be born to do it, God only knows." God, who made Man in His own Image, never makes any man in the exact image of his fellow. Robinson's book has never been completed on the lines which he laid down, but, while Dr. Hitchcock was speaking, a Scotch lad, barely seven years old, was beginning the studies which in later days led him into the great region opened up by the American Pioneer. George Adam Smith's "Historical Geography of the Holy Land" has not the mass of systematized detail that would have characterized the vast work planned by Robinson, but the power to illustrate the interaction of forces, physical and historical, a subject requiring not only knowledge based on personal investigation and wide reading, but a handling at once vigorous, subtle, and sympathetic, is all his own. On him willingly would Robinson have cast his mantle.

[48] Physical Geography of the Holy Land. By Edward Robinson. Boston, 1865.

2. Robinson's Biblical Researches

The following brief excerpts from Robinson's first volume give some insights into the spirit and flavor of his three-volume work, which remains a massive landmark in biblical scholarship. The way the love of the Bible motivated archaeological and geographical work has rarely been more clearly stated. The bulk of the work is a detailed account, enlivened by personal anecdotes, of the discoveries he made.

Robinson's companion, Eli Smith, was a former pupil who had long been a missionary in Syria; and whose knowledge of Arabic was especially helpful. Later researches have, of course, corrected aspects of this monumental contribution, yet remain indebted to it.

Source: Edward Robinson, *Biblical Researches in Palestine, Mount Sinai and Arabia Petraea: A Journal of Travels in the Year 1838 by E. Robinson and E. Smith, Undertaken in Reference to Biblical Geography*, 3 vols. (Boston: Crocker & Brewster, 1841; reprinted by Arno Press, 1977), 1:46–48, 152–58, 371–78. See also the follow-up volume, *Later Biblical Researches in Palestine, and in the Adjacent Regions, by E. Robinson, E. Smith, and Others* (Boston: Crocker & Brewster, 1856; reprinted by Arno Press, 1977).

In respect to our further journey, it may be proper to remark, that I entered upon it without the slightest anticipation of the results to which we were providentially led. My first motive had been simply the gratification of personal feelings. As in the case of most of my countrymen, especially in New England, the scenes of the Bible had made a deep impression upon my mind from the earliest childhood; and afterwards in riper years this feeling had grown into a strong desire to visit in person the places so remarkable in the history of the human race. Indeed in no country of the world, perhaps, is such a feeling more widely diffused than in New England; in no country are the Scriptures better known, or more highly prized. From his earliest years the child is there accustomed not only to read the Bible for himself; but he also reads or listens to it in the morning and evening devotions of the family, in the daily village-school, in the Sunday-school and Bible-class, and in the weekly ministrations of the sanctuary. Hence, as he grows up, the names of Sinai, Jerusalem, Bethlehem, the Promised Land, become associated with his earliest recollections and holiest feelings.—With all this, in my own case, there had subsequently become connected a scientific motive. I had long meditated the preparation of a work on Biblical Geography; and wished to satisfy myself by personal observation, as to many points on which I could find no information in the books of travellers. This indeed grew to be the main object of our journey—the nucleus around which all our inquiries and observations clustered. But I never thought of adding any thing to the former stock of knowledge on these subjects; I never dreamed of any thing like discoveries in this field. Palestine had for centuries been visited by many travellers; and I knew that Schubert had just preceded us, to explore the country in its physical aspects, its botany and geology; and we could hope to add nothing to what he and others had observed.

Under the influence of these impressions, we carried with us no instruments, except an ordinary surveyor's and two pocket compasses, a thermometer, telescopes, and measuring-tapes; expecting to take only such bearings and measurements as might occur to us upon the road, without going out of our way to seek for them. But as we came to Sinai, and saw how much former travellers had left undescribed; and then crossed the great desert through a region hitherto almost unknown, and found the names and sites of long-forgotten cities; we became convinced that there "yet remained much land to be possessed," and determined to do what we could with our limited means towards supplying the deficiency. Both Mr. Smith and myself kept separate journals; each taking pencil-notes upon the spot of every thing we wished to record, and writing them out in full usually the same evening; but we never compared our notes. These journals are now in my hands; and from them the following work has been compiled. On thus comparing them for the first time, I have been surprised and gratified at their almost entire coincidence. My own notes were in general more full in specifications of time, the course, the features of the country, and personal incidents; while those of my companion were necessarily my sole dependence in respect to Arabic names and their orthography, and chiefly so as to all information derived orally from the Arabs. The bearings also were mostly taken by Mr. Smith; since it often required a great deal of questioning and cross-examination, in order to extract the necessary information from the Arabs as to distant places and their names. This department therefore naturally fell to him; while I contented myself usually with taking the bearings of such places as were already known to us. It is only since my return, that I became aware of the value of the materials thus collected, in a geographical point of view, from the judgment passed on them by eminent geographers; and I look back with painful regret on the circumstances, which prevented me from taking along more perfect instruments, and from obtaining a more exact knowledge of the observations necessary for the trigonometrical construction of a map. . . .

This little plain [near Mt. Sinai] is about twelve or thirteen hundred feet above the vallies below, extending quite across the ridge; and from it towards the West a path descends to the convent el-Arba'în in Wady el-Leja. On the right, clusters of rocks and peaks from two to four hundred feet higher than this basin, extend for nearly two miles towards the N.N.W. and terminate in the bold front which overhangs the plain er-Râhah N. of the convent. This is the present Horeb of Christians. On the left, due S. from the well, rises the higher peak of Sinai, or Jebel Musa, about seven hundred feet above the basin and nearly a mile distant. A few rods from the well, where the ascent of Sinai begins, is a low rude building containing the chapels of Elijah and Elisha. Here was evidently once a small monastery; and the older travellers speak also of a chapel of the Virgin. In that of Elijah the monks show near the altar a hole just large enough for a man's body, which they say is the cave where the prophet dwelt in Horeb.[1] Tapers were lighted and incense burnt in both these chapels. The ascent hence is steeper, though not difficult. There are steps for a great part of the way, merely rough stones thrown together; and in no part of the ascent of the whole mountain are they hewn, or cut in the rock, as is said by Burckhardt.[2]

Leaving the chapels at half past 9 o'clock, we ascended slowly, not failing to see the track of Muhammed's camel in the rock by the way; and reached the summit of Jebel Mûsa at twenty minutes past ten. Here is a small area of huge rocks, about eighty feet in diameter, highest towards the East, where is a little chapel almost in ruins, formerly divided between the Greeks and Latins; while towards the S.W. about forty feet distant stands a small ruined mosk. The summit and also the body of this part of the mountain are of coarse gray granite.[3] On the rocks are many inscriptions in Arabic, Greek, and Armenian, the work of pilgrims. In the chapel are the names of many travellers; and I found here a pencil note of Rüppell's observations, May 7th, 1831; marking the time 12[h] 15'; Barom. 21' 7."6; Therm. 13¼° R. or 62° F. At half past ten o'clock my Thermometer stood in the chapel at 60° F.—The height of this peak above the sea,

[1] 1 Kings xix. 8, 9. The elevation of this building above the convent in the valley below, is given by Schubert at 1400 Paris feet.
[2] Page 565.
[3] Pococke correctly remarks, that the "north part of Sinai (Jebel Mûsa) is of red granite for above half way up; all the rest being a granite of a yellowish ground, with small black grains in it, and the mountain at a distance appears of two colours;" I. p. 147. fol. This difference of colour is especially striking as seen from the valley el-Leja.

according to the observations of Rüppell, compared with simultaneous ones at Tür, is 7035 Paris feet; and its elevation above the convent el-Arba'în about 1670 feet.[4] From it the peak of St. Catharine bears S. 44° W. a thousand feet higher; and Râs es-Sŭfsâfeh, the highest among the peaks near the front of Horeb, N. 22° W.[5]

My first and predominant feeling while upon this summit, was that of disappointment. Although from our examination of the plain er-Râhah below, and its correspondence to the scriptural narrative, we had arrived at the general conviction that the people of Israel must have been collected on it to receive the law; yet we still had cherished a lingering hope or feeling, that there might after all be some foundation for the long series of monkish tradition, which for at least fifteen centuries has pointed out the summit on which we now stood, as the spot where the ten commandments were so awfully proclaimed. But Scriptural narrative and monkish tradition are very different things; and while the former has a distinctness and definiteness, which through all our journeyings rendered the Bible our best guide-book, we found the latter not less usually and almost regularly to be but a baseless fabric. In the present case, there is not the slightest reason for supposing that Moses had any thing to do with the summit which now bears his name. It is three miles distant from the plain on which the Israelites must have stood; and hidden from it by the intervening peaks of the modern Horeb. No part of the plain is visible from the summit; nor are the bottoms of the adjacent vallies; nor is any spot to be seen around it, where the people could have been assembled. The only point in which it is not immediately surrounded by high mountains, is towards the S.E. where it sinks down precipitously to a tract of naked gravelly hills. Here, just at its foot, is the head of a small valley, Wady es-Sebâ'îyeh, running toward the N.E. beyond the Mount of the Cross into Wady esh-Sheikh; and of another not larger, called el-Wa'rah, running S.E. to the Wady Nŭsb of the Gulf of 'Akabah; but both of these together hardly afford a tenth part of the space contained in er-Râhah and Wady esh-Sheikh. In the same

---

[4]Rüppell's Reise in Abyssinien, I. pp. 118, 124. I follow here Rüppell's measurements throughout, because they alone are founded on corresponding observations on the sea-coast at Tûr. Schubert gives the height of Sinai at 6794.4 Paris feet, or 2071 feet above the convent in Wady Shu'eib; Russegger at 7097 Paris feet, or 1982 feet above the same convent.
[5]Other bearings from Jebel Mûsa were as follows: Um Lauz, a peak beyond Wady Sebâ'îyeh, N. 40° E. Um 'Alawy, connected with smaller peaks running towards the eastern gulf, N. 73° E. Abu Mas'ûd, west of Wady Wa'rah S. 36° E. Jebel Humr, S. 87° W. Jebel Tînia, or Sŭmr et-Tînia, N. 62° W. Jebel Fureia', north end, N. 23° W. Jebel ed-Deir N. 21° E. Jebel ez-Zebîr, east end, N. 35° W. el-Benât, or el-Jauzeh, N. 45° W. Island of Tîrân, S. 31° E.

direction is seen the route to Shŭrm; and, beyond, a portion of the Gulf of 'Akabah and the little island Tîrân; while more to the right and close at hand is the head of el-Leja among the hills. No other part of the Gulf of 'Akabah is visible; though the mountains beyond it are seen.[6]

Towards the S.W. and W. tower the ridges of St. Catharine and Tînia, cutting off the view of the Gulf of Suez and the whole Western region; so that neither Serbâl on the right, nor the loftier Um Shaumer towards the left, are at all visible from this peak of Sinai.[7] Indeed in almost every respect the view from this point is confined, and is far less extensive and imposing than that from the summit of St. Catharine. Only the table-land on the Mountain of the Cross, is here seen nearer and to better advantage across the narrow valley of Shu'eib. Neither the convent from which we had come, nor that of el-Arba'în, both lying in the deep vallies below, were visible. To add to our disappointment, old 'Aîd, the head-guide, who had been selected expressly in order to tell us the names of the mountains and objects around, proved to know very little about them, and often answered at random. In short, the visit to the summit of Jebel Mûsa, was to me the least satisfactory incident in our whole sojourn at Mount Sinai.

We remained upon the summit nearly two and a half hours. Leaving it at 12¾ o'clock, we returned to the cypress-tree and well near the chapel of Elijah. From this point a path leads South of West over the little plain, and descends partly by steps to the convent el-Arba'în in Wady el-Leja. We determined, however, to visit the northern brow of Horeb, which overlooks the plain er-Râhah; and took a route towards the N.N.W. in order to reach it. As we left the well for this purpose at 1¼ o'clock, the clouds which had been gathering for some time, threatened to drench us with a shower of rain. The drops began to fall thinly but heavily; and for a while we hoped that Beshârah's entreaties for rain might have been fulfilled; even at the expense of our being counted as prophets by the Arabs, and getting a wet skin for ourselves. But the clouds soon passed away, and the desert remained parched and thirsty as before.

---

[6] Brown speaks of having seen the whole length of the Gulf of 'Akabah from Sinai; but this is an impossibility. Travels, chap. XIV. p. 179.

[7] Yet Laborde professes to have seen from it Serbâl, Um Shaumer, and the mountains of Africa beyond. It must have been with 'the mind's eye.' Voyage en Arab. Pet. p. 68. Engl. p. 252. A similar exaggerated account is given by Russegger; see Berghaus' Annalen, März 1839, p. 420, seq.—Rüppell correctly remarks: "The prospect from the peak of Sinai is limited in the East, South, and West, by higher mountains; and only towards the North, one looks out over a widely extended landscape;" Reise in Abyssinien, I. p. 118. Burckhardt was prevented by a thick fog from seeing even the nearest mountains; Travels, etc. p. 566.

The path was wild and rugged, leading over rocks and winding through ravines among low peaks. In fifteen minutes we came to a small round basin among the hills, with a bed of soil full of shrubs; where also were a holly-hock and hawthorn, and evident traces of an artificial reservoir for water, which was said formerly to have been carried down to the convent. Here stands a small chapel of St. John the Baptist. Not far off are the cells of several anchorites cut in the rock. Twenty minutes further is another larger basin, surrounded by twelve peaks, and the bottom enclosed by a low wall; showing that it was once tilled as a garden. At 2 o'clock we reached a third basin, still deeper and more romantic, surrounded by a like number of higher peaks, one of which is Râs es-Sufsâfeh, the highest in this part of the mountain. A narrow fissure runs out northward from this basin towards the plain, through which the mountain may be ascended. Here a willow and two hawthorns were growing, with many shrubs; and in all this part of the mountains were great quantities of the fragrant plant *Ja'deh*, which the monks call hyssop. Here is a small chapel dedicated to the Virgin of the Zone. Near by we found a pair of horns of the Beden or Ibex, left behind perhaps by some hunter.

While the monks were here employed in lighting tapers and burning incense, we determined to scale the almost inaccessible peak of es-Sŭfsâfeh before us, in order to look out upon the plain, and judge for ourselves as to the adaptedness of this part of the mount to the circumstances of the Scriptural history. This cliff rises some five hundred feet above the basin; and the distance to the summit is more than half a mile. We first attempted to climb the side in a direct course; but found the rock so smooth and precipitous, that after some falls and more exposures, we were obliged to give it up, and clamber upwards along a steep ravine by a more northern and circuitous course. From the head of this ravine, we were able to climb around the face of the northern precipice and reach the top, along the deep hollows worn in the granite by the weather during the lapse of ages, which give to this part, as seen from below, the appearance of architectural ornament.

The extreme difficulty and even danger of the ascent, was well rewarded by the prospect that now opened before us. The whole plain er-Râhah lay spread out beneath our feet, with the adjacent Wadys and mountains; while Wady esh-Sheikh on the right, and the recess on the left, both connected with, and opening broadly from er-Râhah, presented an area which serves nearly to double that of the plain. Our conviction was strengthened, that here or on some one of the adjacent cliffs was the spot, where the Lord "descended in fire" and proclaimed the law. Here lay the plain where the whole congregation might be assembled; here was the mount that could be approached and touched, if not forbidden; and here the mountain brow, where alone the lightnings and the thick cloud would be visible, and the thunders and the voice of the trump be heard, when the Lord "came down in the sight of all the people upon Mount Sinai." We gave ourselves up to the impressions of the awful scene; and read with a feeling that will never be forgotten, the sublime account of the transaction and the commandments there promulgated, in the original words as recorded by the great Hebrew legislator.[8] . . .

Jerusalem.
Topography and Antiquities.

We enter here upon a more detailed description of the Holy City, and its remains of antiquity. In doing this, I must request the reader to bear in mind, that for the lapse of more than fifteen centuries, Jerusalem has been the abode not only of mistaken piety, but also of credulous superstition, not unmingled with pious fraud. During the second and third centuries after the Christian era, the city remained under heathen sway; and the Christian church existed there, if at all, only by sufferance. But when, in the beginning of the fourth century, Christianity became triumphant in the person of Constantine; and at his instigation, aided by the presence and zeal of his mother Helena, the first great attempt was made in A. D. 326, to fix and beautify the places connected with the crucifixion and resurrection of the Saviour; it then, almost as a matter of course, became a passion among the multitudes of priests and monks, who afterwards resorted to the Holy City, to trace out and assign the site of every event, however trivial or legendary, which could be brought into connection with the Scriptures or with pious tradition. The fourth century appears to have been particularly fruitful in the fixing of these localities, and in the dressing out of the traditions or rather legends, which were attached to them.[9] But the

[8] Exod. xix. 9-25. xx.1-21.
[9] The *Itinerarium Hierosol.* A. D. 333, mentions the palm-tree as still standing on the side of Mount Olivet, from which the people broke off branches to strew before Jesus. Cyrill also speaks of it in the same century; Cat. X. 19. The column to which Christ was bound and scourged, was already found; but the blood upon it is first mentioned by Jerome nearly a century afterwards. The *Coenaculum* connected with it was the work of a still later age; as we have already had occasion to remark. See p. 357, above.

invention of succeeding ages continued to build upon these foundations;[10] until, in the seventh century, the Muhammedan conquest and subsequent oppressions confined the attention of the Church more exclusively to the circumstances of her present distress; and drew off in part the minds of the clergy and monks from the contemplation and embellishment of Scriptural history. Thus the fabric of tradition was left to become fixed and stationary as to its main points; in much the same condition, indeed, in which it has come down to our day. The more fervid zeal of the ages of the crusades, only filled out and completed the fabric in minor particulars.[11]

It must be further borne in mind, that as these localities were assigned, and the traditions respecting them for the most part brought forward, by a credulous and unenlightened zeal, well meant, indeed, but not uninterested; so all the reports and accounts we have of the Holy City and its sacred places, have come to us from the same impure source. The fathers of the Church in Palestine, and their imitators the monks, were themselves for the most part not natives of the country. They knew in general little of its topography; and were unacquainted with the Aramaean, the vernacular language of the common people.[12] They have related only what was transmitted to them by their predecessors, also foreigners; or have given opinions of their own, adopted without critical inquiry and usually without much knowledge. The visitors of the Holy Land in the earlier

[10] Thus the traditions respecting the house of Caiaphas, Gethsemane, and various other sites, although slight traces of them are found quite early, appear to have been decked out with new circumstances, as centuries rolled on. In A. D. 870 the monk Bernard speaks of a church on the side of the Mount of Olives, on the spot where the Pharisees brought to Jesus the woman taken in adultery. In the church was preserved a marble tablet, with the writing which our Lord there wrote upon the ground! Itinerar. 13, in Acta Sanctor. Ord. Benedict. Saec. III. Pars II. p. 525.

[11] A multitude of the minor legends, such as those relating to the place where Peter's cock crew, the houses of the Rich Man and Lazarus, and the like, were probably the work of more modern times. Even the *Via dolorosa* seems to have been first got up during or after the times of the crusades; see above, p. 344.

[12] Though the Greek language was understood and spoken by the inhabitants in general, yet there is reason to believe that the real mother-tongue of the common people was still the Aramaean. Origen and Jerome appear to have been the only fathers in Palestine who understood Hebrew. The latter, who died in Palestine A. D. 420, made it a particular study, in order to translate the Bible. He mentions the Punic dialect, by which he probably means the Phoenician, as a spoken language; Quaest. ad Gen. xxxvi. 24 ad voce [Yamin]. See Gesenius *Script. et Linguae Phoenic. Monumenta* pp. 331, 337. In his Comm. in Esa. xix. 18, Jerome also speaks expressly of a *"lingua Canantide, quae inter Aegyptian et Hebraeam media est et Hebraeae magna ex parte confinis."* Various other circumstances go also to show the long continuance of the Aramaean among the common people. The subject is worthy of a more particular investigation than has yet been bestowed upon it.

centuries, as well as the crusaders, all went thither in the character of pilgrims; and looked upon Jerusalem and its environs, and upon the land, only through the medium of the traditions of the Church. And since the time of the crusades, from the fourteenth century onwards to the present day, all travellers, whether pilgrims or visitors, have usually taken up their abode in Jerusalem in the convents; and have beheld the city only through the eyes of their monastic entertainers. European visitors, in particular, have ever lodged, and still lodge, almost exclusively, in the Latin convent; and the Latin monks have in general been their sole guides.

In this way and from all these causes, there has been grafted upon Jerusalem and the Holy Land a vast mass of tradition, foreign in its source and doubtful in its character; which has flourished luxuriantly and spread itself out widely over the western world. Palestine, the Holy City, and its sacred places, have been again and again portrayed according to the topography of the monks; and according to them alone. Whether travellers were Catholics or Protestants, has made little difference. All have drawn their information from the great storehouse of the convents; and, with few exceptions, all report it apparently with like faith, though with various fidelity. In looking through the long series of descriptions, which have been given of Jerusalem by the many travellers since the fourteenth century, it is curious to observe, how very slightly the accounts differ in their topographical and traditional details. There are indeed occasional discrepancies in minor points; though very few of the travellers have ventured to depart from the general authority of their monastic guides. Or even if they sometimes venture to call in question the value of this whole mass of tradition; yet they nevertheless repeat in like manner the stories of the convents; or at least give nothing better in their place.[13]

Whoever has had occasion to look into these matters for himself, will not be slow to admit, that the views here expressed are in no degree overcharged. It follows from them,—and this is the point to which I would particularly direct the reader's attention,—that *all ecclesiastical tradition respecting the ancient places in and around Jerusalem and throughout Palestine, is of no value, except so far as it is supported by circumstances known to us from the Scriptures*

---

[13] Even Maundrell, shrewd and accurate as he is elsewhere, gives in Jerusalem little more than what he heard from the monks. Of other travellers, Rauwolf was one of the most independent; and the accounts of Cotovicus (Kootwyk) sometimes vary from the usual form. The independence of Dr. Clarke is sufficiently manifest; but it led him over into an opposite extreme of extravagant hypothesis.

or from other contemporary testimony. The Thus one of the very earliest traditions on record, that which points out the place of our Lord's ascension on the summit of the Mount of Olives, and which certainly existed in the third century, long before the visit of Helena, is obviously false; because it stands in contradiction to the Scriptural account, which relates that Christ led out his disciples "as far as to Bethany," and there ascended from them into heaven.[14] On the other hand, I would not venture to disturb the traditional location of Rachel's grave on the way towards Bethlehem; for although this is first mentioned by the *Itin. Hieros.* and by Jerome in the fourth century, yet the Scriptural narrative necessarily limits the spot to that vicinity.[15]

On the same general principle, that important work the *Onomasticon*, the production of the successive labours of Eusebius and Jerome, which gives the names and describes the situation of places in the Holy Land, can be regarded in an historical respect, only as a record of the traditions current in their day. The names thus preserved are of the highest importance; but the value of the traditions connected with them, must be proved in the same manner as all others; although in general they were then far less corrupted than in the lapse of subsequent centuries.

The preceding remarks apply more particularly to Jerusalem, and to those parts of Palestine with which the fathers of the Church and the hosts of monks have chiefly occupied themselves. But there is in Palestine another kind of tradition, with which the monasteries have had nothing to do; and of which they have apparently in every age known little or nothing, I mean, *the preservation of the ancient names of places among the common people.* This is a truly national and native tradition; not derived in any degree from the influence of foreign convents or masters; but drawn in by the peasant with his mother's milk, and deeply seated in the genius of the Semitic languages. The Hebrew names of places continued current in their Aramaean form long after the times of the New Testament; and maintained themselves in the mouths of the common people, in spite of the efforts made by Greeks and Romans to supplant them by others derived from their own tongues.[16] After the Muhammedan conquest, when the

[14]Luke xxiv. 50, 51. Compare Acts i. 12, where it is only said, that the disciples *returned* from Mount Olivet; not that Christ ascended from it.—the tradition alluded to in the text is mentioned by Eusebius, Demonstr. Evang. VI. 18. p. 288. Col. Agr. This work, according to Valesius, was written about A. D. 315, ten years or more before the visit of Helena to Palestine. De Vit. et. Script. Euseb.

Aramaean language gradually gave place to the kindred Arabic, the proper names of places, which the Greeks could never bend to their orthography, found here a ready entrance; and have thus lived on upon the lips of the Arabs, whether Christian or Muslim, townsmen or Bedawîn, even unto our own day, almost in the same form in which they have also been transmitted to us in the Hebrew Scriptures.[17]

The nature of the long series of foreign tradition has sometimes been recognised and lamented by travellers and others; while that of the native Arab population has been for the most part overlooked, and its existence almost unknown.[18] Travellers have in general been ignorant of the Arabic language, and unable to communicate with the common people except through the medium of illiterate interpreters; they have mostly followed only beaten paths, where monkish tradition had already marked out all the localities they sought; and in this way few have ever thought of seeking for information among the Arab peasantry. Yet the example of Seetzen and Burckhardt in the countries East of the Jordan might have pointed out a better course; and the multitude of ancient names which they found still current in those regions, where monastic influence had more rarely penetrated, might have stimulated to like researches in western Palestine. Yet this had never been done; and in consequence of this neglect, and of the circumstances alluded to above, it had become a singular, though notorious fact, that notwithstanding the multitude of travellers who have swarmed through Palestine, the countries East of the Jordan were in many respects more accurately and distinctly known, than those upon the West.

[15]Gen. xxxv. 16—20. See above, pp. 322, 323.
[16]It is sufficient to mention here the sounding names Diospolis, Nicopolis, Ptolemais, and Antipatris, which have perished for centuries; while the more ancient ones which they were intended to supplant, are still current among the people, Ludd (Lydda), 'Amwâs (Emmaus), 'Akka, and Kefr Sâba. Yet a few Greek names thus imposed have maintained themselves instead of the ancient ones; as Nabulus (Neapolis) for Shechem, and Sebŭstieh (Sebaste) for Samaria.
[17]The Semitic letter *'Ain* in particular, so unpronounceable by other nations, has a remarkable tenacity. Of the very many Hebrew names containing this letter, that still survive in Arabic, our lists exhibit only two or three in which it has been dropped; and perhaps none in which it has been exchanged for another letter.
[18]It may perhaps be asked, whether there does not exist a Jewish tradition, which would also be trustworthy? Not in respect to Jerusalem itself; for the Jews for centuries could approach the Holy City only to weep over it; see p. 350, above. In other parts of Palestine, a regular Jewish tradition could not well be different from that handed down among the common people. Their early written accounts, as is well known, are not less legendary than those of the Christians.

In view of this state of things, we early adopted two general principles, by which to govern ourselves in our examination of the Holy Land. The *first* was, to avoid as far as possible all contact with the convents and the authority of the monks; to examine everywhere for ourselves with the Scriptures in our hands; and to apply for information solely to the native Arab population. The *second* was, to leave as much as possible the beaten track, and direct our journies and researches to those portions of the country which had been least visited. By acting upon these two principles, we were able to arrive at many results that to us were new and unexpected; and it is these results alone, which give a value (if any it have) to the present work.

3. The Land Illumines the Bible

While many teachers of the Bible, such as Robinson, engaged in serious scholarly research in the Holy Land, others used their experiences there to enrich and enliven their biblical teaching and exegetical work. Horatio B. Hackett (1808-75), a graduate of Amherst College and Andover Theological Seminary, where he studied under Edward Robinson, was ordained a Baptist minister and taught at Brown University, first in the field of Latin and German languages, then as professor of Hebrew literature. He then served many years (1839-68) as professor of biblical literature and interpretation at the Newton Theological Institute in Massachusetts. In 1852 he traveled in the Holy Land, and wrote a well-received book showing how acquaintance with the land illumined the message of the Bible. There were many books of that type, not all of them written by persons as well-prepared as Hackett, whose book went into a second edition.

Source; Horatio B. Hackett, *Illustrations of Scripture: Suggested by a Tour through the Holy Land* (Boston: William Heath, 1857), pp. 73-75, 171-74.

Praying on the House-top.

The roofs of the larger houses have usually a wall or balustrade around them, three or four feet high; so that a person there, while he has a view of surrounding objects, does not expose himself necessarily to the observation of others. Without considering this fact, it might strike one that the apostle Peter hardly acted in the spirit of the Saviour's precept (Matthew 6, 6), in repairing to the house-top for the performance of his devotions. See Acts 10, 9, sq. The roof in this instance, however, may have had a protection like that mentioned above, and the apostle may have chosen this retreat because he could be secure there both from interruption and from public notice. Indeed, at Jaffa, the ancient Joppa, where Peter was residing at the time of his vision on the house-top, I observed houses, furnished with a wall around the roof, within which a person could sit or kneel, without any exposure to the view of others, whether on the adjacent houses or in the streets. At Jerusalem, I entered the house of a Jew early one morning, and found a member of the family, sitting secluded and alone on one of the lower roofs, engaged in reading the Scriptures and offering his prayers.

The Mahommedans, it is true, make no scruple about performing their religious duties in public,—they desire rather than shun the observation of others; and we know that the Jews of old were ever prone to the same ostentation. But our Lord enjoined a different rule. His direction was: "When thou prayest, enter into thy closet, and when thou hast shut the door, pray to thy Father in secret, and thy Father which seeth in secret shall reward thee openly."

Dwelling on the House-top.

On the roof of the house in which I lodged at Damascus were chambers and rooms along the side and at the corners of the open space or terrace, which constitutes often a sort of upper story. I observed the same thing in connection with other houses. At Deburieh, a little village at the foot of Mount Tabor, probably the Daberath of the Old Testament (Joshua 19, 12), I noticed small booths, made of the branches and leaves of trees, on some of the roofs. Peter exclaimed at the time of the transfiguration: "It is good for us to be here; and let us make three tabernacles" or booths; "one for thee, and one for Moses, and one for Elias." (Matthew 17, 4.) As I was then approaching Tabor, the reputed (though I suppose not the actual) scene of that event, it was certainly striking, at least, as a coincidence with the subject of my thoughts at the moment, to see those booths in such a place.

Pococke, who spent a night at Tiberias, says: "We supped on the top of the house, for coolness, according to their custom, and lodged there likewise, in a sort of closet about eight feet square, of wicker-work, plastered round toward the bottom, but without any door." Such places, though very agreeable as a retreat from the sun in summer, and cooler than the interior of the house, would be very undesirable as a constant abode, especially in the rainy season and during the winter. Any rooms so exposed as those on the roof, and comparatively so narrow and confined, would be inferior to the lower and ordinary apartments of the house. To such places of retreat on the roof we may suppose the proverb to refer which says: "Better to dwell in the corner of the house-top than with a brawling woman in a wide house," (Proverbs 21, 9.) . . .

Chapter Five.
Geographical Accuracy of the Bible.

Under this title I propose to mention some instances in which the observations of the traveler in Palestine enable him to verify the accuracy of the sacred writers in the geographical notices and local allusions which occur on almost every page of the Bible. The subject is an extensive one, and admits of a limited illustration only within the compass of a work like the present. I shall restrict myself to a few examples of an incidental character, which stand in some special relation to my own journey.

Value of Such Accuracy

Before entering on my immediate object here, I would premise a remark or two respecting the value of this agreement between the Scriptures and the geography of the holy land, as a testimony to the truth of the Bible. Regarded in the light of such testimony, it has both a negative and a positive side. It not only frees the Bible from a class of objections which might be and have been urged against its claims to veracity, but, in so far as the agreement can be shown to be obviously unstudied, incidental, it furnishes a direct proof of the truthful character of the sacred Word.

The following supposition will illustrate this statement: We read in the book of Genesis that when Sodom and Gomorrah were destroyed by fire from heaven, Abraham was dwelling in his tent by the oaks of Mamre, near Hebron (Genesis 18, 1). On the morning after that awful catastrophe, it is said that "he looked toward" the site of those cities, "and all the land of the plain, and beheld, and lo, the smoke of the country went up as the smoke of a furnace" (Genesis 19, 28). Suppose travelers now had returned from the East, saying that the region of the Dead Sea is not visible from the neighborhood of Hebron, and that Abraham, therefore, could never have seen any rising smoke from that position, what a shock would this give to our confidence in the Bible! Every one feels that such a representation, if true, would encumber the Scriptures with a serious difficulty. If such errors are to be found in them, if the writers betray such ignorance of the relative situation of the places which they mention, they would incur the suspicion of having recorded not facts but inventions of their own, or mythic traditions in which they could no longer distinguish the true and the false from each other. If convicted of mistakes here, who could resist the impression that they may be fallible also as religious teachers, and thus forfeit the character from which they claim their authority over the faith and consciences of men? Hence, to show that objections of this nature have no proper foundation subserves a two-fold purpose; it turns back one of the weapons with which opposers have assailed the truth of the Scriptures, and, at the same time, strengthens our confidence in them as authentic, reliable, and capable of receiving fresh confirmation from the results of all true progress in investigation and knowledge.

I presented just now an imaginary case, for the purpose of illustration. I return to that to say that the geography of the Pentateuch, so far from being involved in any contradiction by what is said of Abraham on the occasion referred to, is confirmed entirely by the testimony of eye-witnesses. From the height which overlooks Hebron, where Abraham stood, as he beheld the proof that the guilty cities had perished, the observer at the present day has an extensive view spread out before him towards the Dead Sea. The hills of Moab, sloping down towards that sea on the east, and a part of Idumea, are all in sight. A cloud of smoke rising from the plain would be visible to a person at Hebron now, and could have been, therefore, to Abraham, as he looked toward Sodom on the morning after its destruction by Jehovah.

I pass now from these preliminary remarks to the proper subject of this chapter of the book.

Notice of Bethel

I spent the night of the twenty-eighth of April at Beitin, the Bethel, in Jacob's history, where he saw the vision of the ladder, with the angels ascending and descending upon it. This village is about twelve miles north of Jerusalem. A brief notice is due to a place of so much interest. The village now there, which has succeeded to the ancient one, stands on the declivity of a hill which slopes towards the south. The highway which led from Judea to Galilee runs a little to the west, and a narrow valley, extremely fertile, lies on the east. Bethel is first mentioned in Genesis 12, 8.

As Abraham stopped there once and again in his pastoral migrations, we may infer that he found the country well adapted to grazing purposes. It answers to that description still. I do not recollect to have seen anywhere so many herds of cattle, and of such fine appearance, as I saw in this particular region. The basin of an immense reservoir still remains at the foot of the hill; the southern wall of which is quite perfect, though the other parts are more or less broken or have disappeared.* No one can see this ruin, and doubt that it belongs to an early Hebrew age; for the size and peculiar shape of the stones afford decisive proof of such an origin. A small pool of water was standing at the east end of the reservoir, in which the frogs were croaking in a lively manner. Two living springs, also, issue from the ground, to which females from the village came down, from time to time, and filled their pitchers. The other ruins there are of a mixed character. Some have thought that they could distinguish among them the remains of churches and military towers built by the crusaders, as well as single stones and heaps of rubbish, which may date back to Jewish times.

---

*The dimensions of the tank are given as three hundred and fourteen feet in length, and two hundred and seventeen feet in breadth.

4. A Minister on Pilgrimage Interprets the Bible

Not all of those who came to the Holy Land and engaged in study of the Bible and its sites were professional scholars of the scriptures. Many were pastors of congregations, as was Harry Emerson Fosdick (1878–1969), who in the 1920s was the minister of the Park Avenue Baptist Church, which later was moved to a towering new edifice on New York's Morningside Heights and was reconstituted as the Riverside Church. A lifelong student and teacher of the Bible, Fosdick wrote (among many books) The Modern Use of the Bible (1924) and A Guide to Understanding the Bible (1938). In his own lengthy journey to the Holy Land in 1926, he was impressed by the way a study of the stage on which the biblical dramas had been played illumined a contemporary reading of the Scriptures. Much of the book that grew out of his pilgrimage is a commentary on biblical passages in the light of his knowledge of their sites. The book was very widely read; it was reprinted four times soon after initial publication, and was reissued in 1935, 1949, and 1977.

Source: Harry Emerson Fosdick, *A Pilgrimage to Palestine* (New York: Macmillan Co., 1927; reprinted by Arno Press, 1977), pp. 9–19.

Another impression immediately made upon the visitor is that the land is small. How tiny and compact it is, no description, however vivid, is likely to make clear to one who has not been there. Many factors encourage one's imagination of a larger country, even though one has memorized the statistics of distances and acreage. For one thing, our Bible-school maps naturally have made Palestine huge and central, with Egypt and Assyria hanging on the edge; for another, our modern life moves in continental areas and does business on a vast scale, so that where much has happened, as in Palestine, one instinctively imagines for it a large setting. From Dan to Beersheba, therefore, has come to sound like a long way; as a matter of fact, it is about 150 miles, and in a day one can traverse the whole length of Palestine in an automobile. The Mediterranean and the Dead Sea are barely fifty miles apart; and as one moves north the distance narrows until the Sea of Galilee is little over twenty-five miles from the Bay of Acre.

In comparison, therefore, with the spaces in which Western life habitually moves, the littleness of the Holy Land is difficult to picture. The state of Connecticut, with an area of 4965 square miles, is one of the smallest in the United States, and yet nearly all the events narrated in the Old Testament happened within an area no larger. Such comparisons, however, fail utterly to explain why Palestine feels so small to the visitor. Connecticut is comparatively flat; little though it is, you cannot see from one end to the other; but Palestine is one of the most dramatically broken countries in the world and there are many points of vantage from which one can practically see all over it. Not only is it small; it feels even smaller than it is.

Jordan rises in the fountains of the north as high as 1700 feet above the sea, born from the snows of Hermon and Lebanon, and, flowing down through the Waters of Merom and the Sea of Galilee, empties at last, nearly 1300 feet below sea-level, into the Dead Sea. That gorge of Jordan, one of the natural marvels of the world, extends from the latitude of Jerusalem on the south to lofty Hermon, which lies outside the northern boundaries of Palestine. But I well remember walking the shores of the Dead Sea, where the Jordan ends, and watching the noble snow-capped peak of Hermon, at whose base the Jordan rises. That is why Palestine seems small; one can see all over it.

When, therefore, the Bible tells us that from Mount Nebo's top Moses was shown the whole of the Promised Land, there is no exaggeration about it. Mount Nebo towers 4000 feet above the very spot on the Dead Sea shore from which I could see Hermon, and from that altitude the eye still can sweep the whole length of Palestine.

A trip to Neby Samwil helps to make clear this dramatic visibility of the Holy Land. The mountain stands nearly 3000 feet high, six miles northwest of Jerusalem, and two and a half hours on donkeys brought us, as comfortably as donkeys permit, to its summit. It used to be considered the site of Mizpah, where Samuel judged Israel,[1] and the reputed tomb of Samuel, a Moslem shrine, still is here. Here the medieval pilgrims caught their first view of the Holy City and called the spot the Mount of Joy. Here Richard the Lion-Hearted, forced to turn back from capturing the city by the disaffection of his allies, refused to look upon the sacred place which he could not seize. The view is glorious. With one turn of the head we could see the whole breadth of Palestine, fifty miles, from Jaffa to the Dead Sea, and beyond that into Moab. To the west the Mediterranean shone clear on the horizon and, moving eastward, the glance swept over the coastal plain with its palm trees and orange groves; then over the Shephelah hills, the old battleground of the Philistines, with their wheat fields and olive trees; then up the bare, rocky ridge of Judea, 2500 feet above the sea, with Jerusalem close at hand and Bethlehem beyond. Then came the abrupt drop into the wilderness of Judea with its ghastly, spectral aspect as of a lunar landscape, until, beyond the abyss of the Dead Sea,

---

[1] I Samuel 7:6.

Moab lifted its great plateau three to four thousand feet from the Dead Sea level, marking the eastern horizon with its towering wall.

From more than one height one thus can take in Palestine at a glance, with its amazing diversity, its unparalleled associations of history and sentiment, compact in a small compass.

The littleness of the land, accentuated by its brokenness and wide visibility, adds light and interest to many a narrative in the Bible. When, in the story of Ruth, Naomi and her family in famine time moved from Bethlehem to Moab, I used to think they traveled a long way.[2] As a matter of fact, Moab can be seen from Bethlehem, the most conspicuous element in the eastern landscape, lifting its towering plateau from the Dead Sea gorge. Naomi went thirty miles to Moab, and Ruth the Moabitess, who came back with her, had often seen Bethlehem from her native hills.

I used to think that when Hannah, who lived at Ramah, took her son Samuel to Shiloh and left him there with Eli, visiting him once a year,[3] she was putting a great distance between them. It was really fifteen miles. One walks the heights about Jerusalem and looks down into the Philistine country as David must have done when he was king. Those chief enemies of his in Ekron and Gath were barely twenty-five miles distant. And when the Master, driven from Nazareth, went to Capernaum to make that the center of his ministry,[4] he walked some twenty miles across the hills. The modern lord of automobiles and airplanes has to readjust his idea of distances to fit this little land.

V

A further impression sure to be made upon one who sees Palestine is its extraordinary diversity. Little as it is, there are as many kinds of climate and landscape there as one could expect to find in a whole continent. That one may swelter in the torrid heat of the Dead Sea while he looks at snow-crowned Hermon is typical. If a traveler starts at Beersheba and moves north along the spinal ridge of Palestine, he will begin on the border of a fiery desert, on portions of which rain never falls, and he will end among the pines and snows of Anti-Lebanon. On that short route—a possible day's trip in an automobile—he will have climbed from a parched

[2] Ruth 1:1-2.
[3] I Samuel 1:19-28 and 2:18-19.
[4] Luke 4:16-31.

wilderness to the cool ridge on which Jerusalem stands, where rains fall in the spring and the snows sometimes lie thick in winter. From that temperate height he will have looked on one side into the blazing, barren gorge of the Dead Sea and on the other into the wheat fields of the moderate Shephelah and the citron groves and palm trees of the hot Philistine plain. As he moves north he will leave the grim rocks of the Judean ridge for the more open and gracious country of Ephraim, with its green valleys, its fig trees and olive groves, and, crossing the plain of Esdraelon, will climb the central ridge again to pass through Galilee, with its oaks and sycamores, to the northern mountains, with their pines and cedars. Whatever else may be true of Palestine, it is never monotonous. In no other country in the world can you pass from thirteen hundred feet below sea-level to nine thousand feet above.

All this brokenness and diversity of the land is constantly reflected in the Bible, but I never felt it until I went there. When I read the Book now I am conscious that it was written in "a land of hills and valleys."[5] The central ridge is all cut up by valleys, slashed into on every side by wadies dry in summer but torrential when it rains. This separation of Palestine into innumerable small pockets helps to explain the tribal nature of its old inhabitants. Those many breeds of Canaanites, from Jebusites to Perizzites, were scattered among these numberless natural pigeonholes along the central ridge. The tribes of Israel also were sundered from each other by these abrupt, sharp boundaries, so that it took at least two centuries after their arrival to make one nation of them, and then this unity lasted at the utmost eighty-five years. It is the easiest country in the world, one traveler assures us, in which to lose oneself. Out of this chopped-up, irregular, diversified land the Bible came. In its pages mountains and valleys are the boundary lines—"from the valley of the Arnon unto mount Hermon"[6]— and the omnipresent wadies of the land enter constantly into the figurative language of the Book. Sometimes they mean what crossing the Rubicon means to us—"the valley of decision";[7] sometimes they are retreats where revelations are given—"the valley of vision";[8] sometimes they are symbols of difficulty—"the valley of the shadow of death";[9] and once, weary of so broken a country, a prophet foretells the happy time when "every valley

[5] Deuteronomy 11:11.
[6] Joshua 12:1.
[7] Joel 3:14.
[8] Isaiah 22:1.
[9] Psalm 23:4.

shall be exalted, and every mountain and hill shall be made low."[10]

To take only one illustration of the land's strange contrasts, we may go, as I have gone more than once, up from the Philistine plain over the Jerusalem ridge to the Judean wilderness upon the other side. It is a trip of hardly more than thirty-five miles, but it presents an astonishing antithesis. The plain reminds one of southern California with its verdant fertility. Its oranges cannot be surpassed; its grain fields are fruitful, and in the season of its beauty even a Westerner will reecho the prophet's praise for the excellency of Sharon. Then in an hour one has climbed a few hundred feet, has passed by the walls of Jerusalem, skirted the flank of Olivet, driven through traditional Bethany, and is plunging down that amazing fourteen miles through the wilderness of Judea toward the Dead Sea. Every vestige of life has vanished except, in the springtime, a few brilliant flowers—"a root out of a dry ground,"[11] as Isaiah said—and a sparse growth of thin weeds, like down on a bald head. By June even this has gone and all is dead, dry, yellow rock and earth—a landscape, I imagine, like the moon, if one could see it at close range.

Somewhere into this arid waste, this weird desolation, slashed by barren wadies and baked in merciless heat, the Master went when he was tempted,[12] and down through this wilderness from Jerusalem to Jericho the victim in the Master's parable was traveling when he fell among thieves.[13] Even yet jackals and hyenas roam here, and many a night I have heard the yelping of jackal bands that had come up from the wilderness to scavenge under the wall of Jerusalem.

When Mark says that the Master during his temptation in the wilderness was "with the wild beasts,"[14] he is speaking literally. Lions and bears are familiar figures in the Bible and they lived in the copses beside Jordan and in this wilderness which leads up from it to the ridge. Here prowled the lion and the bear that David, the shepherd lad, slew;[15] and up from here came the lion that Benaiah caught and killed in a pit on a snowy day.[16] "Where else than in Palestine," exclaims one commentator, "could lions and snow thus come together?"

[10] Isaiah 40-4.
[11] Isaiah 53:2.
[12] Matthew 4:1-11.
[13] Luke 10:29-35.
[14] Mark 1:13.
[15] I Samuel 17:34-35.
[16] II Samuel 23:20.

Such wild life was known in the wilderness well on into the Christian era. We hear of no lions there after the crusades. In Medeba, an ancient town of Moab, celebrated in the taunt-song which the early Hebrews chanted against their fallen foes,

> . . . we ravaged till war's fire
> was blown to Medeba,[17]

a large, mosaic map of Palestine was recently uncovered in the floor of an old church. The map was made in the fifth century A.D. and has already settled more than one disputed site for the archeologists. It is a quaint, old-fashioned map with huge fish in the rivers to show that they are rivers and huge ships on the sea to show that it is sea, and up from the thicket of Jordan, through the wilderness, we could discern in the mosaic a lion chasing a stag.

Only the year before our visit two students, who should have known better, figuring that the distance from Jericho to Mar Saba through the wilderness was only a few miles, started off across the waterless, trackless waste. The distance was short as the bee flies, but before they had well started they were as lost as compassless sailors in a thick fog. The Bedouin found one of them unconscious and brought him to Jerusalem. All that was found of the other was a few bones and buttons in a jackal's den. And all this below the very gates of Jerusalem and within a few miles of orange groves as lovely as earth can boast!

Only one important qualification can I think of to the endless variety of Palestine: the Great Sea is always a stranger, alien to the life of the land. In Greece the sea is everywhere intimate and alluring: in numberless bays and estuaries of an infinitely broken coast it beckons and invites, and sprinkles its islands like stepping stones across the Aegean to tempt even landsmen to seamanship. But in Palestine the sea is always distant, strange, foreign. Long ago a psalmist stood on the Judean ridge and, looking westward, sang,

> Yonder the sea lies, vast and broad,
>   with its countless swarms,
>   with creatures small and great,
>   with fleets of the nautilus,
>   with leviathan at his play.[18]

[17] Numbers 21:30 M.
[18] Psalm 104:25-26 M.

Always to the Jews the sea is thus a marvel, not a neighbor; they gaze from afar upon it but they do not sail it; and whenever the test of choice comes they still are Bedouin of the desert and not seamen.

Nor is the reason difficult to understand. Opposite Judea and Samaria there is not a harbor on the seacoast worthy of the name—only a long, straight, inhospitable lee shore with the prevailing southwest winds blowing in upon it. No maritime people ever could come from such a coast or ever did come. When, therefore, in the old allegory, Jonah flees from God by way of the sea to distant Tarshish,[19] perhaps in Spain, that is as desperate a venture as he could try, and when, in the prophets, the vision of God's kingdom becomes so comprehensive that "the isles shall wait for his law,"[20] that is the Jews' widest imagination of a universal reign.

Amazingly varied the Holy Land is for so small a country, but there is one limitation—the sea, while in the picture, is not of it. The Jew was a landsman.

[19]Jonah 1:3.
[20]Isaiah 42:4.

5. The American School of Oriental Research in Jerusalem

Throughout the twentieth century, many American students have had an opportunity to study at this institution, and many professors have taught there and cooperated in its extensive programs of archaeological research. Others centered their activity at a sister school in Baghdad, founded in 1921. The schools developed an ecumenical outreach, as Catholic and Jewish scholars and institutions cooperated in the work.

The July 7, 1929 issue of the New York Times *carried an informative description of the school in Jerusalem written by the Jerusalem correspondent, Joseph M. Levy, which was reprinted in the schools'* Bulletin. *The attitudes of many Americans toward the Holy Land were considerably influenced by the experiences of those who had been related to the ASOR and who wrote articles and books based on what they saw and did there.*

Source: "The 'New York Times' Correspondent Describes the School in Jerusalem," *Bulletin of the American Schools of Oriental Research* 35 (October 1929):18–21.

Jerusalem, June 4—The 1929 term of the American School of Oriental Research in Jerusalem has ended. The many American students, a large majority of whom are young ministers and rabbis, have practically all departed for home. The ending of this term marks the close of another successful year in the history of the school, which, although devoted mostly to archaeological work throughout the Near East, is also an institution for biblical research, receiving its support through the coöperation of Catholics, Protestants and Jews, both liberals and Fundamentalists.

To one who reads and hears constantly about the bitter strife between different religions and sects, and between conservative and liberal members of each sect, the very existence of such an institution may seem incredible. Yet such an American institution is now approaching its thirtieth anniversary, after a history unmarred by a single dispute of a religious nature.

The school was founded in 1900 for the purpose of conducting research and giving instruction in the archaeology, geography and history of Palestine in Bible times. It is supported mainly by annual contributions from more than fifty different American and Canadian institutions. Among them are universities like Harvard, Yale, Princeton, Pennsylvania, and Chicago, and theological seminaries of many different denominations. The Catholic University of America and the four leading Jewish rabbinical seminaries are also among the contributing institutions. The president of the board of trustees is Professor J. A. Montgomery of the University of

Pennsylvania; two of the trustees are Jews and one is a Catholic.

From the start, inter-religious cooperation has been stressed. Among the former directors and annual professors have been such eminent scholars as Torrey of Yale, Lyon of Harvard, McCurdy of Toronto, Montgomery of Pennsylvania, President Brown of Union Theological Seminary, Gottheil of Columbia and Margolis of Dropsie College.

The present director of the school, Dr. W. F. Albright, has just completed ten years of service at Jerusalem and has been called to Johns Hopkins University to become the head of the Department of Semitics there, following the late Paul Haupt. Dr. Albright intends to continue his archaeological work in Palestine, coming at regular intervals from America for that purpose. During his directorship the American School has maintained very close relations with the European archaeological institutions in Jerusalem.

While connected with the school, the late Professor Clay of Yale University founded the Palestine Oriental Society, now a flourishing organization in its tenth year, with an excellent journal. The society meets four times a year, nearly always at the American School, and papers on Biblical and Palestinian topics are presented in various languages. This year the Director of Antiquities of the Palestine Government, Mr. Richmond, is president, while a French Dominican Father and an American archaeologist are vice presidents. An Anglican authority on Jewish literature is secretary, the head of the German Protestant Mission is treasurer, while the three directors are, respectively, an Arab physician, who is the leading authority on the folklore of Palestine; a French Dominican Father, and a Jewish rabbi, who is also an eminent authority on Palestinian topography. The American School is not only responsible for the creation of this society but has also played the chief part in maintaining it.

An interesting phase of the recent development of the school is the close relations established with Palestinian scholars, both Jewish and Arab. Thanks to the assistance given to a little group of Arabs interested in folklore, a great deal of the fast disappearing folklore of the country has been collected and published in the Journal of the Palestine Oriental Society. This folklore has great interest to students of the Bible, as well as to anthropologists.

The relations established with Jewish scholars have been particularly close. Dr. Albright frequently lectures before Jewish audiences in Hebrew on archaeological and Biblical topics. In the original plan for the Institute for Jewish Studies he was slated for the lectureship on Egyptology, and after the foundation of the Hebrew University he was twice invited to a chair in it, once for Egyptology, and once for Oriental archaeology.

Dr. Albright's place as director is being taken in July by Dean C. C. McCown of the Pacific School of Religion in Berkeley, Calif. Dean McCown has written extensively on comparative religion, the New Testament, Palestinian geography and folklore, and is well equipped to maintain the inter-religious and international character of the school. Every year some twenty young scholars, Christian and Jewish, return from the school in Jerusalem to disseminate in America the new international and interconfessional ideals of scholarship which they have learned to know in Jerusalem. With them they bring a first-hand knowledge of Palestine and its antiquities, which is of the greatest value in vivifying their teaching. They also bring ideals of scholarship and research which raise them above the narrow limitations of sect and denomination.

The primary task of the school is to advance the knowledge of the historic past of Palestine. The vast number of discoveries made under its auspices have thrown light on every phase of the history and geography of Palestine. In several expeditions evidence has been collected to prove that the earliest civilization of Palestine arose in the Jordan Valley, where there was once, before the time of Abraham, an elaborate system of irrigation. With the coming of the Hebrews the old civilization was destroyed, the irrigation works fell into ruin, and malaria came into the valley with the swamps which arose in consequence.

It was the American school which discovered the ruins of the great City of the Moon, on the Sea of Galilee, destroyed before the time of Abraham. In another expedition of the school ruins were found, southeast of the Dead Sea, which established the essential truth of the Biblical traditions of Sodom and Gomorrah. Other archaeological undertakings have thrown light on many different phases of Old and New Testament history, and have revolutionized our knowledge of the social and industrial life of ancient Palestine.

Four years ago the American School in Jerusalem moved into its present building, erected with money left by the late Dr. James B. Nies of Brooklyn in his will in memory of his wife, Jane Dows Nies. But the school is now in a precarious financial condition, since it does not possess an endowment, and is supported almost entirely by the annual contributions of its fifty-three supporting institutions. The American School in

Jerusalem is practically the only institution of its kind which is without an endowment, and its remarkable work has only been performed at the cost of the strictest economy and the utmost self-sacrifice on the part of the staff.

6. Albright and Palestinian Archaeology During the Mandate

American involvement in archaeological work in the Holy Land increased significantly in the 1920s and 1930s. Conditions under the British mandate were favorable for scholarly expeditions, and, as the following excerpt explains, some impressive new institutions concerned with Palestinian archaeology were founded. Immediately following World War I, strong leadership in the American School of Oriental Research in Jerusalem was provided by an industrious and prolific scholar, William Foxwell Albright (1891–1971). Born in Chile, the son of Methodist missionary parents, Albright graduated from Upper Iowa University and Johns Hopkins University, from which he received a Ph.D. in 1916. He served in Jerusalem as director of the ASOR through the 1920s and continued to be involved in its work during nearly thirty years as professor of Semitic languages at Johns Hopkins.

Albright's leadership was not only in the technical work of archaeological exploration; he was also an able interpreter of the work for lay audiences. He delivered the Richards lectures at the University of Virginia in 1931, from whose published version the following selections have been chosen, one summarizing developments in archaeology during the 1920s, the other commenting on a topic dear to many Americans—how archaeology informs biblical interpretation.

Source: William Foxwell Albright, *The Archaeology of Palestine and the Bible* (New York: Fleming H. Revell Co., 1932), pp. 13–18, 127–34.

Chapter I.
Recent Progress in Palestinian Archaeology

In the years since the close of the World War, there has been a striking revival of interest in archaeological research. It is not our purpose to investigate the ultimate causes of this movement, in which America shares with the European nations. In part it may be parallel to the triumphant emergence of romanticism in art and literature, after a long eclipse. Wearied of an intellectual life which culminated in the mechanistic philosophy of war years, people of culture have altered their point of view so as to admit humanistic factors. The study of man, his past and his present, has gained a new importance, which is now expressing itself in the steady increase of endowments and foundations devoted primarily to it. Compared to these obscure, but irresistible tendencies of the day, other factors in the increase of interest in archaeology are of minor importance. It is fortunate for archaeology that American men of wealth have devoted themselves so widely to the collection of archaeological objects; it is a happy coincidence that popular interest in the field was stimulated at so critical a period by the discovery of the tomb of Tut-ankh-aman. Yet events and tendencies like these are symptoms rather than causes.

Be that as it may, Biblical archaeology has not been by any means the last to profit by the tendency of the times. In fact, it may be said to have profited by an exceptionally favourable combination of circumstances: the establishment of the British mandatory, with a well-organized Department of Antiquities and a liberal Antiquities Ordinance; the active interest taken by Mr. John D. Rockefeller, Jr., which has led to the excavation of Megiddo and the foundation of a magnificent Palestine Museum; the inauguration of a broad policy of coöperation on the part of the American School of Oriental Research in Jerusalem, which has greatly stimulated the launching of minor enterprises. The fact that Palestine is now governed as a British colony means that public security is generally better than in Ottoman times, and that the need of bribery in dealing with officials is very greatly reduced. Even more important to the archaeologist is the presence of a certain number of men of high education and lofty ideals, which leavens the bureaucratic mass. The Department of Antiquities, supported by the international Archaeological Advisory Board, controls the scientific responsibility of the scholars and institutions which conduct the work of excavation, and prevents native exploitation of ancient remains as far as possible. The first Director of Antiquities, Professor John Garstang of the University of Liverpool, himself an archaeologist, directed several small excavations in person during his tenure of office. Since leaving the post, his interest in Palestine excavation has not flagged, but has shown itself in most fruitful researches and excavations, notably at Jericho. As a practical excavator, Garstang was able to understand the problems of the archaeologist and to sympathize with his difficulties. His assistance to excavators greatly eased their task, and is gratefully remembered by all who dug in Palestine between the years 1920 and 1926. In 1927 he was followed by E. T. Richmond, Esq., who had won his spurs in administration rather than in archaeology, though his work in the field of historical architecture and of Islamic art is of value. Shortly after Mr. Richmond's installation came the munificent Rockefeller gift of $2,000,000 for the establishment of a Palestine Museum of Archaeology in Jerusalem. The construction and organization of this museum could not have fallen into better hands than those of Mr. Richmond. The administrative skill of the latter is also responsible for the solid organization of the Department of Antiquities along the lines marked out by Professor Garstang.

The second of the three circumstances which, as we observed, have combined to advance the cause of Biblical archaeology in Palestine, is the attraction of Mr. Rockefeller's interest to archaeology by Professor J. H. Breasted. Starting as an Egyptologist, the latter achieved an eminence in his chosen field which has brought him more international recognition than has ever before been accorded an American Orientalist. It was not until then that he founded the Oriental Institute of the University of Chicago, for which he received, in 1919, an annual subvention from Mr. Rockefeller. Thanks to Breasted's remarkable capacity for organization, as well as to his equally unusual ability to interest laymen in archaeology, the Oriental Institute has continued to develop, with the aid of princely gifts from the Chicago Maecenas, until it is now the most elaborate organization of its kind in the world, without even a remote competitor. Biblical archaeology has benefited directly so far by the organization of the Megiddo excavation in 1925, followed in 1927 by the announcement of the gift for the Palestine Museum. This gift is divided into two parts: a million dollars for building, library, and equipment; a second million for endowment, since Palestine is much too poor to carry the operating expenses of so elaborate an institution without outside aid. It is expected that other enterprises will be launched by the Oriental Institute in Palestine and Syria during the coming years.[1]

Third in importance comes, we venture to maintain, the work of the American School in Jerusalem, which has directly stimulated the launching of a number of most productive minor undertakings, such as the excavations at Tell Beit Mirsim, Tell en-Nasbeh, Bethshemesh, and Gerasa, to mention only a few. In 1929 this institution, together with its sister school in Baghdad, received the promise of half a million dollars from the Rockefeller Foundation. Half of this sum is to be paid to the Schools, to enable them to carry on their work on a much more solid basis during the years 1930-36, and the other half will be given to them as an endowment, at the expiration of this period, provided that an equal sum is contributed from outside for this purpose. Practically all American Oriental archaeologists of standing, aside from the Egyptologists, are now directly or indirectly affiliated with the American Schools of Oriental Research. There can be no doubt that the further development of the Schools will greatly assist in the maintenance of high standards of archaeological research.[2] It will also help materially to prevent the formation of a most undesirable cleavage between field archaeologists and Oriental philogists, whose constant coöperation is essential to the progress of our research.

From this encouraging survey of the recent expansion and the future promise of the field of Palestinian archaeology, let us turn to consider its intrinsic possibilities. First we must sketch its history, for without historical perspective, or as the natural scientists are coming to say, without a four-dimensional treatment, it is impossible to comprehend the evolution and the present tendencies of any science. Our title for this lecture, "The Discovery of Ancient Palestine," is not thoughtlessly purloined from the domain of physical geography. On the contrary, we describe the real discovery of the unknown past of the Holy Land. Like all lands of the Near East, its present is so very different from the historical past, that it is quite impossible to obtain a correct idea of any phase of the latter from the unaided study of the former. Except for the work of the last century, and especially of the last generation, it would be impossible to reconstruct the ancient social, political, or religious history, material civilization, arts and crafts, etc., since our chief documentary source, the Bible, invariably requires archaeological elucidation before it becomes completely intelligible from any of these points of view.

The discovery of ancient Palestine is a two-fold task, which involves both surface exploration and excavation. The technique and methods employed by both types of archaeological work have improved immeasurably since the beginning of scientific exploration in 1838, and of excavation in 1851. This first phase came to a close with the beginning of scientific excavation in 1890. The second phase, which lasted until the outbreak of the War in 1914, was, as we shall see, a period of collection and publication of material, which was not dated or classified with sufficient accuracy to make it of much value to the historian. During the third phase, since the close of the War, scientific method in the archaeology of Palestine has improved so remarkably, and the amount of work accomplished has so increased that archaeological data which were quite meaningless now yield important historical information. The progress of the linguistic study of ancient scripts and languages, not one of which could be read a century ago, has made it possible for the trained scholar to decipher all inscriptions found in Palestine, though written in many different scripts and an even greater number of tongues. . . .

Chapter III.
The Bible In The Light Of Archaelogy.
The Bearing of Archaeology on Biblical Problems.

Archaeological research in Palestine and neighbouring lands during the past century has completely transformed our knowledge of the historical and literary background of the Bible. It no longer appears as an absolutely isolated monument of the past, as a phenomenon without relation to its environment. It now takes its place in a context which is becoming better known every year. Seen against the background of the ancient Near East, innumerable obscurities become clear, and we begin to comprehend the organic development of Hebrew society and culture. However, the uniqueness of the Bible, both as a masterpiece of literature and as a religious document, has not been lessened, and nothing tending to disturb the religious faith of Jew or Christian has been discovered.

As will be shown in the following pages, there has been a distinct gain to theology from this research. On the one hand, the excessive skepticism shown toward the Bible by important historical schools of the eighteenth and nineteenth centuries, certain phases of which still appear periodically, has been progressively discredited. Discovery after discovery has established the accuracy of innumerable details, and has brought increased recognition of the value of the Bible as a source of history. On the other hand, the theory of verbal inspiration—sometimes miscalled a doctrine—has been proved to be erroneous. The discovery that conceptions and practises evolve through many stages has led the leading Catholic and Protestant theologians to adopt a revised interpretation of the doctrine of progressive revelation, a line of defense behind which theology is secure from further encroachments on the part of the archaeologist and the historian.

The most practical way in which to illustrate the importance of archaeology for the better comprehension of the Bible is to select several outstanding problems of Hebrew history, and to discuss them in chronological order, in order to make their relation clearer. We shall, accordingly, choose the following topics for our discussions: the Age of the Patriarchs as described in Genesis; the Mosaic Law; the period of the Exile and the Restoration. It would hardly be advantageous, with the limited time at our disposal, to describe the innumerable archaeological confirmations of the historical record of Joshua, Judges, Samuel, and Kings. A very interesting and important theme is that which deals with the new light on the social and economic background of the prophetic movement of the eighth and seventh centuries, but since we must select, let us choose the topics listed above. As will be seen, they are all storm-centers in the long struggle between Biblical critics, and there is no general agreement among scholars as to the interpretation of our data. However, recent archaeological discoveries in Palestine and neighbouring lands speak with no uncertain voice, so that it is high time for the scholar who is in touch with them to express his views, even if they may sometimes appear rash.

The Age of the Patriarchs in the Light of Archaeology

The orthodox critical attitude toward the traditions of the Patriarchs was summed up by the gifted founder of this school, Julius Wellhausen, in the following words: "From the patriarchal narratives it is impossible to obtain any historical information with regard to the Patriarchs; we can only learn something about the time in which the stories about them were first told by the Israelite people. This later period, with all its essential and superficial characteristics, was unintentionally projected back into hoary antiquity, and is reflected there like a transfigured mirage."[1] In other words, the account given in Genesis of the life of the Patriarchs is a faithful picture of the life of Israelites at the time when this account was composed, *i.e.*, according to the view of the dominant critical school, in the ninth and the eighth centuries B.C. The nomadic touches were derived, it is supposed, from the life of the Arab nomads of the day—or perhaps from the life of the Judaean nomadic tribes of the Negeb. Practically all of the Old Testament scholars of standing in Europe and America held these or similar views until very recently. Now, however, the situation is changing with the greatest rapidity, since the theory of Wellhausen will not bear the test of archaeological examination.[2] The opposition to this theory began in the camp of Assyriology, where the gauntlet was thrown by Sayce, Hommel, and Winckler,[3] but the methods employed by these scholars were so fanciful, and the knowledge of ancient Palestine (apart from the Bible) which then existed was so slight, that they were not taken seriously by their antagonists.

As an illustration of the changing attitude, let me call attention to the recent brochure by Professor Böhl of Leyden, *Das Zeitalter Abrahams* (Leipzig, 1930).[4] In this little book, Böhl, a successor of Kuenen, Wellhausen's lieutenant, maintains the essential historicity of the Patriarchs, and closes with the words: "Just as the Homeric Age stands at the beginning of Greek history, so does the Age of the Patriarchs in Israelite. Through the mist of ages we greet the figure of Abraham, whom Christians, Jews, and Mohammedans reverence as a 'friend of God' and as the 'father of all who believe.'" Another illustration is the monograph by Professor Alt of Leipzig on *Der Gott der Väter* (Stuttgart, 1929), in which the brilliant author shows that the patriarchal religion, as described in Genesis, is not an artificial construction of priestly historians of a later day, but actually reflects pre-Mosaic conditions: "Abraham, Isaac, and Jacob remain on the other side of Moses; but the lines which lead from their gods to the God of Israel have become distinct."[5] Shades of Wellhausen and Kuenen!

In Genesis the Patriarchs are portrayed as semi-nomadic, *i.e.,* as devoting themselves partly to sheep-raising and cattle-breeding, and partly to agriculture. They are, moreover, represented as wandering slowly about the country, but as having definite bases, to which they invariably return. They always wander about the hill-country or the extreme north of the Negeb, never on the coastal plains or in the desert. Were this description of their life a late invention, we should have the greatest difficulty in finding an adequate explanation of its origin, since it does not agree at all with conditions in any part of Palestine in the Iron Age, to say nothing of Early Iron II. Wellhausen and his followers did not even recognize the difficulty, because of their ignorance of modern Palestine and adjoining lands. The Arabs of to-day distinguish sharply between *Fellāhîn*, "peasants," *'Arab*, "semi-nomadic Arabs," and *Bédū*, "nomads." All the Arabs who are entirely sedentary are called *fellāhîn*, even if they only remain in their village during two or three months of the year, as at Dūrā and Beit Feddjâr.[6] If, however, they live entirely, or almost entirely in tents, and yet do not move outside of their own restricted district, which they till regularly, they are *'Arab*, like the 'Azâzmeh around Beersheba, or the Ta'âmreh about Tekoa. True nomads, who despise agriculture, and preserve the noble traditions—and poverty—of the desert, like the 'Anezeh and the Ruwâlā, are called *Bédū, i.e.,* Bedouins. It is clear that the Patriarchs come under the category of *'Arab*. Yet they do not correspond exactly to the *'Arab*. Their scope of wandering, which extends from Mesopotamia through Syria into central and southern Palestine, is much greater, and they wander between fortified towns and districts occupied by a purely sedentary population, engaging in trade relations with the latter. In the Early Iron Age there was no true analogy, since the Kenites were a very highly specialized group.[7]

Here archaeology provides the necessary explanation. In the Middle and Late Bronze Ages the hill-country was still but sparsely peopled, and almost the entire sedentary population occupied the coastal plains, Esdraelon, and the Jordan Valley. The plains and broad valleys were dotted with towns, as shown by the innumerable mounds which remain to mark them. Occupation in these regions was considerably denser than it was in the Iron Age, or than it is to-day. A century ago the plains and the Jordan Valley were largely occupied by *'Arab*, while the sedentary population (outside of Gaza, Jaffa, Acre, etc.) was almost entirely in the hill-country—a curious reversal of conditions in the Bronze Age. The mountains of Palestine were then heavily forested on the watershed ridge and the western slopes, so that little space was left for agriculture. Moreover, cisterns had not then come into general use, so there were no settlements except where good springs were located just under a low hill, suitable for defense, with meadows or broader valleys near by, to ensure a supply of food. Between these fortified towns, most of which were situated on the watershed ridge or near it, there was ample room for semi-nomadic tribes, which have left abundant traces of their existence in cemeteries containing Middle and Late Bronze [Age] pottery, but too far from towns to have been employed by the sedentary population. In Genesis also we are told that the Patriarchs buried their dead in the Cave of Machpelah, following the customs of the settled inhabitants of the land. The Amarna Tablets call these semi-nomadic people the Khabiru, a name which is probably to be identified with Biblical "Hebrew."[8] The Khabiru correspond closely, at all events, to the Hebrews of the patriarchal period in many important respects; in their independence of towns, in their geographical localization in Palestine, in their warlike spirit. At least once we learn of a Canaanite coalition to resist their encroachments.

According to the Wellhausen school, the association of certain towns with the history of the Patriarchs is due simply to the fact that cult-legends relating to them were attached to these places in much later times. If we consider the situation in the light of the topographical and archaeological researches of the past few years, we will discover the interesting fact that practically every town mentioned in the narratives of the Patriarchs was in existence in the Middle Bronze Age. Examples are Shechem,[9] Bethel,[10] Ai,[11] Jerusalem (Salem),[12] Gerar,[13] Dothan,[14] Beersheba.[15] Aside from the case of the Cities of the Plain, which we shall take up presently, there is only Hebron whose existence at that time cannot be established archaeologically.[16] From its situation in an extremely fruitful and well-watered valley, there can be no reasonable doubt that Hebron was occupied at a very early date, especially since neighbouring cemeteries, plundered by the Arabs, have yielded a great many Middle Bronze [Age] remains.[17] If the patriarchal stories were first told as we have them in the Iron Age, we should expect to find references to Israelite settlements like Mizpah and Gibeah, etc., etc.

The story of the Cities of the Plain is still obscure in many respects. However, the tradition that the Plain of the Jordan, where these towns were located, was exceedingly fruitful and well peopled at the time of the first entrance of the Hebrews into the country, but that it was shortly afterwards abandoned, is absolutely in accord with the archaeological facts.

As recently as 1928 the famous ancient historian, Eduard Meyer, knowing nothing of the researches of the American School in the Jordan Valley, was able to say of this region in the fifteenth century B.C.:"Absolutely barren lay also the Jordan Valley south of Beth-shan and Pella, burning hot between the mountain walls on both sides, through which it cut its broad and deep way. . . . Here the attempt was never made to utilize the soil and to make it productive by systematic irrigation, as was done in the Nile Valley under essentially the same conditions(!)."[18] From about 1922 on, the writer has carried on explorations in the Jordan Valley, culminating in an expedition undertaken with the coöperation of Dr. M. G. Kyle in 1924, for the purpose of studying the archaeological remains of the southern Ghôr (Jordan Valley).[19] These researches and those of Père Mallon and other scholars[20] have proved that the most prosperous period of the history of this valley was in the Early Bronze Age, and that the density of its occupation gradually declined until it reached its lowest point in the Early Iron II, after the tenth century B.C.Except in the Turkish period (before the Jewish colonization began toward the end of the nineteenth century A.D.) this was the age of least occupation in the valley's history. Yet we are asked by some to believe that the traditions of its pristine fertility arose in the Iron Age!

APPENDIX

Notes on Chapter I

1. For the launching of the Oriental Institute and its original programme see Breasted, *Oriental Institute Communications* No. 1 (=AJSL 38, 233–328); for its subsequent development see especially the *General Circulars*. The most important publications for our purpose appear in two series: *Oriental Institute Communications*, a series of preliminary reports, in popular form; *Oriental Institute Publications*, which include definitive publications. There is now a steady stream of publications, all characterized by the highest standards of method and precision.

2. For the work of the Schools see the *Bulletin*, a quarterly describing in concise and popular fashion what the Schools are doing in the archaeological field; it is edited by the writer. More elaborate preliminary reports, as well as some definitive publications, appear in the *Annual* (Vol. I, 1920). Other series of publications have been launched, but do not, so far, touch our field so closely. For information one should write to Professor J. A. Montgomery, University of Pennsylvania, Philadelphia (president of the Schools), or to Professor Mary I. Hussey, Mount Holyoke College, South Hadley, Mass. (A dollar sent to Miss Hussey will secure a year's subscription to the *Bulletin*.) The present director of the School in Jerusalem is Professor Millar Burrows.

Notes On Chapter III

1. See Wellhausen, *Prolegomena*, 3rd ed., p. 331.

2. The change is particularly noticeable in Germany, where the growing opposition to Wellhausenism, though generally with full recognition of the importance of Wellhausen's own contribution, centers around the extremely influential school of Kittel. The latter gave expression to his point of view regarding Wellhausenism in the following pungent words, spoken in his address at the first German Alttestamentlertag, which was held at Leipzig in 1921 (ZAW 1921, 86): "Es fehlte dem Gebäude das Fundament, und es fehlten den Baumeistern die Massstäbe," *i.e.*, The structure (of the Wellhausen school) lacked a foundation, and the builders were without measuring rods.

3. Sayce and Hommel are neither strictly conservative, as is sometimes supposed; their views depart far enough at times from traditional lines.

Both are characterized by an originality which generally overshoots the mark, so that very few of their innumerable observations have stood the test of time. Winckler represents an entirely different point of view. He was the real founder of the astral-mythological or pan-Babylonian school, once very influential, but now almost extinct; Alfred Jeremias is the only active living exponent of it. Winckler, however, possessed marked philosophical ability, and he was the first to understand the nature of the oral transmission of history, and to recognize that it is quite possible for a given element to be history and folklore at the same time.

4. This brochure is the expanded form of his article in the new edition of the *Encyclopaedia Britannica*, Vol. I, p. 59 f.

5. *Op. cit.*, p. 73.

6. Beit Feddjâr is the village nearest the site of Tekoa, the home of Amos. It is interesting to note that a similar environment forced Amos to spend part of the year abroad as a hired labourer.

7. There is no reason to doubt the common view that the Kenites (*Qênîm* from *qain, qên,* "smith") were travelling coppersmiths, especially since their original home was in Sinai and Midian, where copper mines had been worked from the earliest times. While in some respects analogous to the modern gypsies (Nâwar or Zuṭṭ) of Palestine, as well as to the Ṣleib in Arabia (see especially Werner Pieper, *Le Monde Orientale*, Vol. 17 [1923], pp. 1-75), the social position of the Kenites was undoubtedly much superior. The smith enjoyed a much greater prestige then than now.

8. The Khabiru problem grows more complicated all the time. The material has been discussed recently by Jirku, *Die Wanderungen der Hebräer*, Leipzig, 1924, and by Landsberger, *Kleinasiatische Forschungen*, Vol. 1, pp. 321-34 (1929), among others. The writer's views are developed JBL 43, 389-92, and JAOS 48, 183-5; he agrees, quite independently, with Landsberger's view that the term *Khabiru* means "condottiere, condottieri." It is now probable that the word is an appellative, like its synonym *khabbatu,* "raider, bandit," as maintained by Landsberger. The way in which the Khabiru are described in the Amarna letters makes it probable that the same people are referred to in the broken Sethos stele of Beth-shan, line 10, where the name is spelled *'Apiru,* written with determinatives meaning "foreign warriors." Since the cuneiform orthography *Kha-BI-ru* may just as well be read *Khapiru* and Canaanite *'ain* is regularly transcribed *kh* in the Amarna tablets, it is difficult to avoid the conclusion that the true form of the name is *'Apiru.* Hebrew *'Eber,* for *'Ibr, 'Ipr* (which is derived from *'Apir* in the same way that late Canaanite *milk,* "king," is derived from older

malik, "prince") is then presumably a specifically Hebrew form with partial assimilation, as in the word *hopshî,* "peasant freeholder," for Canaanite (*awîl*) *khubshî,* "peasant (bound to the soil)," etc. The relation between the collective *'Ibr* and the gentilic *'Ibrî* is exactly that between *Khubshu* and *Hopshi.* The sense "condottiere" was early lost, and has left no trace in the classical Hebrew use of the name. Khabiru names mentioned in the cuneiform inscriptions belong to several languages, and there is no reason to believe that the designation was then peculiar to a single ethnic group. The form *'Apiru,* if correct, suggests a Canaanite or Amorite origin, and the name may have belonged originally (*i.e.,* in very early times) to some nomadic group like the Midianite tribe of the same name (Gen. 25:4). The writer expects to discuss this complicated subject elsewhere at length.

9. While the German excavations have not yet disclosed the building level of MB I, sherds from this period have been found in abundance in the lowest stratum. Shechem is mentioned in an Egyptian inscription of the nineteenth century B.C. (JPOS 8, 226 f.; 233).

10. See *Bulletin,* No. 29, p. 10.

11. The pottery of et-Tell (Ai) covers the latter part of EB, all MB (apparently), and the beginning of LB; cf. ZAW 1929, 12.

12. Cf. *Jewish Quarterly Review,* Vol. 21 (1930), 165 f.

13. See Petrie, *Gerar,* London, 1928, and Hempel, ZAW 1929, 63 f. Isolated Middle Bronze [Age] sherds were found in the excavation.

14. Middle Bronze [Age] sherds occur on the slopes of the mound.

15. Beersheba is not certain; the writer has not actually found any pottery antedating the Early Iron [Age] on Tell el-Imshash. Yet the mound is fairly high, and many of the mounds in the Negeb go back to the Middle Bronze [Age] or earlier, so an MB date for Beersheba must be considered probable.

16. On the hill er-Rumeideh, just above the town, are the cyclopaean walls of an ancient town, which apparently was never occupied, to judge from the absence of early pottery. The Bronze Age mound lies presumably under the modern town in the valley.

17. In the story of Judah (Gen. 38), the town of Adullam is mentioned. While this story may not belong to the primary patriarchal cycle, it is curious to find that Adullam was also occupied during the Age of the Patriarchs. On a visit to its site, modern Khirbet esh-Sheikh Madhkûr, with Garstang, in 1928, we picked up several characteristic sherds from the Middle Bronze [Age], both MB I and MB II, at the foot of the mound.

18. See *Geschichte des Altertums,* Vol. II, 1, 2nd ed., p. 96.
19. See *Bulletin,* No. 14; *Annual,* Vol. VI, pp. 56 ff.; Mallon in *Biblica,* Vol. 5, pp. 413–55. A very interesting popular account is given by Kyle in his book *Explorations at Sodom,* New York, 1928. The full report of our expedition is in course of preparation.
20. See especially *Biblica,* 1929, p. 95 ff., 21; ff.; 1930, p. 3 ff.

7. Ancient Sodom in the Light of Modern Research

A conspicuous example of the way American biblical scholars actively participated in archaeological exploration in the Holy Land is provided by Melvin Grove Kyle (1858-1933). He was born in Ohio, and educated at Muskingum College and Allegheny Theological Seminary, from which he graduated in 1885. A clergyman of the United Presbyterian Church, he began teaching at Xenia (later Pittsburgh) Theological Seminary in 1908, becoming professor of biblical theology and archaeology and serving as president for nearly a decade. He was lecturer at the American School of Oriental Research in 1921 and returned frequently for shorter periods until his death in 1933.

He led an expedition sponsored by Xenia in cooperation with the American School into the land of Moab to probe into the mysteries of the destruction of Sodom. Letters written on the trip appeared in various periodicals and finally in book form. The selections that follow describe the personnel of the expedition, stressing its interfaith aspects, and summarize some of the main conclusions of the expedition. A conservative theologically, Kyle sought to demonstrate the trustworthiness of the ancient documents of the Bible.

Source: Melvin Grove Kyle, *Explorations at Sodom: The Story of Ancient Sodom in the Light of Modern Research* (New York: Fleming H. Revell Co., 1928; reprinted by Arno Press, 1977), pp. 23-26, 122-30.

It was a most beautiful morning, February the fourteenth, on which we loaded our four Ford cars even to the mud-guards, said goodbye to loved ones as cheerfully as we could, and dashed off down the Jericho road on the way to the Land of Moab. A letter from a far-off friend the evening before had brought a story of answered prayer not surpassed since the days of Peter and Cornelius, and a sweet peace of faith so filled the soul as to banish all the lurid imaginings concerning the mysterious land to which we journeyed.

The Jericho road is too much a part of civilization, since the war times turned it into one of the finest highways of the world, to enter into an account of a journey to such an out-of-the-world place as the Cities of the Plain. So while we rush down, down, down, by the Apostles' Spring and the Good Samaritan Inn and the Brook Cherith, I will introduce the members of the staff organized for this expedition of Xenia Theological Seminary, in coöperation with the American School of Oriental Research at Jerusalem, that it may appear clearly that there was nothing sectarian in the expedition and that the strictly scientific character of the work may be assured. This, to the end that the results of the expedition may meet with acceptance in every part of the Biblical world.

The President of the staff was the President of Xenia Theological

Seminary, Saint Louis, Missouri, U.S.A., who happens to be a United Presbyterian. The director of field operations was Director Albright of the American School of Oriental Research at Jerusalem. Dr. Albright is a Methodist, the son of a South American missionary near Santiago, Chile. He received his university training at Johns Hopkins. He was appointed to his position, one of the most important in the archaeological world, because of his unusual qualifications as an archaeologist and philologist. Our geologist was Professor Alfred Day of Beirut College, Syria, a man of long years' experience in the land and thoroughly familiar with the geology of the particular region to which we were going, having made two or three previous expeditions into the same region for geological work.

The proto-archaeologist of the staff, the flint and old stone expert, was Père Mallon, a Jesuit priest, of Ratisbon, Jerusalem. He is a well-known specialist in this field of research with many years of experience in Bible lands. He aided also materially in furnishing out the expedition and in securing us accommodations at the Parish House in Kerak, whence this letter is written. Na'im Makhouli, a representative of the Department of Antiquities of the Palestinian government, gave a semi-official character to our expedition and by his technical knowledge and his perfect acquaintance with the vernacular rendered invaluable assistance. Mr. Makhouli is a member of the Greek Catholic Church in Palestine.

Two Fellows assisted also in the work; William Carroll, the Thayer Fellow of the American School, was a graduate of Yale Divinity School and a member of the Church of God in Ohio. Herbert H. Tay, a Fellow of Xenia Theological Seminary, belongs to the Brethren of California. Two students accompanied us, Mr. Homer B. Kent of Xenia Theological Seminary, also of the Brethren of California, and Mr. E. L. Sukenik, a Russian Jew educated at Berlin. He was our surveyor and field botanist. We had in addition the advice of Mr. Dinsmore of Jerusalem, of the American Colony, the most expert botanist in Palestine. Upon our return, we submitted our evidence to the judgment of Père Vincent, the foremost Palestinian scholar in the world, and professor in L'Ecole Saint Etienne, Jerusalem, and also to Phythian-Adams of the Palestine Exploration Society who was just being ordained to the priesthood in the Anglican Church.

This unusual combination of faiths certainly relieves the expedition of any possible suspicion of sectarianism. All these were men of devout reverence for the Old Testament Scriptures, which represents the field of our operations. It is a pleasure to say that we worked together in the greatest harmony, and our conclusions were, I think without exception, unanimous. . . .

Chapter V.
The Story of Ancient Sodom in the Light of Modern Science.
Letter Ten: on the Dead Sea.

"Of the catastrophe which destroyed the city and the district of Sodom, we can hardly hope ever to form a satisfactory conception."[1]

"The pottery from Bab-ed-Dra'a is all older than the eighteenth century B.C., at the latest, since none of the characteristic Middle Bronze [Age] or Hyksos types appear, and everything is 'first Semitic.' . . . The data we have fixed for the catastrophe of Sodom and Gomorrah, about the early part of the eighteenth century B.C., seems to be exceedingly probable. In any case, there was a great convulsion of nature which destroyed the towns of the Southern Ghor, and made an ineffaceable impression upon the survivors."[2]

These contrasting statements show how great has been the advance in Biblical knowledge in the last fifty years and how absolutely also this advance has been toward the verification of the ancient records. So much for the Light of Modern Science. In fact, as we are now to see in the summing up of the evidence, every item of the story of Sodom and Gomorrah has been certified by scientific evidence.

It is an interesting, though rather tedious, day's ride up from Mezra'ah at El Lisan to the Port of Jericho. Come sit beside me, on the little promenade deck of the old motorboat, that we may talk over what we have seen. Now that the missing link of evidence has been found, we must put all the links together into a complete chain. Probably many who read these letters have already done this, but others will not have done so. It is always helpful clearly to state conclusions. Some of the evidence in this case is the result of the labors of others, and has been known for many years; some is the result of this expedition. All must be put together for a complete understanding of the case. This is the task before us now.

---

[1]George Grove, *Smith's Bible Dictionary*, Ed. 1887, p. 3069.
[2]Dr. W.F. Albright, *The Annual of the American Schools of Oriental Research*, Vol. VI., 1924-5, p. 66.

1. It has been established that there was here a Canaanite civilization of the Early Bronze Age, the time of Abraham and Lot, and of Sodom and Gomorrah, Cities of the Plain, at the southern end of the Dead Sea, and that this Civilization ceased about the time of Abraham, and was not resumed, nor even succeeded by any other, certainly until the time of Ezekiel, and probably not until Byzantine times. This is the very important conclusion established by the Expedition of Xenia Theological Seminary in coöperation with the American School at Jerusalem to the Cities of the Plain.

The pottery from the graves along the eastern edge of the Plain, the fine old pottery of the Early Bronze Age, together with the primitive Canaanite High Place discovered in connection with these graves, reveals unmistakably the civilization of Palestine at that time. Pieces of bronze were rare and small, a fact pointing to the *beginning* of the Bronze Age, and the same conclusion as to date forces itself on one from the characteristic Early Bronze [Age] type of the potsherds. The flint artifacts are naturally contemporaneous with the pottery and bronze; and belong, accordingly, to the so-called aeneolithic period, by definition. During this intermediate period, after the discovery of metal working, men still continued to use some of the stone implements with which they had hitherto been content, though employing copper and an alloy of copper and tin (bronze) for more solid and resistant instruments. This was the dawn of metallurgy.

This is the first time we have found in Palestine a large station of the early period in the open air and on the surface, with a mixture of flint artifacts, potsherds, and objects of bronze. These finds are similar to those which have been made in the oldest levels of the ancient Canaanite cities so far excavated; Tell el-Hesi (Lachish), Gezer, Megiddo, and especially Tell es-Sultan (Jericho). But there the objects found were buried deep under débris, and the stratification was more or less confused by later foundations and pits, so that one might often be uncertain whether given flints and potsherds were *really contemporaneous*. The station of Bab-ed-Dra'a is thus of extreme importance for the comparative study of the ceramics, flint industry, and bronze culture in the second half of the third millennium.

Then, the careful and painstaking search of the Plain north, south, east, and west, and the examination of ruins down to virgin sand and gravel has failed to reveal any trace of any civilization in twenty-five later centuries. This is negative evidence, it is true; but there are times when negative evidence comes to have all the force of positive evidence, and this is one such instance. For the absolute silence of Scripture concerning any civilization on this Plain from the time of Abraham onward, certainly to the time of Ezekiel, and most probably to the end of the period of Old Testament revelation, finds its counterpart and confirmation in this like silence in the testimony of the ruins on the Plain, in the period during which the prophets cited the condition of Sodom as a warning. Thus science and revelation tell here the same story.

2. The next thing in order concerning this Plain is that the only correct description of the natural conditions of life here is that given in the Bible, "Even as the Garden of the Lord, before the Lord destroyed Sodom and Gomorrah." It is quite easy to realize as we sit on the deck of our motor-boat in the boiling sun of March what the heat on the Plain must be in July. But it is so in many places in the tropics. Heat and cold are comparative terms to express climatic conditions. Natives of India have been known to perish of cold when caught out over night in time of light frost. We would doubtless find the summer heat on the Plain intolerable, yet it means tropical luxuriousness. Altogether, now that the captivity of Sodom has been restored, and climatic action has fully washed out the salt and sulphur from the Plain, the only correct description of the natural conditions of life on the Plain is in fact as set out in the words of Scripture, "Like the Garden of the Lord."

3. Having verified the Canaanite civilization on the Plain for the time of Abraham and Lot and having discovered the natural conditions of life there, now that the effects of the great tragedy have passed away, we come to the heart of the Story of Ancient Sodom in the Light of Modern Science; the great catastrophe did take place exactly as narrated in the Bible. We are just now passing Messada there on the left and coming toward the gorge at the mouth of the Arnon there on the right, while the sugar-loaf of Jebel Usdum is sinking to the horizon yonder in the South. It is a favourable occasion for a careful survey of all the evidence of that tragedy.

The Biblical story is from the standpoint of divine Providence; it draws aside the curtain to let us see what God was doing. Science examines only the remaining evidence of what happened, what the geologists are able to tell us of the natural remains of what took place: the Biblical writers tell of the divine agency; the geologists know the effects. This expedition only collated and confirmed this evidence.

According to the Biblical story the Plain and all the inhabitants of it and all that grew out of the ground were destroyed by a rain of fire and brimstone from heaven. The account indicates also that salt was mixed with the descending fiery rain; one of the refugees, like some of those at Pompeii, tarried too much and was caught in the descending deluge and incrusted with salt, as indeed the mountain peaks near by are to this day. Thus the whole region was ruined and rendered uninhabitable for two millenniums and more. The Biblical account shows how the timing of the events was entirely in the hands of God which held the fire in leash till Lot be gotten out. It is also made known that a vast column of smoke, as from a furnace up to heaven, was seen by Abraham from far-off Hebron. So far the Bible.

But the Biblical account does not tell us the original source of the sulphur and the salt, whether natural or supernatural, though these elements as finished products are set forth here in the event as real salt and sulphur. Nor does the Bible say how they came to be up in the sky, or what kindled the fire, or caused the smoke. Concerning all these things we must turn to the findings of the geologists from their examination of things as they are on the Plain.

This region was found by the geologists to be a burned-out region of oil and asphalt, of which material, indeed, there is again an accumulation that will soon be exploited, even now, as I write, such exploitation is being reported. Now wherever these conditions exist there is an accumulation of gases, and the geologists tell us that here, at some time which they cannot exactly fix, these gases were ignited by some means, also to them unknown, and there was a great explosion, with first an upheaval, and then a subsidence of the strata.

The character of the ruptured strata has also been determined, with most interesting conclusions. There is along the lower part of this Plain a great stratum of rock salt, which on the western side of the Plain shows itself in that great salt mountain, now known as Jebel Usdum. At its base is a stratum of rock salt about one hundred and fifty feet thick. It is almost pure salt, but lies in layers of varying thickness. Mixed with the layers of salt, and falling down over them also, is a marl in which is much free sulphur, lumps of which we picked up along the sea. When the explosion of the gases took place, this stratum of salt mixed with sulphur was ruptured with the other strata, and the salt and sulphur carried up into the heavens red-hot, and so rained down upon Sodom and Gomorrah and over the whole region, exactly as the Scripture describes the rain of fire and brimstone from heaven. Mixed with the salt and sulphur was also the asphalt, heated to a high degree.

Now, what makes a greater smoke than a vat of boiling asphalt at work on the street? Thus we have an exact accounting for the smoke up to heaven, "as the smoke of a furnace." A low place in the hills toward Hebron opened the way for Abraham to see this distinctly from that distant point.

Thus the geologists have found in nature exactly what the Biblical record describes in Providence. The sacred writer draws aside the veil and lets us see the immediate working of the hand of God; the geologist looks upon the materials upon which the hand of God was employed, and shows us what was done. We have thus a scientific account of the miracle, and at the same time its confirmation. Thus, while only in the Bible do we get an explanation of the events, science is able to certify that the events took place.

II

The Missionary Venture

8. American Protestant Missionary Pioneers in the Holy Land

Early in the surge of missionary enthusiasm that swept across the Protestant world in the nineteenth century, a major missionary agency was founded in 1810, the American Board of Commissioners for Foreign Missions. Supported mainly by the Congregational Churches, but with assistance in the early years from other denominations of the Reformed or Calvinist tradition, the ABCFM was soon carrying out extensive mission enterprises across the world. In 1818 the board determined to undertake a mission to the Holy Land and launched it by sending two appointees, Levi Parsons and Pliny Fisk, to Palestine. Their assignment was to witness first to the Oriental churches, believed to be archaic and static, and second to Muslims. Both natives of western Massachusetts, the pair had been classmates at Middlebury College and Andover Seminary. Both were sent on preaching tours in the United States to enlist enthusiasm and support for their mission.

On the eve of departure, they delivered sermons in which their hopes and dreams for the new venture were stated. Levi Parsons (1792–1822), part of whose sermon is reproduced, stated his belief that ancient prophecies as to the restoration of the Jews to the Holy Land would be literally fulfilled. He soon became a modern missionary "martyr"; overcome by illness he died in Alexandria in 1822. Back home, his reports and letters had captured many imaginations, and his death was widely lamented. The mission to Jerusalem did not turn out to be successful in the long run, and later was given up by the ABCFM; Protestant missions had greater success in what is today Lebanon and Syria.

Source: Levi Parsons, *The Dereliction and Restoration of the Jews: A Sermon, Preached in Park-Street Church Boston, Sabbath, Oct. 31, 1819, just before the Departure of the Palestine Mission* (Boston: Samuel T. Armstrong, 1819; reprinted in Arno Press anthology, *Holy Land Missions and Missionaries*, 1977), pp. 3–6, 9–12, 16–20.

Sermon

For the children of Israel shall abide many days without a King, and without a Prince, and without a sacrifice, and without an image, and without an ephod, and without teraphim. Afterward shall the children of Israel return, and seek the Lord their God, and David their king; and shall fear the Lord and his goodness, in the latter days.— Hosea iii, 4, 5.

Many circumstances, connected with this prophecy, render it one of the most interesting and remarkable. It was left on sacred record 780 years previous to the advent of our Savior; refers, as commentators agree, to the *present* captivity of the Jews; represents, in the most impressive language, the degradation and misery which were hastening upon this once beloved people; and follows them, through a long and dreary night, to the dawn of that blessed morning, which will shed down upon them the light of an eternal day. It developes a series of events, in the system of divine providence, the most instructive and sublime: in view of which, St. Paul was led to exclaim, *"O the depth of the riches, both of the wisdom and knowledge of God: how unsearchable are his judgments and his ways past finding out."*

The prophecy relates exclusively to the Jewish nation, the seed of Abraham, the friend of God. It is this: *The children of Israel shall abide many days,* WITHOUT A KING, AND WITHOUT A PRINCE; predicting very evidently the utter subversion of their *civil* institutions, the extermination of their political state: WITHOUT A SACRIFICE; alluding to the mediatorial service of the High Priest in the Sanctuary; a service, which commanded the highest veneration, as it included all their hopes of the divine favor, and blessing: WITHOUT AN IMAGE, AND WITHOUT AN EPHOD, AND WITHOUT TERAPHIM. This clause seems to be added to convey a more lively impression of the extent and aggravation of their ruin. It predicts a complete dissolution of their ecclesiastical establishment, a removal of all their sacred utensils, their idols, and indeed *every object* attached to their religious institutions. And is it not a remarkable fact, that during the present captivity, the Children of Israel have abode without an *image*, without any vestige of idolatry, even while urged to this sin by the most alluring temptations.

Afterwards THEY SHALL RETURN, be reinstated in all the privileges included in the covenant with Abraham, and be again a peculiar people, a royal priesthood, a chosen generation.

To such scenes and events this interesting prophecy refers. It must be the language of inspiration, the prediction of one, who was enabled to look through the vale of futurity, and describe, with minuteness, the designs of Jehovah. It is now more than *eighteen centuries* since this prophecy has begun to unfold; and it will continue to unfold, to an admiring world, until its accomplishment shall be complete, and triumphant; until the Jews shall be gathered in from their present dispersions, and there shall be one fold, and one shepherd.

But permit me to speak, more particularly, of the *present captivity of the Children of Israel, of their final restoration, and of their claims upon the Gentile church.*

I. THEIR CAPTIVITY.

After their hands were imbued in the blood of the Son of God, the judgments of heaven were not long suspended. In less than forty years, Jerusalem was given up to be plundered; the city was demolished, and a ploughshare drawn over it as a sign of perpetual desolation. On the 17th of July, A.D. 71, as testified by Josephus, *the daily sacrifices ceased*; and, as the temple was the only place for sacrificing, they have not been, and cannot be, renewed. On the 10th of August, of the same year, the Temple was wrapped in one general conflagration—the Sanctuary of God, the wonder of the world, was laid in ruins. Agreeably to the prediction of our Saviour, not one stone was left upon another which was not cast down. Mount Zion was literally ploughed like a field. As Lot fled from Sodom, so the followers of Christ fled from this city devoted to destruction. No prophet raised his voice of admonition, or of prayer. The messengers of salvation preached their farewell sermon, and turned to the Gentiles. No angel was seen there with a message of mercy. The Holy Spirit departed from the maddened people forever. The God of their Fathers forsook them. The door of hope was closed; the day of probation past; and these wretched beings were shut up in the darkness of an eternal night.

O Jerusalem, Jerusalem! how often would I have gathered thy children together, as a hen doth gather her brood under her wings, but ye would not.—BEHOLD YOUR HOUSE IS LEFT UNTO YOU DESOLATE.

The remnant, who escaped this awful catastrophe, were utterly dispersed; their political existence was annihilated; and they have ever since abode without a king, and without a prince; have been a *proverb* and a *byword* among all the nations of the earth.

Their lands in Judea were sold. They were reduced to abject slavery; exposed, in vast multitudes, to public sale; subjected to most rigorous corporeal [sic] punishment; and, at last, they were not permitted to tread upon that spot where Jerusalem stood; nor to shed their tears upon that ground, where they crucified the Lord of glory.

From that period, the condition of the Jews in Judea has been miserable beyond description. They have waited for the Messiah, but waited in vain. They have attempted to reestablish the religion of their Fathers, but every attempt has been marked with *sword, bloodshed, and death.* To this day they remain the objects of universal abhorrence, and contempt. Thus the *blood* of *Jesus* has been upon them, and upon their *children*; thus for ages they have been suffering the vengeance of an incensed Judge.

Time will not permit a *particular* detail of their sufferings in *other* countries. It will be sufficient to notice a *few* instruments employed in the execution of this memorable prediction. . . .

II. THEIR FINAL RESTORATION.

Upon this subject, the promise is explicit, and decisive, *Afterwards they shall return.*
But does this imply both a *literal* and spiritual restoration? The simple word of God is our safest guide. Let us compare the language in which the two events, their return from Babylon, and their final restoration, are recorded.

In the 29th chapter of Jeremiah, we have the following account of the return from the *Babylonish* captivity. *For thus saith the Lord, after seventy years are accomplished at Babylon, I will visit you, and will perform my good word towards you in causing you to return to* THIS PLACE, *and I will gather you from all nations and from all places, whither I have driven you, saith the Lord, and I will bring you again* into the place, whence I caused you to be carried away captive.*

Compare with this the description given in Ezekiel of the *final* return of the Jews. I say *final*, because it is so considered by the Apostle Paul in his Epistle to the Hebrews. *I will take the Children of Israel from among the heathen, whither they be gone, and will gather them on every side, and bring them into their* OWN LAND. AND THEY SHALL DWELL IN THE LAND THAT I HAVE GIVEN UNTO JACOB, MY SERVANT, WHEREIN YOUR FATHERS HAVE DWELT, AND THEY SHALL DWELL THEREIN, *even they and their children, and their children's children, forever and ever. And my Servant David shall be their Prince forever.*

Let these two predictions fall into the hands of a Jew, contemporary with the prophet Jeremiah. He reads the *former*, and says, 'My brethren are to be captives at Babylon, seventy years; after that they are to return to their own land, and be a beloved people.' He reads the *latter*, 'My Brethren are to go again into captivity, so long a captivity that it will be said of Jerusalem, it has *been always waste*; they shall be cast out from God, excluded from all their religious, and civil privileges even till the latter days; then they shall *return* to the land which was given to our *Father Abraham.* God himself will dwell with them, and establish with them an everlasting covenant which shall never be forgotten.'

Place the same predictions in the hands of a Christian, who has the advantage of looking back upon the accomplishment of one of them. Does he object to a literal interpretation of the latter, because there is *figurative* language attached to it. He finds figurative language in the other; yet the Jews did *literally* return. Would not an impartial examination of these two

*Jer. xxxii, 20.

predictions, recorded precisely in the same terms, constrain him to adopt the sentiment, that as one was *literally* fulfilled, the other must be. The outcasts of Israel will yet be gathered to their own land.

Besides, what was the opinion of the prophet? Did he design to inform the Jewish nation, that one prediction was literal, and the other not, and yet employ the same language in the latter, that was used in the former? How could the reader discover the *truth*, when no intimation is given of this change? Is it credible that the prophet should conceal a point of so much magnitude, as he considered this to be, in a phraseology altogether unintelligible. Would he keep the world in darkness upon a doctrine, which he designed to present in the light of day.

It will be acknowledged by all, that the prophecy relating to the present captivity of the Jews has thus far received a *literal* accomplishment. The children of Israel have literally remained without a King and without a Prince; they are carried away captive; and are strangers in a strange land. Can we adopt the opinion that it is *literal* language till the close of the captivity; and the rest of it figurative.

But the objection is made, if there be a literal restoration, the whole Jewish economy will be re-established. Is this a *necessary* consequence? The description given us of heaven is highly figurative; yet no one doubts of the existence of such a place, in distinction from the world of despair. No one will say, if there be a heaven, and an assembly of saints, there must be there mountains, rivers, trees, and a temple a thousand miles square.

The description given us of the *millennium* is figurative; yet it will be admitted by all, that such expressions as these are literal, *The greatness of the Kingdom under the whole heaven shall be given to the people of the saints. Knowledge shall be increased. Nation shall not lift up sword against nation, neither shall they learn war any more.*

Why may we not apply the same principle to the subject under consideration? Admit that the Jews are to be restored to their own land, and that the description given of their civil, and religious state *afterwards*, is designed to raise our conceptions of the glory and blessedness which are in reserve for them under the Gospel dispensation.

Beside, there still exists in the breast of every Jew an unconquerable desire to inhabit the land which was given to their Fathers; a desire, which even a conversion to Christianity does not eradicate. Destroy, then, the Ottoman Empire, and nothing but a *miracle* would prevent their immediate return from the four winds of heaven.

It is objected, again, that the land will not support the inhabitants. But it will be recollected, that the Jews are not now so numerous as they were when they dwelt in the land of Canaan. And is there not a promise that, when God blesses his people, he will bless the land for their sakes, and cause it to bring forth abundantly. . . .

With these facts before us, we cannot for a moment hesitate? Surely the day so long desired by the people of God is beginning to dawn! The darkness and gloom of this long and dismal night are retiring before the light of truth. The blessed Gospel has commenced its gradual, yet *irresistible* progress. The Holy Spirit is carrying on among them a work of grace. The sacred Scriptures are circulated, and *received*, with the most animating prospect of success. Jewish children are receiving a Christian education; and are thus secured from the most bitter prejudices against the name of Jesus.

Encouraged by these events, the Christian world are awaking from their long and criminal slumbers, and are inquiring, with deep solicitude, "Lord, what wilt thou have us to do."

This leads me to the *third* particular in the discourse,

III. THEIR CLAIMS UPON THE GENTILE CHURCH.

If any individual, in this assembly, should inquire, what part can I bear, what duties can I discharge? To such I reply,

1. Let the Jews be the subject of your *prayers*. We ask you not to imitate the example of the crusaders, those deluded champions of the cross. The battles of the Lord are not fought with these carnal weapons. But we do request your unceasing intercessions. Most earnestly do we request you to cherish the spirit of Daniel, and of Nehemiah. Who can read the prayer of Daniel for Jerusalem, without mourning over his own unbelief. That good man prayed, because God had *promised* to build the walls of Zion. His faith was unshaken, although that city had been *seventy years* a desolation. And *every* good man will pray, because God has *promised* to restore the lost tribes of Israel. O where is the faith of Nehemiah, and of Daniel? Where do we hear the language of St. Paul, *My heart's desire, and prayer to God, for Israel is, that they may be saved.* We must forever despair of the conversion of the house of Israel, unless there be a revival of the spirit of the prophets and apostles. God will be inquired of by his people, before he accomplishes his great work.

Often did the Jewish saints pray for *us;* for our *families,* for our churches. They toiled, and suffered, and died, in defence of *our* holy religion. *Our* God was *their* God, *our* heaven is *their* heaven. This *Holy Bible* they faithfully handed down to us, secure from the assaults of infidelity. All our seasons of communion with God, all our hopes of glory, are come to us through the instrumentality of the Jewish saints. *Gratitude* demands a suitable return for these invaluable favors.

The duty of prayer is enjoined upon us by the great Head of the Church. Are the Jews obdurate? We will weep for them. Did they *crucify* our Lord? He himself prayed, Father, forgive them. Every *Christian* will adopt the same prayer. In the sincerity of his heart, he will plead for their forgiveness, and restoration to the privileges of the Gospel.

As I may not again plead the cause of Israel, in this place, I earnestly commend them to your prayers in *secret;* to your prayers in your *families;* to your prayers in *this house,* consecrated to the worship of God. Do you wish to see the dispersed Tribes gathered into the fold of Christ? Pray for them. Do you wish to hear them crying, Hosanna to the Son of David? Pray for them. And let it be the resolution of every Christian, *If I forget thee, O Jerusalem, let my right hand forget her cunning; if I do not remember thee, let my tongue cleave to the roof of my mouth; if I do not prefer Jerusalem above my chief joy.*

But, brethren, this is not *all* we have to do. Our prayers and our *alms* must ascend together as a memorial before God.

2. The Jews have *special* claims upon our *charity.*

As a benevolent people, the Jews held a high and important station. Observe the conduct of the first Jewish Christians! They brought their substance, and laid it at the apostles feet. The love of *Christ constrained* them. Their religion was a religion of *benevolence.* They sought not their own, but the things which are Jesus Christ's. And, to exceed all this, behold the first Missionaries of the Cross relinquishing every earthly interest, for the salvation of the *Gentiles.* Even while we were pagans, sitting in darkness and in the shadow of death, they suffered perils by land, and by sea; if by any means they might save some of us. O when shall we, Gentiles, imitate this blessed example! When shall we repay this unmeasured benevolence? when be as faithful to them as they were to us! They who taught us the way to salvation were *Jews.* And what is more, *infinitely* more than all this, your Lord and your Savior, as concerning the flesh, was a Jew. Yes, brethren, he who now intercedes for you before the throne of God, as concerning the flesh, is a Jew! And his last command was, *Go into* ALL *the world and preach the Gospel.*

We do not expect the conversion of the Jews by a *miracle.* The means which God hath appointed must be employed. The millions of Jews must be furnished with the *word of God,* and with the instruction of *Missionaries.*

But this cannot be done without *charity;* without the *liberal,* and *persevering* efforts of the Christian world. Say then, brethren, shall we bear a part in this work of benevolence, or must it be accomplished without us.

Our assistance is now particularly solicited. Many of the Jews are willing to receive the New Testament. Conversions to Christianity are rapidly increasing. A general movement is taking place. Every eye is fixed upon Jerusalem. There they believe the Messiah will come, and turn away ungodliness from Jacob. And if our Savior should revive his work within those consecrated walls, the good resulting would, probably, surpass all calculation. The dispersed abroad, fixing their attention upon this event, might renounce their fatal delusion, and receive him, who was crucified on calvary, as the Lamb of God who taketh away the sins of the world.

Many of you expect soon to enter into the joy of our Lord. As you enter the gates of the New Jerusalem, will you not be greeted by Abraham, Isaac, and Jacob; by Moses, and the Prophets; by Peter and Paul, and their fellow Disciples. And may you not hear the inquiry, where are our degenerate children? We toiled, and suffered for you, but our children have been left to famish for the bread of life. O my brethren, as you value the privileges of the Gospel, as you desire the universal diffusion of the word of life, let me entreat you to regard with compassion that people, *beloved for the fathers' sake.* Carry back to them the blessings which, through their hands, have been so richly conferred upon you. Take them by the hand and lead them to Mount Calvary. For Zion's sake let us not hold our peace, for Jerusalem's sake let us not rest, until the righteousness thereof go forth as brightness, and the salvation thereof as a lamp that burneth.

Finally, *we beseech you, brethren, for the Lord Jesus Christ's sake, and for the love of the Spirit, that ye strive together with us, in your prayers to God for us, that we may be delivered from them that do not believe in Judea, and that the service which we have for Jerusalem, may be accepted of the saints.* AMEN.

9. An Indigenous Denomination's Mission to Jerusalem

Hoping to restore "primitive Christianity" as a means of unifying Christianity, the Christian Churches (Disciples of Christ) were formed in 1832 when the followers of Alexander Campbell and Barton Stone merged in Kentucky. Campbell emerged as the central figure in the new movement, in part because of his power as preacher, author, and editor. In his journal, The Millennial Harbinger, *he called for a mission to the Holy City:*

> *We strongly incline to the opinion, that, of all the foreign fields that claim our attention, to which our energies can be directed, and our means employed, Jerusalem, that great centre of attraction, that great point of rendezvous—visited by men of all climes and of all tongues—demands our first efforts and our earliest attention. It is, moreover, quite practicable. We can find a missionary and a Christian family to locate there, possessing such accomplishments for the station and work to be accomplished, as warrant our confidence in the undertaking. In this view of the premises and great object, we expect a liberal response, in the form of contributions, from all the friends of foreign and domestic missions, sent forward to the Treasurer, at Cincinnati, and their earliest convenience.[1]*

The missionary who was found was a physician, James T. Barclay, who arrived in Jerusalem in February, 1851, full of hope for winning converts among Jews and Mohammedans and for reforming the Oriental Christian "sects" there. He soon discovered that "there is no worse missionary ground in all the earth than this same city"; he gathered few converts and found himself in sharp controversy with the older Christian churches. He returned home after three and a half years. A by-product of his residence was a major work, The City of the Great King.

The story of the mission's origin and early efforts was compiled by D. S. Burnet out of the letters, reports, and journals of Dr. Barclay. The first selection here is from an "anonymous" article, understood to be from Barclay's pen; the second from the doctor's annual report of the Jerusalem mission for 1851.

Source: D. S. Burnet, compiler, *The Jerusalem Mission: Under the Direction of the American Christian Missionary Society* (Cincinnati: American Christian Publication Society, 1853; reprinted by Arno Press, 1977), pp. 15–20, 224–29. See also J. T. Barclay, *The City of the Great King: or, Jerusalem as it was, as it is, and as it is to be* (Philadelphia: J. Challen & Sons, 1858; reprinted by Arno Press, 1977).

The signs of the times are altogether auspicious too, for the immediate fulfillment of the glorious prophecies relating to this once covenant people of the Lord. Tired of looking for another Messiah, they seem at last, willing to investigate the claims of Jesus of Nazareth to the Messiahship.

---

[1] Alexander Campbell, in *The Millennial Harbinger* 20 (1850):87.

According to recent accounts there are many of these outcasts of Israel who have arrived at the conclusion, that the once despised Nazarene is indeed the Son of God. It is an augury full of hope to Israel, that they are everywhere paying more attention to literature, and less regard to the Talmud and Rabbinical tradition.

Then verily if we have rightly discerned the signs of the times, God hath not utterly cast away his people whom formerly he acknowledged; and neither should we. So much interested were the apostles in behalf of the Jews, that even after having preached the Gospel exclusively to them for twelve years, when they were at last specially summoned by the Holy Spirit to the work of Foreign Missions among the Heathen, we discover that it was still their uniform practice, wherever they found Jews, first to propose the Gospel to *them*. And so important did they deem *their* conversion, that after they had been fifteen years thus engaged in missionary operations among the Gentiles, they still deemed it expedient to send special missionaries to the Jews. The first three years of Paul's missionary career, were devoted to one branch of the Abrahamic family, and the last we hear of him, he is still pleading with God's chosen people. Perhaps we could not do better than to imitate this example of the apostles, in their decided preference for the seed of Abraham. Did an apostle feel such great heaviness and continual sorrow, that he could even wish himself accursed for his brethren, the Jews! and shall we feel no peculiar interest in this noble race to whom pertain the adoption, and the glory, and the covenants, and the giving of the Law, and the promises; whose are the Father's and of whom as concerning the flesh, Christ came, who is over all, God blessed forever? The evangelization of Israel becomes invested with tenfold interest, when it is considered, that without their conversion, vain are our hopes with regard to the consummation of many of the great events, so dear to the friends of Zion. But slight them as we may, this much is certain, that let what will happen, the conversion of God's ancient people is clearly predicted, and must be accomplished, and that too, as an event preliminary and indispensable to the general prevalence of the empire of Truth. An additional reason for making the Jews a special object of missionary effort is found in the fact that other nations, when evangelized, may be speedily enslaved or even exterminated by some more powerful nation, or like the South Sea Islanders, and some of our own Indian tribes, dwindle to nothing, and thus their auxiliary agency be lost to the cause of missions; but this peculiar nation is absolutely indestructible by all the combined powers of earth, because preserved by the arm of Omnipotence for the wisest purposes. Many a Gentile will doubtless yet be glad to take hold of the skirt of the despised Jews, saying, "we will go with you, for we have heard that the Lord is with you."

Admitting that the Jews are the people to whom we should first send the Gospel, where should the mission be located for their benefit? for they are found dispersed abroad "in every nation under heaven." Perhaps they are to be found in greater numbers in Salonica, than in any other city in the world; and, (as we learn by the late arrivals), "these (inhabitants of Salonica) are more noble than were those of Thessalonica, (its ancient name) in that they search the Scriptures," and throwing aside their antiquated parchments, receive, as genuine, the Old Testament, which the colporteur of the Bible Society has carried them. They are also very numerous in Constantinople, Smyrna, and other Mediterranean cities; yet without doubt the Holy Land is the place where we should first establish a mission, for their special benefit, for the Jews there, are very accessible, and a blow struck on this great center of sympathies would be felt much more sensibly than anywhere else. They are there found congregated in various cities in sufficient numbers to justify the settlement of a missionary among them, and are composed of such as are most interested on the subject of religion—are the least money-loving, time-serving, and over-reaching; (for it is not to be concealed that being almost invariably disfranchised and persecuted by the Gentiles, too many of them have attempted to compensate their civil disabilities by the acquisition of wealth obtained too often by "wiles not justified by honor"). They are already quite numerous in Palestine—that glory of all lands—and now that many long-existing obstacles to their return are removed, and they are permitted by the sultan to build a temple on Mount Zion, they will doubtless soon be found there in greater numbers than in any other quarter of the globe. Believing, as they universally do, in their literal and speedy restoration to the Land of their Fathers, and ardently desiring to return thither, the removal of that despotic embargo which for eighteen centuries has been scattering them to the four winds, will cause them to flock to Judea, "as doves to their windows."

The Mohammedan portion of the population of Judea, are very generally impressed with the belief received by tradition from their fathers, and riveted by their doctrine of fatalism, that the "Franks," as they term Protestant Christians, will soon possess that country, and indeed, all the Ottoman Empire; and the Ishmaelitish part of them especially, ardently desire it, as we learn from the reports of late travelers. Perhaps no event whatever, furnishes a happier augury for the speedy triumph of Christianity, than the present attitude of the Turkish government toward the Christian religion: for whereas, but a few years ago, there still existed that obstinate bigotry and unrelenting spirit of persecution which had ever characterized the followers of the false prophet, there is now perfect toleration! Even twelve moons ago, apostasy from Islamism to Christianity, was punished with death and confiscation—*now* such encouragement is offered to "Franks," as almost to constitute a premium for Christianity. The "Crescent truly is rapidly waning," and "the Euphrates fast drying up!" Here then is a great and (must needs be) effectual door opening (through the sublime Porte) for the establishment of a mission, in reference to Mohammedanism. The last sands of the prophetic period assigned to the Moslem Desolater, are now running out! The "Little Horn of the East" shall gore no more! and no more shall the desolating abomination "practice and prosper!" "Lo! what God hath wrought!" Mr. Thompson, who has recently returned from the Syrian mission, remarked at a late missionary meeting, that "just before embarking for the United States, he had preached before a congregation of Arabs, at their own request, in Joppa."

The place whence the Gospel started on its westward mission to us eighteen hundred years ago, is now waiting for us to send it back to its inhabitants. When he was about to leave, they came and threw their arms around his neck, and told him to tell Christians in America to pray for them, and send them missionaries. Some of them followed him several miles on his journey, and bathing his hands with their tears, begged that missionaries might be sent. They do not ask for our money, but they want our sons and daughters; "and somehow," said Mr. T., "I thought they ought to have them!" From what part of Heathendom does there come such a Macedonian cry as from these swarthy sons of Ishmael, residing at this old port of Jerusalem? Surely we should not be indifferent to the fact that the Father of the faithful—the friend of God, prayed so earnestly for these Bedouin "dwellers in the desert," in the person of their progenitor Ishmael—"O! that Ishmael might live before God"—a prayer too, that the Lord has promised abundantly to answer! . . .

The state of society in the "Holy" City (the city of three *Sabbath* days per week), is deplorable in the extreme; and it would seem that there are few places on all the earth where the propagation of Christianity (even when somewhat accommodated to the taste of the age, by a liberal admixture of philosophy, Judaism and Paganism) is attended with greater difficulties than at this same Jerusalem, where it succeeded so triumphantly at first. In proof of this, I need only refer to the vast expenditure of treasure and effort here on the part of several powerful missionary societies. The American Board of Commissioners for Foreign Missions sent two missionaries here as long ago as 1821; and their mission was well sustained (with occasional interruptions) by a strong band of most excellent, devoted and talented men, till about four or five years ago, during all which time three converts were all the fruits of this great outlay. The persevering efforts of the Lutherans have been still more barren of good results. The London Jews' Society have had missionaries here, more or less constantly, for more than a quarter of a century; and in 1834 they established a regular mission on a very extensive scale, which has been lavishly supplied with chaplains, missionaries, colporteurs, helps, governments, etc., under its learned "Lord Bishops." A splendid church edifice has been erected, at a total cost, as I am informed by the architect, of £70,000; an extensive and well-conducted Hospital established; well-endowed literary and manual-labor institutions founded, and money funded for the purpose of "aiding inquiring Jews," "assisting to establish converts in business," etc. Beside the money already so extensively invested in real estate by the society, thirty or forty thousand dollars are annually expended in support of the missions, which is not only under the auspices of that powerful and wealthy society, (one of whose patrons alone has recently given it $300,000), but is under the special care and patronage of two of the most enlightened and potent monarchs in Europe, (Victoria and Frederick William), both of whom maintain able consuls in the city, for the special protection of its members. And yet, during the thirty years' labors of its various well-sustained and energetic agents, the number of converts made in this city, even with all the worldly inducements set before them, amounts to only a score or two, more than three-fourths of whom are retained in the service of the society at salaries far more than adequate to their support.

Not a single convert from Mohammedism has been made by either of these denominations, nor by the combined efforts of the dozen different Christian sects of Jerusalem; but on the contrary, several Christans have actually gone over to the Moslems and Jews!

And yet, notwithstanding all these great discouragements, I can but regard Jerusalem as one of the most important missionary stations on earth; and cannot help believing that "the faith once delivered to the saints" would soon number its converts here by hundreds, but for one main difficulty, which, although we have not the power to remove entirely, can yet be counteracted to a considerable extent. The site originally selected by Divine Providence as the grand radiating point of the light of salvation, possesses all the advantages now that it ever did, for enlightening the greatest possible number of the benighted sons and daughters of Adam; for hither, as to no other place on earth, the tribes, not only of Jews but of Gentiles of every nation still resort for religious purposes. With Africa, the dwelling-place of the children of Ham, on one side, and Asia, the hive-like abode of Shem's descendants, on the other, and in front the Mediterranean (that great highway to the everywhere-dwelling sons of Japhet) dividing, yet uniting, the lands of Shem and Ham, and the Isles of the Gentiles, what spot could be more admirably situated for the wide and speedy diffusion of truth! Be it, then, that "the city is walled up to heaven," and the children of Anak dwell here—drawing our resources alone from the armory of Heaven, are we not able to fully rescue "the city of the Great King" from its Canaanitish oppressors, by whom it is trodden under foot—whether open enemies or pretended friends? The great obstacle to which I alluded as so formidably opposed to the revival of pure religion in this city, and upon which I wish to say a few words, is confessedly one of some delicacy; but the importance of the subject, I trust, will sufficiently plead my apology for using so much plainness of speech only as will enable me to make myself understood by you. I allude to the practice of *supporting converts*, which prevails here, to a greater or less extent, among all professions of religion—Christians, Jewish and Mohammedan? But as this assertion may sound rather strangely and uncharitably if unsustained by evidence, I beg leave to adduce the testimony of several persons (at least so far as Christian converts are concerned), whose character and position constitute them unimpeachable witnesses. Mr. Spencer, an Episcopal minister who spent some time here in 1849, remarks, (page 275—"Sketches of Travel in Palestine," etc.), when speaking of the Luthero-Episcopal mission here, that "the mission to the Jews has not only got to convince them of their guilt and perversity in rejecting the Messiah, but, on their professing Christianity, is obliged to undertake their temporal support also, as a necessary consequence."

Mr. Williams, chaplain to this same Prussio-Anglican mission, observes (page 570, vol. 2, of his "Holy City,") when speaking of the proselytes made by the missionaries of the American Board of Commissioners for Foreign Missions, that "there were three of these men—I believe not more. The Missionaries have taken charge of their families, as they were bound to do." Dr. Tischendorf, in his "Travels in the East," page 159, goes so far as to say that "conversions in Jerusalem are framed to an accommodation with the most modern Judaism, and six thousand piasters (about £50), with other advantages, are offered to the converts as a premium." Now, while I cannot believe that the gravest item of this charge is literally true, yet I lament to say, there is far too much of truth in it; for it is undeniably true that worldly inducements of a very tempting character are held forth, the effect of which (not to say design), is both to make proselytes and to retain them in ecclesiastical connection, upon principles not countenanced by the Word of God. It is a matter deeply to be regretted, that gentlemen so worthy as I know some of the members of this Mission to be, should have fallen into a practice so unfavorable to the interests of pure religion. The existence of a custom so fraught with evil tendencies, renders great circumspection necessary on the part of the evangelist, who would have his converts influenced alone by moral principle, apart from all worldly motives. And in this time-serving latitude, nothing seems better calculated to render his efforts abortive, than the necessity (imposed upon him by such a state of things), of frequently and solemnly protesting against a practice so congenial to the vitiated taste of a crooked and perverse generation; and especially when, as in the present instance, his meaning is perverted, and undue advantage of his protestation is taken, to create the impression that the opposite course argues not only a want of interest in the temporal, but spiritual welfare of the convert!

10. A Cooperative Approach to Missionary Policy

One of the most respected and extensive of the Christian missionary efforts in Jerusalem by the early twentieth century was that of the Anglican communion, centering in St. George's Cathedral and related institutions, many of them educational. Both by sending personnel and contributing financially, the Protestant Episcopal Church in the U.S.A. was an active participant in the work, which sought to be cooperative with the ancient Eastern churches, with other Protestant denominations, and with the YMCA and relief agencies.

An interesting "window" on this effort was provided by a pamphlet issued in the early 1930s by the National Council of the Episcopal Church. "The Story of Our Work" was told by the Rev. Charles T. Bridgeman (1893–1967), educational chaplain in Jerusalem. Mr. Bridgeman, a graduate of St. Stephens (Bard) College and the General Theological Seminary, had begun his work in Jerusalem in 1924 as liaison officer for relations with the Eastern churches on behalf of the American Episcopal church. In the pamphlet, his account was followed by brief testimonies to the value of the work being done, and by a statement of the influence of this Anglican approach on general American missionary policy, written by John R. Voris, a Presbyterian then serving as an executive with Near East Relief.

Source: *Our Church's Work in the Levant* (New York: The National Council, Episcopal Church, 1932), pp. 3–7, 9, 12.

The Story of Our Work

The active resumption by our Church of its century-old interest in the Near East Christian world, signifies a deeper appreciation of her duty as a part of the Church universal. *Jerusalem,* where the Saviour preached the Gospel of His sacrificial death and life-giving resurrection; *Athens* which provided the intellectual terms in which the Gospel was carried to the world; and *Mosul* (the ancient Nineveh) from which the Syrian missionaries first evangelized India and China, are brought into contact with every parish in the United States through the work which our Church is doing in the reawakened Levant.

As I leave St. George's Cathedral close for my daily walk to the Armenian Theological School inside the crenelated walls of the old city I pass in rapid review civilizations centuries apart which co-exist in the Jerusalem of today.

The Palestinian *fellahin* or peasants who pass me in chattering groups going to and from the markets come from the unchanged countryside where Biblical conditions still obtain. Their mincing donkeys, the fat old sheikhs astride them, the sturdy women with high piled baskets on their heads, the sedate, haughty camels, all seem to be of bygone days. Near St. George's the villagers strike the asphalt road of modern times and go the last half mile to the city gates in company with a mad scurry of motor cars that drive them dust-covered to the very edge of the roadway.

As I go cityward with these companions I find myself before the Bab-el-Amoud or Damascus gate. Here mediaeval Jerusalem is unfolded. From blinding sunlight I enter the cool dark passageway of the gate tower where sit weary travelers, a fortune-teller catching the curious, the public letter writer, and village fathers chatting over a *narghile* and coffee cup.

Inside the wall an inclined cobbled street filled with donkeys, merchants, screaming water-carriers with their clinking brazen cups carries me into the Khan-es-Zeit or olive market. The thronged streets through which I pick my way across the city are a kaleidoscopic medley of the East: Arabs from the country, town-dwelling Jews with long curls, Europeanized natives of every race, mullahs, rabbis, Christian monks and priests—an endless variety.

Had my path been outside instead of inside the walls I should have passed through the modern part of the city where asphalt streets, filled with cars, neat European shops of every type, and hotels, more or less modern, suggest the western influences which are making so rapid a change in the life of the country. The modern city is neat but banal. I am always glad to leave it behind and plunge into the quieter old world atmosphere within the walls.

An essential part of the mediaeval Jerusalem is its scores of monasteries where the manifold needs of the local Christians are met, for the monasteries are not merely places of meditation. Work of varied kind is done. There the poor find shelter, the children a school. The printing presses are still part of the monks' duties. Pilgrims look for rooms in the cool chambers provided to accommodate them. Art is at home in the monastery. In fact the monastery is the microcosm which the Middle Ages knew; a world in itself, apart from, yet ministering to the world in which it is set.

At School on Mt. Zion

The Armenian Monastery of St. James where my work lies is a city within a city. Occupying the southwest corner of the ancient town where stood Herod's palace, the monastery is walled off from the world at large and protected by great iron gates which in the troubled past were no needless luxury. Within is the tenth century church built on the site of the burial place of St. James' head (St. James the Apostle). Its cool interior has echoed for centuries to the sonorous litanies of the devout Armenians.

Other churches and numerous chapels are found in the great barrack-like quarters. Some forty monks under the leadership of their abbot, the Armenian Patriarch, are the local religious community. Accommodations for more than two thousand pilgrims are provided. There in the prosperous pre-war days came the hosts of Armenian pilgrims, certain of entertainment. Since the war the doors of the monastery have been thrown open to refugees, of whom more than three thousand were once housed there, while half that number still count it their home. Children throng the courtyard. The men and women go in and out about their business in the outside city. When the schoolbell rings in the morning some three hundred or four hundred children go to the day school provided by the community in the heart of the big monastery. The rattle and bang of the printing presses tell of other activities.

A special part of the monastery is set apart for the residence and classrooms of the forty theological students. In a little world of their own they study in Armenian the lore of their great race, and through English and French glean some knowledge of the outside world. After a five-year preparatory course the best-fitted are given the option of studying for Orders. Such a step is signalized by their letting the beard grow, though they may be but eighteen or nineteen years old, and taking deacons orders.

The theological classes which face me each morning are interesting groups. For all their bearded dignity and long ecclesiastical robes they are but youths who love a rough game of football or practical jokes among themselves. But in the classroom they are serious students aflame with zeal to bring to their people the comfort of the eternal Gospel and the Church's manifold ministrations. Discussions of Old and New Testament history, of theology, of sociology and practical parochial work, of philosophy and ethics are serious affairs to which they bring their best.

The individual histories of the men are interesting. Most of this generation are from that reservoir of Armenian youth, the Near East orphanages which rescued the homeless victims of countless deportations. One young man remembers little of his early youth except that he was a camel herder for a group of Bedouins in the Syrian desert, a waif rescued by them from starvation and kept till picked up by the relief committee. Another remembers his native village where his father was a peasant. He says he often used to look with awe at the village priest as at one far above him in education and position. He wonders at himself when he realizes that he too is to come to that same position. Individual capacities quickly manifest themselves. A deacon who is good at music finds himself the leader and instructor of the others in the important rôle of choir master. The artistic gifts of another are likewise used to advantage.

In intellectual interest the men differ greatly. Some of them take quickly to English, while others find French or Arabic more interesting, and so also with the various studies. No one of them but has some outstanding ability or trait of character which will stand him in good stead in the manifold work of the Church. Two of our recent graduates have done such excellent work that they have been sent by the Patriarch to England for further study. They will return better equipped in Biblical scholarship, Church history, and pedagogy to strengthen our teaching staff. We hope in time to send others abroad for similar postgraduate study.

The surroundings of the school are most inspiring. From the classrooms we look out on the walls of the old city and in the distance across the gray hills of the barren Judean wilderness a little patch of the Dead Sea is visible, with the purple hills of Moab beyond. The Mount of Olives rises to the northeast. A few minutes' walk away are the place of the Last Supper and the sepulchre of our blessed Lord. Frequent visits to these and other places make the study of the Bible a living experience.

The monastery is under the guidance of that modern saint, scholar, poet and statesman, His Beatitude Elisse Tourian, Armenian Patriarch of Jerusalem. Its theological school is the only one now remaining for the whole scattered Armenian Church. I have been teaching there for the past five years in response to the Patriarch's desire that something of western practicality and modernity be added to the traditional curriculum of the Armenian Church. Through these students, the new leaders of the Armenian Church, we hope to make a deep impression on the spiritual life of the whole Armenian nation. It is a precious trust that has been given us: the delicate task of infusing western ideas into an ancient Church in such a way as not to harm its apostolic traditions and national customs.

The invitation of the head of the Old Syrian (Jacobite) Church of northern Mesopotamia and India to do the same for his young theological students in Jerusalem has opened another door. These young monks and candidates for Holy Orders whom I teach give us the same opportunity to help strengthen their Church's life.

The Native Christians

Jerusalem, the City of Peace, is indeed a center for nearly all the Christian Churches which trace their history back to apostolic times, but it is more than that. In our attention to the conflict of Jews and Moslems we are apt to forget that ten per cent of the population of Palestine is Christian. The large majority of these belong to the Orthodox Church, the great Mother Church of the East. In language they are Arabic-speaking like their Moslem neighbors, but they are not Arabs; rather a mixed race in which Jewish, Greek, and European blood is found. They are all that remain of the once dominant Christian population which was conquered by the Moslem invaders in the seventh century. Many Christians went over to Islam, but these have been staunchly loyal to the Cross of Christ, veritably carrying a daily cross of oppression and even persecution.

The native Christians live in the large Christian towns of Jerusalem, Bethlehem, Nazareth, Ramallah, and in dozens of small villages far off on the stony hills of Palestine and Trans-Jordan. In the latter country, under a Moslem Emir, but also a British protectorate, the Christian remnant is often seen in the sordid villages which stand in the ruins of the once flourishing Byzantine towns, where churchless and schoolless they gaze upon the broken columns and earthquake-shattered walls of their ancestors' beautiful shrines. They wonder if there is to be any return to their former happiness.

The two needs of the Orthodox people of Palestine are for a better educated village priesthood, and Christian schools for the boys and girls. We are trying now to help the Church in her program for village education. The Orthodox Church has in Palestine but fifteen schools with fifty-three teachers and 1,165 pupils. The schools are badly equipped, inconvenient and staffed by poorly paid teachers. They cannot meet the needs of the six or seven thousand Orthodox children. In Trans-Jordan the case is yet more pathetic. The sixteen village schools with their twenty-seven teachers and seven hundred children are even more needy. There through the generous benefactions of kindly people we are beginning to help, offering to match dollar for dollar.

The promotion of daily vacation Bible schools among the Orthodox through their own archbishops and priests, in coöperation with the World's Sunday School Association in promoting Sunday religious education among those who have no religious instruction in the week day school, are other methods by which we are trying to aid.

The Orthodox Church in Palestine has two great functions: The care and beautification of the holy places of our Lord's incarnate life, and the nurture of the yet more precious souls for whom He died. The Church has been greatly impoverished since the War with the loss of her great friend, the devout Russian nation. Both her tasks languish for lack of help. For the shrines which the visitor goes to see it is easier to get help than for the needy sheep on a hundred barren hills whom the tourist rarely meets.

The work of the Anglican Bishop of Jerusalem, the Right Rev. Rennie MacInnes, which our Church, along with the rest of the Anglican Communion, helps support by part of the Good Friday Offering under the name of the Jerusalem and the East Mission, is another story in itself. His educational and medical work in Palestine, Syria and Cyprus, aimed to show Moslems and Jews the glories of the Christ and to aid native Christians, is something we may be proud to share.

The four stated objects of the mission are work among the Jews, the Moslems, our own people and the Eastern Churches. There is a staff of thirty Anglicans and many more native workers. The institutions are: in Jerusalem, the Cathedral, Pilgrim Hostel, College for Men, College for Women, St. George's School for Boys; in Bethany, a school; at Haifa, St. Luke's Hospital and a Girls' High School; at Ain Anoub the mixed school for Druse boys and girls.

Bishop MacInnes says in his report:

"All those who come, receive religious instruction. We do not try to over-persuade any boy or girl, but we do try to make known to them— that is our first job—the truths and beauties of the Christian faith." . . .

Testimony To the Value of Our Work

The church in Jerusalem is the only mission where the entire Anglican Communion is united in supporting the work. St. George's Cathedral in Jerusalem is one of the best known places in Christendom. Among the five hundred students in our schools and colleges, are Christians of every name. Mohammedans and Jews, working, and living together in brotherhood, thus making a valuable contribution to distracted Palestine."—BISHOP GARLAND of Pennsylvania, Episcopal Canon of St. George's Cathedral, Jerusalem.

"My impressions during a brief visit to Jerusalem were very definite. First, the Jerusalem and the East Mission, while teeming with difficulties, has tremendous value both as an evangelistic agency and a unifying force. Second, the contribution made by our American Church both in money and in Mr. Bridgeman is of real worth. Third, an associate for Mr. Bridgeman is urgently needed."—BISHOP FRANCIS of Indianapolis.

"Those of us who lived at the American School of Oriental Research, which is just across the way, used the services of the Cathedral regularly.

The work of the Bishop Gobat School, the Jerusalem Girls' College and St. George's School, impressed me as very solid. I also visited the hospital and dispensary in Hebron, the seat of Moslem fanaticism, whence the Jewish Hadasseh work has been withdrawn since the August riots. It is now the only medical center in that ancient city. My sister, Dr. James of Wuchang, gave it a close inspection and told me afterward that she found it carried on in a very efficient way."—Professor Fleming James, *Old Testament and Ethics, Berkeley Divinity School.*

Influence on American Missionary Policy

Out of the work of Mr. Bridgeman in Jerusalem and Mr. Panfil in Mosul, no new sect is appearing. Those who receive inspiration from them are not inspired to leave their own churches.

"The theory of the Protestant Episcopal Church in the United States (as of the Anglican Church) in respect to the Eastern Churches is that of a friendly, coöperative relationship based upon mutual understanding, appreciation, and consciousness of kinship. It is not a proselytizing relationship.

"The theory of the Congregational and Presbyterian Foreign Mission Boards when they first began work in the Near East, and again at the present time, is the same. But due to a number of circumstances these Communions were not entirely successful in reaching a coöperative relationship with the Eastern Churches. Instead there developed, contrary to their underlying theory, an 'evangelical' church, largely westernized in its theological and ecclesiastical expression. The application of the theory showed that some important element was lacking.

"The whole problem of coöperative relationships hinges upon that one concept, mutual confidence. Without it the West cannot give to the East that peculiar contribution of practical ethics which it has to give, nor can the West receive the mystical sense of communion with God, which the East has to give. Confidence must be not alone between institutions, it must reside in persons.

"The work of the American Episcopal Church in the Near East with but two representatives may seem very small in the light of the extensive programs of some of the American Communions in these eastern lands. The American Board (Congregational) has a dozen or more representatives; the Presbyterian has more than a hundred. The Christian Associations must have not less than eight or ten in the Christian lands of the Near East.

"If this work of the Episcopal Church chaplains were merely another missionary effort by American Protestantism, rivaling and interfering with the older work of the Communions on the field for so long a time, I should call it not only unnecessary, but pernicious. Already we have too many sectarian movements on foreign fields.

"But the work of these representatives of the Episcopal Church in America is significant. It is a new venture in friendly relationships. These men have been given to the Eastern Churches to work entirely with and under their direction, in the upbuilding of the life of those Churches. They are furnishing a type, and an incentive to other Communions to render a like service. They are demonstrating that a theory of coöperation can work, provided that theory is perfectly sound, and is interpreted by representatives who know how to make it work.

"I believe this attitude of the Episcopal Church has already accomplished far more than most of its adherents realize. It has been one of the important factors in making Near East Relief a genuinely non-proselytizing organization with a constructive program of religious education in relation to the Eastern Churches. It has been an incentive to the Presbyterian and Congregational Churches to announce unofficially, through their American leaders, their desire to work coöperatively with these ancient Churches of the East. It has stimulated the Y.M.C.A. to better work along these same lines of cooperation and the World's Sunday School Association to undertake a coöperative relationship in religious education.

"I doubt if anywhere in the world the Episcopal Church has made a greater contribution through a few personalities than it has made through these rather unknown 'missionaries' or 'educational chaplains' or prophets in the Near East."—REV. JOHN R. VORIS, *an authority on the Levant, Presbyterian, Near East Relief Executive.*

11. An Evangelical Witness in the Heart of the Levant

By the middle of the twentieth century, the Southern Baptist Convention had grown to be the largest single American Protestant denomination. Though not without its own inner diversities and tensions, the convention as a whole was characterized by a strongly conservative, evangelical, and missionary spirit. In its missionary drive, it spread to all the American states and conducted overseas missions in many parts of the world.

Its characteristic approaches can be seen in its missionary work in Palestine, described in this selection as it was in the mid-1930s. Informing a communion about the details of its foreign work is one of the tasks mission boards must regularly undertake in order to maintain enthusiasm and support for the work; as a result of this process, the attitudes of its constituents toward distant lands are often significantly influenced. The following brief account was part of a mission study book. It was written by J. McKee Adams (1886–1945), a graduate of Wake Forest College and the Southern Baptist Theological Seminary in Louisville, where he earned a Ph.D. in 1929. After service in the pastorate, he served as professor of biblical introduction at Louisville. The selection describes the denomination's mission in Palestine; much of the rest of the book is given to an informed discussion of the land and its people, with an informal description of cultural and political trends.

Source: J. McKee Adams, *The Heart of the Levant, Palestine-Syria: A Survey of Ancient Countries in the Interest of Modern Missions* (Richmond: Foreign Mission Board, Southern Baptist Convention, 1937), pp. 62–74.

Baptist Work in Palestine

Southern Baptists are beginning to fulfill in Palestine their historic mission as a great missionary denomination. Successful work is now being conducted on several fronts, mainly at Nazareth, Jerusalem, and Haifa. Our missionary efforts relate both to the Jews and to the Arabs. In our actual contacts we are touching effectively the life of the people in all of these places with promise of growing success. Plans are now being made for enlargement of our sphere of influence in various parts of the country, particularly that the Galilean district, once hallowed by the footsteps of the Master, might hear again His message of the abundant life. Judea and Jerusalem will continue to rejoice in the Good News, and even Samaria will come to know the long expected Messiah. Throughout the country the fields are white unto the harvest, just as promising and inviting as they were in the days of Jesus. The fundamental nature of Palestinians, whether Galileans, Samaritans, Judeans, Arabs, Jews, or Gentiles, has not changed, nor has the power of the Gospel, to meet the deepest needs of the heart and life, been changed. One recalls the thrilling narratives of the New Testament, the vivid description of the ministry of Jesus and the disciples, how they touched city, village, and rural life in the early days, bringing the fuller, the deeper, and the richer life. Through the eye of faith one may dare to expect with confidence the dawning of another day in which the milling multitudes will throng the ministry of His heralds of love and peace. It is rather easy to sit in the seat of harsh and summary judgment with regard to Palestine, to think of it as already overstocked with religion, and as irresponsive to a new call to the old and sublimer faith. Many have spoken and written stern words of condemnation and impatience in view of the apparent abundance of religious forms and practices which reveal little of genuine Christianity and the deeper aspects of the spiritual life. But we never make any real progress by destructive attacks and methods, by determination to tear down another's dwelling to build our own. If we feel that Palestinians have had little opportunity to experience or to observe the fruits of a vital, spiritual life in Christ, in all sincerity we might venture a step forward and ask just what have *we* done to afford them a better opportunity? If we are inclined to condemn others because they have largely succeeded in *concealing* Christ through forms and sacraments, are we bold enough to question our own hearts as to what we have done in Palestine to *reveal* Him through the years?

Now these are bold and pertinent questions put forward with no purpose to humiliate us nor to condemn us, but simply to remind us that the present religious situation in Palestine was not produced over-night, but that it is the result of centuries of growth and entrenchment. If Southern Baptists had been laboring in Palestine earnestly and aggressively through the years we believe that conditions would have appeared in far better light. If we labor faithfully and intelligently, progressively and unselfishly during the present we believe that future conditions will set forth real triumphs of grace in multitudes won from sin and saved to useful Christian service. Let us face the fact frankly: we are *beginning* to fulfill our mission in Palestine, the full accomplishment of which shall not be witnessed until Jesus comes! But we have begun and propose to press on in a worthy manner, to share with all Palestinians the radiance of the life in Christ. We now present in outline some of the more important phases of our work in Palestine of today. From this review we will be able to picture the real progress that has been made, and it will encourage us in regard to the promise and hopefulness of added zeal and effort in our sacred cause.

Nazareth. Nestling in the hills of Lower Galilee, about 1800 feet above the Mediterranean, lies the little town of Nazareth with a population of approximately 10,000. In the New Testament period the reputation of

Nazareth was far from good, according to the statement of Nathanael, but the name of Jesus of Nazareth has lifted its fame to glory and it will ever wear that illustrious crown! From its elevated hills one can get a beautiful view of the Mediterranean and Mt. Carmel, the great plain of Esdraelon, and majestic Mt. Hermon. In these wonderful environs Jesus grew up from childhood to manhood, leaving the city when He was about 30 years of age to begin His public ministry. About nineteen hundred years after that remarkable ministry of love and sacrifice, Rev. M. S. Musa, a native of the Near East, began our Baptist work in Nazareth, assisted by his devoted wife. For many years the work prospered and the church grew in an encouraging way. Great assistance in this forward movement was rendered by Mr. and Mrs. George W. Bottoms, of Texarkana, Arkansas, and other generous Southern Baptists, who gave a splendid church building to the Nazareth Christians. This commodious plant is now used not only for regular services but for other interests in connection with Bible School and the Daily Vacation Bible School. After long years of consecrated service, Brother Musa was called to his heavenly reward, being succeeded by his nephew, Rev. L. V. Hannah, also a son of the Near East, and Mrs. Hannah, a native of Texas. Both have had theological training in America and are prepared to do splendid service. During the past several years Mrs. Hannah and Mrs. Musa have done very good work with the children of the church and congregation which argues well for the future. On the other hand, with the phenomenal development of Haifa, only a few miles away, the Nazareth church has lost some of its members and now faces a real struggle for existence. Here is a work about which we are prayerfully concerned and fully believe that in this town of the Master the work should be adequately supported and encouraged. And, as in other days when Jesus and the disciples went throughout the towns and villages of Galilee preaching, teaching, and healing, so today our Baptist Evangel should make his impact on Galilean communities in the interest of the Kingdom of God. If one is looking for difficulties he will find plenty of them through all this territory, but he will also find that the "prospects are just as bright as the promises of God."

Jerusalem. Here in the religious capital of the world, and amid every type of religion imaginable, Southern Baptists are bearing testimony to the simple and abiding claims of the Gospel. Inseparably connected with every phase of Hebrew history and the redemptive purpose of God which came to its consummation in the Holy City, Jerusalem offers probably our most difficult field but, likewise, our most successful work in Palestine hitherto. One cannot think of this sacred place apart from its hallowed associations with the long line of Israel's great men and women, from the time of Abraham to the days of Jesus and His apostles. In this city where God chose to put His name, we follow in the train of prophets, priests, and kings, sensing always the eternal purpose back of every event in the national life and moving always toward the goal of that greatest of all events when Jesus came unto His own. Through these hills and valleys He moved, walked the ancient streets of the city of the Great King, wept over its destiny, hallowed its Temple by His presence and work, plead for the salvation of the people, only to be rejected and to be crucified on the shameful cross. But the crowning glory of the Saviour's earthly mission broke forth from the Empty Tomb outside the city wall. Here then in Jerusalem Jesus moved in devoted service; here He died, rose again, and ascended to His Father. On the last day of His resurrection appearance He laid on the hearts of His people: "Ye shall receive power, when the Holy Spirit is come upon you: and ye shall be my witnesses both in Jerusalem, and in all Judaea and Samaria, and unto the uttermost part of the world." Accordingly, it was from Jerusalem that the light commenced to break until the whole Gentile world began to share in its love, its liberty, and its law. The heralds of the Good News went forth from its sacred gates with the proclamation of peace and good will to all men. In the modern age we are making a return journey to the place of His Cross, His Tomb, and His Commission. One instinctively feels that it is good for us to be here with gratitude and with earnest service, that we may announce to all what great things Jesus has done for us! And to plead for a heartfelt reception of Him on their part! Indeed, that is what we are doing, and the blessings of the Father are seen on every hand.

Our work in Jerusalem is now being conducted by most capable and consecrated missionaries: Miss Elsie Clor, a Christian Jewess; Miss Eunice Fenderson, and Rev. H. Leo Eddleman. Our church property, consisting of church, mission house, and recreational grounds, is the gift of some Northern Baptist friends and the Woman's Missionary Union of the Southern Baptist Convention. The church is located in a very desirable section of modern Jerusalem, almost in the heart of Jewish life and thought, as well as being in close contact with Arab interests. It is a great center of missionary activity conducted along the lines of a symmetrical ministry. Here is a successful Good Will Center operated largely for Jewish children, though the work is open also to Arab children who are heartily welcomed. On Saturday there is held a Sabbath School for Jewish children, and on Sunday a Sunday School for all nationalities. In addition, preaching services are held and the Good News lovingly proclaimed to all hearts. At other periods during the week our missionaries engage in helpful service that includes club work for boys and girls and Bible classes for women. Brother Eddleman has oversight of the work in Jerusalem and surrounding territory, giving most of his time to the Jews. Some converts have been won. These have come into the church which now has a membership of twenty. The work in Jerusalem is the most promising that we have in Palestine and should be reinforced as speedily as possible. Our achievements thus far, under the blessings of God, are real trophies of grace. Privations on the part of our missionaries have been many, dangers seen and unseen have surrounded them, threats of violence and acts of hostility have been their lot, but at no time have they faltered nor feared. In special ways God has cared for His consecrated workers and their work. The outlook is bright, triumphs are assured, and we must continue to advance. For example, Brother Eddleman tells us in a recent letter: "The Saturday after Christmas it was my privilege to preach to more than a hundred Jews in the morning, mostly children, with about forty adults. In the same afternoon I preached to more than seventy adult Jews. It was said that that was by far more Jews to be gathered together in Palestine to hear the Gospel and in their own language, the Hebrew, than in eighteen centuries." All of this is wonderful and serves in blessed manner to assure us that God has not abandoned interest in His people, whether Jews, Arabs, or Gentiles, and that some day we might expect another Jerusalem Pentecost in which *every man* shall hear the things of God in his own language.

Haifa. Haifa, beautifully situated at the foot of Mt. Carmel, and at the haven of the Sea, is the chief seaport of Palestine and destined to be the principal gateway to all of the Near and Middle East. Thronged with nationals from many lands, its streets echoing with the languages of widely separated peoples, Haifa today appears as a metropolitan and cosmopolitan center born almost overnight. Industrial activity is seen on every hand; in the harbor are anchored merchant vessels from over the seas; import trade is growing by leaps and bounds, while exports show the increasing importance of Near East countries in world markets. Clearly, it is the purpose of the British Government to convert Haifa into one of the principal cities of the Eastern Mediterranean world. To this end millions of dollars have already been expended. At present we can think of Haifa's population as the third in rank among Palestine's urban communities, the order of enumeration being Tel-Aviv, Jerusalem, and Haifa, but as an emporium it ranks first, its connections looking to the three great continents of Europe, Asia, and Africa. To win Haifa for Christ would be a far step in evangelization of a vast territory that includes many races, many tongues, and many conditions.

Alert to the alluring possibilities of this great seaport city, with its racial make-up of legion, Southern Baptists have established a most promising work under the leadership and direction of Rev. and Mrs. Roswell E. Owens. These progressive and consecrated young workers completed their first term of service in 1935. Alert to the ever-pressing needs of their exacting field and jealous for their maximum mental and spiritual equipment for the tasks, they are spending their furlough days in arduous study. They spent their first year of service in Jerusalem and Nazareth, engaged mainly in language study, but subsequently moved to Haifa where Brother Owens is preaching regularly to Arabs in their own language. Two of these mission stations are offering the way of life in Christ to all who will hear and receive. God has blessed the work of our missionaries in Haifa. Soon a Baptist church will be organized at Haifa, consisting of those who have accepted Jesus as the Saviour and Lord of their lives.

Among these new disciples there are two young men who give promise of usefulness in preaching the Gospel. It is clear that the one hope of establishing the work securely in Haifa and elsewhere in Palestine, is to raise up and train a native ministry who will be far more effective in preaching the Gospel to their own people than any American missionaries that we could send to them. It is the hope of the Foreign Board that a beginning in this direction of a trained Palestinian ministry may soon be made. Indeed, our leaders are already perfecting plans whereby these two young men of promise may devote one half of their time in study under Brother Owens and the remainder in secular employment to defray their expenses. It is confidently expected that this arrangement will go into effect at an early date. Thus the work goes forward, outward, and upward. Our missionaries at Haifa in their pioneering work certainly deserve and will receive our heartiest cooperation and sincerest prayers for divine blessings and approval upon the labors of their heads, hearts, and hands.

From this brief summary of peoples and conditions in Syria and Palestine it will be seen that the fields are barely touched, that numerous cities and open spaces thronged with nomad hordes remain to be evangelized. In the days of the Master similar throngs pressed upon Him. He looked with deep emotion on the great multitudes as so many sheep without a shepherd. Today the Near East looks toward the horizon of the west for the messengers of peace, the heralds of the Good News.

III

Pilgrims And Travelers

12. Tent Life in the Holy Land

During the nineteenth and twentieth centuries, increasing numbers of Americans of all religious persuasions journeyed to the Holy Land. Many of them wrote letters, articles, and books describing their experiences and feelings, and this flood of literature did much to shape the opinions of Americans concerning the land so important to three historic religions. One of the most devout of such reports was penned by an evangelical layman who clearly understood himself to be a pilgrim, William C. Prime (1825–1905). A graduate of Princeton, he practiced law and then served as editor-in-chief of the New York Journal of Commerce. *Following a journey to Palestine in 1855–56, he wrote* Tent Life in the Holy Land, *a rather sentimental but widely-read account. Mark Twain used the book as a guide when he traveled there a dozen years later, and in* The Innocents Abroad *poked fun at its pious author as "Grimes." The two selections that follow are drawn from the latter part of the book, one reflecting Prime's experiences as he prepared to leave Jerusalem, the other expressing his feelings at the Sea of Galilee—a special place of pilgrimage for many Protestants.*

Source: William C. Prime, *Tent Life in the Holy Land* (New York: Harper & Bros., 1857; reprinted by Arno Press, 1977), pp. 313–16, 366–69.

18.
If I Forget Thee, O Jerusalem!

At length our pilgrimage was accomplished. I had washed in the Jordan, and had prayed at the Sepulchre of the Lord. I had laved my eyes in the Fountain of Siloam, whose waters go softly, and had bathed my forehead in the dews that fell at evening in Gethsemane.

But my face was not yet set homeward. I had before me a journey to the banks of the Tigris. I intended visiting Nineveh and Babylon, and dropping down the Euphrates to the gulf, where I hoped to find a steamer to take me to Madras, or to Aden, so that I could return to Cairo, and thence reach Constantinople in the autumn. My route was, accordingly, to Damascus, visiting the sacred places of northern Palestine in the way. We therefore made our farewell visits to the places of deepest interest, and ordered our men to be ready at nine in the morning for the grand start.

Father Joseph gave to Miriam and myself separate certificates of our accomplished pilgrimage, notwithstanding he knew our Protestantism, and he positively refused a farthing in exchange. It was the last courtesy we received from the monks in Jerusalem, and in character with all we had seen of them.

Thus ended my rest in Jerusalem.

Think not lightly of this, my friend, for it is no light matter to have seen the Holy City. I hesitated much before I visited the Holy Land. I had always reasoned somewhat in this way. If I were taught that the Son of God descended to this earth, assuming the form of a child, and was the reputed son of a carpenter in an American village; that he lived here, walked these streets, preached at these corners, slept in the nights on the hills of Long Island and New Jersey, and was finally mobbed in the public places, tried for some alleged crime, condemned and executed here; if, I say, all this were taught me, I should find it much more difficult to believe than I now do the story of his life and death in a distant land, over which tradition and history have cast a holy radiance. I therefore feared much that when I had walked the streets of Jerusalem, had climbed the sides of Olivet, had rested in the garden of Gethsemane, and visited the Holy Sepulchre, my faith in the divinity of the Saviour, and the authenticity of his mission, might be seriously impaired.

Far otherwise was the reality.

Every step that I advanced on the soil of Palestine offered some new and startling evidence of the truth of the sacred story. Every hour we were exclaiming that the history must be true, so perfect was the proof before our eyes. The Bible was a new book, faith in which seemed now to have passed into actual sight, and every page of its record shone out with new, and a thousand-fold increased lustre.

The Bible had, of course, been our only guide-book. There is no other— and the publication of another will tend materially to decrease the interest of travel in Syria. He who shall visit Holy Soil with Murray's proposed red book in his hands, will know nothing of the keen pleasure that we experienced in studying out for ourselves the localities of sacred incident, or the intense delight that flashed across our minds when we found those startling confirmations of the truth of the story—startling, because unexpected and wholly original.

Sitting on the side of Mount Moriah, it was with new force we read that exquisite passage in the 46th Psalm, "There is a river the streams whereof shall make glad the city of God, the holy place of the tabernacles of the Most High;" which had its origin unquestionably in the beautiful fountain that springs under the very rocks of Moriah, the site of the ancient temple, more beautiful just here where fountains are so rare, and whose waters supplying Siloam, and thence "going softly" down the valley of Jehoshaphat, have in all times been the type of the salvation that God devised in Jerusalem for the races of men. The vision of Ezekiel, which promises a river flowing out of the sanctuary to the eastward, and giving life even to the terrible death of the Dead Sea, was startling when read on the slope of Moriah, whence those sweet waters flow down the valley of the Kedron, failing now, indeed, to reach the far depths of Engeddi, much less the waters of the Lake of Death.

That mournful procession, in which David, flying from his rebellious son, went up the Mount of Olives, weeping as he went, was before us like a picture as we sat outside the gate of St. Stephen, among the Moslem tombs, and looked into the valley and across at the steep slope of the hill of the Lord's ascension. Right well we knew what the passage meant, which likened the guardianship of the Father to the watch kept by the mountains around Jerusalem, when we saw the city, set on a hill itself, yet commanded on the north, east, south, and west by much higher hills, over whose summits the blue sky curves downward with that close embrace that one might well expect from the heavens above the city of the Sepulchre.

With these thoughts, new and fresh, and crowding on our minds every hour, it is not to be wondered at that we were willing to linger in Jerusalem, even after we had visited every one of its interesting points again and again. I should never weary of that walk over the Mount of Olives to Bethany, if I walked it every day until the sky opened above me, as it opened above the Lord. I should never satisfy my thirst for the waters of Siloam, if I drank them daily, and were forbidden evermore even the golden wine of Lebanon. I shall never cease in my soul to visit with pilgrim footsteps, day by day, the Sepulchre of the Saviour of men. . . .

There, far down below us, supremely beautiful, lay the sea of Galilee, a sapphire set in emeralds.

We were five hundred feet above it, and the descent was steep and difficult. Right underneath us was Tiberias, with its ruined walls and falling houses, a melancholy wreck of former beauty and splendor. Our tents were pitched on the shore just outside of the walls on the south side of the city. The blue water rippled up to the edge of the canvas, and the path of the rising moon lay across it, as if we could see the very footsteps of the Lord.

We walked along the shore till nearly midnight, throwing pebbles into the sea, and watching the circles spreading over the lake. What scene on earth's surface can be imagined more divinely beautiful than moonlight on the sea of Galilee. The hushed air seemed heavy with the presence of angels. The very heavens bent down, as if they loved the spot, and the stars came low to look on their own thrones reflected in its calm surface.

In times of tempestuous sorrow, such as all men have known, I had dreamed of the sea of Galilee. In hours of passion, such as human nature is liable to fall into, I had hushed my heart by the fancied voices of the wind over its waves. In feverish visions, when the phantoms of disease made my brain wild, and all manner of hideous imaginings came to frighten and madden me, when the faces of friends assumed the features of devils, and even the best beloved of faces put on a worse than Medusa-like countenance, I have calmed the fever and restored the healthy action of my brain, by simple firmness in thinking of the murmur of the ripples that broke on its beach, whose music, I have often thought, must be nearer the sounds of heaven than any other this side the upper blue. And now I found it even so; and as we sat down by the shore of the sea that night and listened in silence to its voice on the pebbles at our feet, all human passions and emotions were at rest, our souls were hushed, the "peace! be still" of his voice was audible as of old, and our hearts heard it and were calm.

Let him who ridicules the idea that there is hallowed ground, sit down by the sea of Galilee in the light of the moon and stars, and if his soul denies the influences that are on the sea, and in the air, around, above, and within him, I am content that he shall take his verdict. The man does not live that can laugh at the story of the Passion, seated in Gethsemane, nor who can forget the blessing of the pure in heart on the moonlit shore of Gennesaret.

When I was a boy in the up-country (how often I wrote that same sentence, and uttered it aloud in Holy Land—it was so strange that I—that boy—was wandering among Bedouins in the land of the Lord), when I was a boy, there was an old man, a good and kind old man, who was accustomed to come once a week to the old house, and always to take me on his lap, and, in a broad Scotch tongue, to say to me, "Wully, Wully" (yes, I was the Willy, I, the black-bearded horseman—whom the Arabs knew as Braheem Effendi—was the boy Willy, who looked in wonderment at the old man who had come from "ayant the seas"); he would say, "Wully, when ye're grawn to be a mon, mayhap ye'll go a wanderin' up and doon the hills of the warld. But doan ye forgit that gin ye're theersty, there's the sea o'Galilee, and gin ye're hungry, there's the loaves that fed feeve thoosand there by the sea, and when ye get tired and tired out, and want to lay your head doon on any stoun and rest it, but the stouns are all hard, there's Heem that sayed on the same sea, 'Cume unto me all ye that labor, and are heevy laden, and I wull geeve ye rest.'"

Through what long years of wandering my memory went back to the old man's voice and the old man's face. Long ago he, having well done the labor of living, entered the promised rest, and found the sea of heaven broader, and deeper, and fuller than even he had dreamed. The wild March winds were blowing over his grave, that grave that holds, as well, the brown locks of his darling Jeannie, Jeannie Stuart of holy memory, and the wail of the tempest among the pine-trees around them does not disturb their profound peace. And I—how changed—with forehead already in early manhood marked with care and sorrow, weary long ago, but for the joy of pleasant company along the uncertain and varying path of life, I sat by the Gennesaret of Galilee on earth and thought of them in the land of eternal, and holy waters: Galilee beyond Jordan of the Gentiles that are saved!

I lay down in my tent to sleep, but the murmur of the waves invited me, and I could not resist. I stepped outside the tent, and all was silent, still, and gloriously beautiful. The white moonlight lay on the ruined walls of Tiberias, and on our group of tents, and on the blue sea. A dozen Bedouins lay sleeping near the camp fire, and the servants and muleteers, rolled up in their heavy bornooses, had forgotten the pilgrims.

I walked slowly down into the sea. The clear water flashed like diamonds around me as I lay down in it, and it closed over me, and then I floated on the motionless surface.

After that baptism, I slept such peaceful sleep as no man can know of that has not done even as I.

13. A Church Historian's Travels in Bible Lands

Swiss-born Philip Schaff (1819–93), educated at the universities of Tubingen, Halle, and Berlin, was called to teach at the seminary of the German Reformed Church in Mercersburg, Pennsylvania, in 1844. During the Civil War he settled in New York and in 1869 began a long term of service at Union Theological Seminary, where he was active until his death in 1893. He taught in several fields, was author of many books, especially of church history, and was the founder of the American Society of Church History.

The death of a daughter in 1876 was the occasion for a trip to the Holy Land, where he went for solace and to find fresh inspiration. The scholarly traveler wrote letters to friends at home, and as happened many times, this correspondence became the basis of a book. His purpose was "to give the general reader a clear idea of the actual condition and prospects of the East by a simple narrative of what I saw and heard and felt on the spot." His knowledge of the Bible was evident as he described the Holy Land of a century ago, but he also surveyed the religious conditions there at the time of his visit, with particular but not exclusive attention to Christian institutions. The passages which follow deal with his first impressions of Palestine, especially at Hebron, and his concluding overall impressions of the Holy Land.

Source: Philip Schaff, *Through Bible Lands: Notes of Travel in Egypt, the Desert, and Palestine* (New York: American Tract Society, 1878; reprinted by Arno Press, 1977), pp. 207–14, 383–90.

Chapter Twenty-One.

Hebron.

Coming from a forty years' wandering in the wilderness, Palestine was indeed to the Israelites a land of promise flowing with milk and honey. Though fearfully desolate and neglected now, we can even yet everywhere see the traces of its former prosperity and its capacities for a future resurrection under a better government and with a better population. Its climate and natural fertility are unsurpassed; its hills and valleys make it a beautiful country, a sort of Switzerland or Wales of the East; while its historical significance, as the classical soil of revelation and the birthplace of the only true and universal religion, raises it above the most highly favored countries of the globe. The disproportion of its small size to its historical greatness reminds one of Greece. Its length from Beersheba in the south to Dan in the north is only about one hundred and eighty miles, its breadth from the Jordan to the sea not much more than fifty miles; and yet this little country has done more for the religious and moral, as Greece has done more for the intellectual, progress of mankind than the vast empires of Assyria, Babylonia, Persia, and Rome. The isolation of

Palestine from idolatrous countries by sea and desert was favorable to the development of the pure monotheistic religion; while its central location between three continents looked to the universal destination and spread of the gospel which was born there.

My first impressions in reaching Palestine from the Desert and in travelling on its southern border from Gaza to Hebron may be briefly summed up in these points: (1) the natural beauty and fertility of the country; (2) the Swiss-like character of the landscape;* (3) the abundance of variegated wild flowers and of grain fields; (4) the absence of rivers and trees; (5) the want of roads, carriages, wagons, wheelbarrows, and every trace of a good government and enterprising population; (6) the semi-barbarous character and condition of the inhabitants, both Moslems and nominal Christians; (7) the richness of Scripture reminiscences and illustrations, which multiply as we proceed. The ruins of cities on the hills remind us of the "city that is set on a hill and cannot be hid" (Matt. 5:14). The luxuriant vineyards and fig-trees at Hebron recall the grapes, pomegranates, and figs which the spies brought from Hebron and the valley or the brook of Eshcol to the camp of Israel in Kadesh-Barnea (Numb. 13:22-25); and as we see the walls around the vineyards and the watch-towers in the corner for the guard, we have a striking illustration of the parable of the vineyard (Matt. 21:33). The Land is a commentary on the Book.

Before we reach Hebron coming from Gaza, we turn off the main road to see the famous OAK (or Terebinth) of ABRAHAM, about two miles west of the city. It has often been photographed. It is a truly majestic and venerable tree, more venerable than any in the world except the olive-trees of Gethsemane. Its trunk measures thirty-two feet in circumference. Its crown divides into four colossal branches spread out like wings. It is now surrounded by a stone wall and owned by the Russians, who bought the surrounding field and built a fine hospice on the hill above. Already in the time of Josephus there was shown, six furlongs from the city, "a very large turpentine-tree, which has continued ever since the creation of the world."† Here "in the plains" (or rather, "the oaks") "of Mamre" father Abraham courteously received and hospitably entertained the three

---

*Miss Martineau and Dean Stanley, hailing from England, were struck "by the Western, almost the English, character of the scenery," and were reminded of the Lowlands of Scotland and Wales.
†See *Bell. Jud.* Book IV., chap. 9. ¶ 7. Josephus, however, does not connect it expressly with Abraham.

mysterious visitors "under the tree," in front of the tent, and was informed
of the future birth of Isaac, the son of promise (Genesis 18:2-9). From here
he accompanied the strangers to a hill from which he could look upon
Sodom and Gomorrah, and interceded with the Lord for the doomed cities,
but in vain, because not even ten righteous persons could be found there
(23-33). And early in the morning, coming to the place where he stood
before the Lord, "he looked toward Sodom and Gomorrah, and toward all
the land of the plain, and beheld, and lo, the smoke of the country went up
as the smoke of a furnace" (Gen. 19:27, 28).

Hebron is mentioned about forty times in the Old Testament, but
nowhere in the New. Like Damascus, it carries us back to the days of
Abraham, as one of the most ancient cities of the world. It was built seven
years before Zoan or Tanis, the capital of the Shepherd Kings in Egypt
(Numb. 13:22). It is the city of Abraham, "the friend of God" (Jas. 2:23),
and in honor of him the Arabs call it *El Khulil* i.e., "the Friend" (of Allah).
Here he built an altar unto the Lord, and walked and communed with him
(Gen. 13:18). Here he bought from Ephron the Hittite the cave and field of
Machpelah, as the final resting-place for his family. Here the patriarchs
spent a large part of their lives. Here David reigned over Judah seven years
and six months before he became sovereign of the whole land and removed
his residence to Jerusalem (2 Sam. 5:5). Here is the pool over which he
hanged up the murderers of his rival Ishbosheth (2 Sam. 4:12). Here he no
doubt composed some of his psalms which still kindle the devotions of the
people of God all over the world. Hebron is one of the four holy cities of
Islam (with Mecca, Medinah, and Jerusalem) and of Judaism (with
Jerusalem, Safed, and Tiberias). It is situated at the foot of a hill in a well-
watered and fertile valley, usually supposed to be the Valley of Eshcol (the
Valley of Grapes), unless this is to be sought further south near Beersheba.*
It is surrounded by vineyards, olive groves, almond, apricot, and fig trees.
It lies 3,029 feet above the sea, about twenty miles or seven hours' ride
south of Jerusalem. It passed into the possession of Islam in the seventh

* See Numb. 13:22-25; 32:9; Deut. 1:24. It is uncertain whether the valley and the brook of
Eshcol (eshkol, a bunch, a cluster, especially of grapes) derived the name from Eshcol, the
brother of Mamre the Amorite, and one of the four chieftains who accompanied Abraham in
his pursuit of the four robber-kings (Gen. 14:13, 14), or whether he derived it from the valley.
It certainly is in the neighborhood of Hebron. Robinson says, "This valley is generally
assumed to be the Eshcol of the Old Testament, whence the spies brought back the cluster of
grapes to Kadesh; and apparently not without reason. The character of its fruit still
corresponds to its ancient celebrity, and pomegranates and figs, as well as apricots, quinces,
and the like, still grow there in abundance."

century. During the Crusades it was for a short time (1167 to 1187) the seat of a Latin bishopric, but after the disastrous defeat of the Crusaders at Tiberias in 1187 it fell into the hands of Saladin, and has since been a hotbed of Mohammedan insolence and fanaticism. Its eight or ten thousand inhabitants are all Moslems, with the exception of five hundred Jews. There is not a single Christian family there. The inhabitants manufacture water-skins from goats' hides, lamps, and colored glass rings for female ornaments. As the Mohammedans drink no wine, they dry the grapes and sell large quantities of raisins, or they boil the juice into *debs*, a kind of thick grape molasses, which is often mentioned in the Bible under the kindred name of *debash*. The houses are built of stone, and many have domes as at Jerusalem.

The most important building is the GREAT MOSQUE (Harâm), a massive and imposing but gloomy structure, about 200 feet long by 150 (according to Tristram, 115) feet wide, and upwards of 50 feet high, with two minarets. It is surrounded by the dwellings of dervishes and the forty hereditary guardians of the mosque. The high wall is supposed to date from the time of David or Solomon. The mosque itself was probably a Byzantine church, like the Great Mosque of Damascus, the Mosque el-Aksa in Jerusalem, and St. Sophia in Constantinople. It owns some of the best lands in Philistia and in the plains of Sharon.

But the object of greatest interest in this mosque is concealed beneath its pavement. It is "the double cave," or MACHPELAH, the oldest known burial-place in the world. Here the three patriarchs and their wives (except Rachel, who is buried beneath a little white mosque near Bethlehem) sleep till the morning of the resurrection. Joseph's body, too, is said to have been removed thither from Shechem, near Jacob's well, where his tomb is still shown. There never has been any doubt about the identity of the spot. Such caves are as everlasting as the hills to which they belong. The story of Machpelah is singularly touching. With what solemnity and carefulness did father Abraham acquire this his only property in the Holy Land from his heathen friend Ephron, and make it sure for ever by that first legal contract recorded in history (Gen. 23:3-20). The scene comes back to us in all its circumstantial details, as Dr. Thomson shows so graphically from his own experience of bargaining among the Orientals of the present day.* How simple and impressive is the record of the successive interments of the patriarchal families, and the burial of enmities between brothers over

---

* *The Land and the Book*, Vol. II., p. 381 seq.

the graves of their fathers: first Sarah was buried (Gen. 23:19), then Abraham by Isaac and Ishmael (25:9, 10), then Isaac by his sons Esau and Jacob (35:27-29); and last we read the dying request of Jacob in Egypt: "And he charged them and said unto them, I am to be gathered unto my people: bury me with my fathers in the cave that is in the field of Ephron the Hittite for a possession of a burial-place. There they buried Abraham and Sarah his wife; there they buried Isaac and Rebekah his wife; and there I buried Leah" (49:29-31). How much of history, how many family joys and family griefs, what bright hopes of immortality and resurrection were gathered in that spot! How strange that no allusion should be made to it in the later books of the Bible. But Josephus mentions beautiful marble monuments of Abraham and his sons in Hebron, and Machpelah was always regarded as one of the most sacred places on earth. . . .

Chapter Thirty-Nine.
Farewell to the Holy Land.

At last I have fulfilled a long-cherished desire to see with my own eyes and to tread with my own feet the most sacred and the most classical land in the world. My only regret is that I could not visit it twenty or thirty years ago, to make earlier use of the experience for Bible studies.

I have been neither favorably nor unfavorably disappointed. I found the country and the people pretty much as I expected, but I trust I understand both better than before. My faith in the Bible has not been shaken, but confirmed. Many facts and scenes, which seem to float ghost-like in the clouds to a distant reader, assume flesh and blood in the land of their birth. There is a marvellous correspondence between the Land and the Book. The Bible is the best handbook for the Holy Land, and the Holy Land is the best commentary on the Bible.*

We began our journey with Egypt, the cradle of the people of Israel, and we found it still a "land of bondage" under new masters, a smiling garden and a dreary desert, covered with the colossal ruins of the Pharaohs. We crossed the Red Sea, and got a better idea of the miraculous passage of the Israelites. We followed their course through "the great and terrible wilderness," and learned to appreciate their trials, and the benefits of this long training-school for their manhood. We stood on Mount Sinai,

---

* "*L'accord frappant des textes et des lieux, la merveilleuse harmonie de l'idéal évangélique avec le paysage qui lui servit de cadre furent pour moi comme une révélation,*" Renan.

the pulpit of Moses proclaiming the law of God for all ages, and we were indelibly impressed with the adaptation of the awfully sublime scenery to the event which took place there. We sat under the venerable oak of Mamre, where the father of the faithful entertained his celestial visitors, and we approached, not without some danger from Moslem fanaticism, the threshold of the Machpelah which conceals the mortal remains of the patriarchs. We descended to the cave of Bethlehem where the Saviour of the world was born, and we walked over the fields where the shepherds heard the music of angels singing, Glory to God and peace on earth. We spent, with mingled feelings of joy and sadness, the Latin and Greek Easter at Jerusalem, the queen of holy cities, still enthroned on her hills, but a lonely widow, "with dust on her forehead and chains at her feet." We walked about Sion, we marked her bulwarks, we considered her palaces, and we found her still "beautiful for situation, the joy of the whole earth" on account of the wonderful things said and done and suffered there for the benefit of mankind. We wept in Gethsemane, where Jesus, overwhelmed with the load of the sins of the world, was "exceeding sorrowful, even unto death;" and we rejoiced on Mount Olivet, where he ascended to his throne of ever-present and all-sufficient grace. We wandered through the ruins of Bethany, where Lazarus and the sisters entertained their divine Lord and witnessed his power over death and the grave. We looked from the heights of Neby Samwil over the battlefield of Gibeon and Beth-horon, the Plain of Sharon, and the orange-groves of Jaffa. We floated on the salt waters of the Dead Sea, in full view of the mountains of Moab, where Jehovah "kissed Moses to death," after showing him the beauties of the Land of Promise. We took a refreshing bath in the swift-flowing waters of the Jordan at the traditional site of the baptism of Christ. We spent a night at Jericho, and barely escaped "falling among robbers." We rested on a stony bed at Bethel, dreaming the dream of Jacob, and seeing the shining staircase of prayer and faith that leads even from the humblest spot on earth to the throne of grace. We saw the ruins of Shiloh, which once sheltered the Ark of the Covenant. We sat on Jacob's Well, where our Lord, weary of travel, but not of his work, offered to a poor woman the water of life, which has since quenched the thirst of innumerable souls. We ascended the ruins of the temple on Mount Gerizim, where the paschal sacrifice is still offered from year to year, according to the letter of the Mosaic law, by the small remnant of the Samaritan sect. We rode over the fruitful fields and hills of Samaria through which Jesus passed on his annual visits to Jerusalem, scattering flowers of holy thoughts and deeds on the way. Our eyes feasted on the Plain of Esdraelon, so often reddened with blood, and spread out like a green carpet of waving grainfields. We drank from the Fountain of Gideon, and heard his battle-cry ringing through the air, "The sword of the Lord and of Gideon." We lamented, in view of Mount Gilboa, with David the death of Jonathan, whose love to him was "wonderful, passing the love of women." We lunched at Nain, where our Lord comforted a widow by raising her only son from the dead. We spent a memorable Sabbath in Nazareth, where the Saviour of the world lived thirty years in quiet waiting and preparation for his work, misunderstood by his own townsmen and kindred. We ascended the lovely Tabor, and the lofty Hermon, where Christ revealed his glory to Moses and Elijah and his beloved disciples. We rode on the lonely banks and sailed on the blue waters of the Lake of Gennesaret, so beautiful even in its desolation, so hallowed by the footsteps of the Master, "Most human and yet most divine, The flower of man and God." We made our way through thistles and briers to the ruins of Tell Hum, and saw the broken columns of the synagogue once resounding with words that will never die. We camped at Caesaraea Philippi, and confessed with Peter, "Lord, to whom shall we go? Thou hast the words of eternal life. And we know and are sure that thou art the Christ, the Son of the living God."

Palestine is a library of revelation engraved on stones. The mountains and hills, the lakes and rivers, the caves and rocks are alive with Biblical stories. The meanest spot records some deep thought or noble deed that inspires the best of men to this day. It is still the old Canaan,

"In all the imploring beauty of decay."

But in no country is the contrast between the glorious past and the miserable present so startling and sad. Take away the ideal element, and the charm is gone. The whole land is a venerable ruin. It is hardly worth visiting except for its reminiscences. Yet even in these ruins it confirms the truth of prophecy. "I beheld, and lo, the fruitful place was a wilderness, and all the cities thereof were broken down at the presence of the Lord, and by his fierce anger. For thus hath the Lord said, The whole land shall be desolate; yet will I not make a full end."* "Upon the land of my people shall come up thorns and briers. . . . until the Spirit be poured upon us from on high, and the wilderness be a fruitful field."†

*Jer. 4:26, 27.
†Isaiah 32:13, 15.

When shall the Lord "bring again the captivity of Jacob's tents, and have mercy on his dwelling-places"? When will the holy city again be "builded upon her own heap"? When will "the voice of joy, and the voice of gladness, the voice of the bridegroom, and the voice of the bride" again be heard in her palaces, singing, "Praise the Lord of hosts, for the Lord is good and his mercy endureth for ever"? When shall "the wilderness and the solitary place be glad, and the desert rejoice and blossom as a rose"? When shall "waters break out in the wilderness and streams in the desert"? When will "the ransomed of the Lord return, and come to Zion with songs and everlasting joy upon their heads"?

"The mills of God grind slowly, but surely and wonderfully fine." *Deus habet suas horas et moras*. But a thousand years for him are as one day. And his promise can never fail.

Palestine needs for its regeneration a good government, an industrious population, capital, and a better religion, even the religion of the Bible, which sprung from its own soil and is now almost unknown. The Turkish government does not even fulfil the first duty of all government—the protection of life and property. It is no government at all, but a system of heartless oppression and incurable corruption. There is no justice and honesty in officials, no encouragement to till the soil, to build houses, to construct roads, to carry on commerce, to establish manufactories. The country is systematically impoverished, the people drained of its best men by conscription, kept in utter ignorance, and ground down by taxation till every vestige of manhood and every hope of improvement are crushed out of them.

But nature cannot be destroyed. The plains of Philistia, of Sharon, of Esdraelon, of Gennesaret, and the Hauran, though overgrown with weeds and overrun by the wild Bedawin, are still there as fertile as ever. The lakes and the rivers and the fountains are there as abundant as ever. The hills and mountains, though denuded of forests, are there as lofty as ever. The same abundance of flowers adorns the earth in spring as when the Saviour drew lessons from the lilies of the field. And what the indolent Turks will never do, the industry and zeal of foreigners will do, and make Palestine once more a land of promise "flowing with milk and honey," where every man may "sit under his own vine and fig-tree."

The process of regeneration has already begun. We see the small but hopeful tokens of a better future in the carriage-road from Jaffa to Jerusalem (the only one so far in Palestine), in the orange and olive groves of recent planting, in the German colonies of Jaffa, Haifa, and Jerusalem, in the fine houses, gardens, churches, schools, and orphanages which the missionary zeal of foreign Protestants has established in Jerusalem, Bethlehem, and Nazareth. Nor ought we to overlook the significant fact of the increasing immigration of the Jews, which was stimulated by the liberal benefactions of Rothschild and Montefiore, and will be still more encouraged by the *coup d'état* of one of their own blood who sits at the helm of Queen Victoria's government. The Turkish misrule is approaching its downfall, and will give way to a new order of things. The old ruins need not be swept away by the tide of civilization, but should be carefully kept and restored, like the English and Scotch abbeys and cathedrals which perpetuate the memory of the venerable past amid the fresh life of the present.

With these hopes of a brighter future we bid farewell to the Holy Land, and board the Austrian steamer in the beautiful harbor of Beirŭt on our homeward course to Europe and America.

"Thou land of Judaea! thrice hallowed of song,
    Where the holiest of memories pilgrim-like throng;
    In the shade of thy palms, by the shores of thy sea,
    On the hills of thy beauty, my heart is with thee.

"With the eye of a spirit I look on that shore,
    Where pilgrim and prophet have lingered before;
    With the glide of a spirit I traverse the sod
    Made bright by the steps of the angels of God.

"I tread where the Twelve in their wayfaring trod;
    I stand where they stood with the CHOSEN OF GOD,
    Where his blessing was heard and his lessons were taught,
    Where the blind was restored and the healing was wrought.

"Oh, here with his flock the sad Wanderer came;
    These hills he toiled over in grief are the same;
    The founts where he drank by the wayside still flow,
    And the same airs are blowing which breathed on his brow!

    *   *   *   *   *   *   *   *

"But wherefore this dream of the earthly abode
    Of Humanity clothed in the brightness of God?
    Were my spirit but turned from the outward and dim,
    It would gaze, even now, on the presence of Him!

"Beloved of the Father, thy Spirit is near
    To the meek and the lowly and penitent here;

And the voice of thy love is the same even now
As at Bethany's tomb or on Olivet's brow.

"Oh, the outward hath gone! but in glory and power
The spirit surviveth the things of an hour;
Unchanged, undercaying, its Pentecost flame
On the heart's secret altar is burning the same!"

WHITTIER

14. A Preacher on Pilgrimage

The last quarter of the nineteenth century is remembered in American Protestant history as (among other things) an age of "princes of the pulpit." In most cities, downtown churches were often led by pulpit giants who had gathered large followings. Schooled in the lore of the Bible, these preachers knew a lot about the Holy Land of biblical times and longed to visit it. Increasing ease and speed of travel made it more possible for them to do so as time went on.

One of the best-known of the pulpit princes of that period was a Presbyterian minister in Brooklyn, T. De Witt Talmage (1832–1902). A graduate of New Brunswick Theological Seminary, he was author of many books, editor of the Christian Herald, and had the distinction of having a sermon published weekly for twenty-nine years. On his return from leading a group of pilgrims to the Holy Land, he preached a series of sermons, on his experiences, later gathered in book form. The first two of his ten sermons, central parts of which follow, disclosed his high expectancy as he approached the sacred soil, his enthusiasm for enlisting others to undertake a pilgrimage, and his anticipation that the Jews would be restored to Jerusalem.

Source: T. De Witt Talmage, *Talmage on Palestine: A Series of Sermons* (Springfield, Ohio: Mast, Crowell & Kirkpatrick, 1890; reprinted by Arno Press, 1977), pp. 6–12, 22–25, 35–37.

Future Explorers.

The chief hindrance for going to Palestine with many is the dreadful sea, and though I have crossed it ten times, it is more dreadful every time, and I fully sympathize with what was said one night when Mr. Beecher and I went over to speak in New York at the Anniversary of the Seamen's Friend Society and the clergyman making the opening prayer quoted from St. John: "There shall be no more sea," and Mr. Beecher, seated beside me, in memory of a recent voyage said "Amen, I am glad of that." By the partial abolition of the Atlantic Ocean and the putting down of rail-tracks across every country in all the world, the most sacred land on earth will come under the observation of so many people, who will be ready to tell of what they saw, that infidelity will be pronounced only another form of insanity, for no honest man can visit the Holy Land and remain an infidel. This Bible from which I preach has almost fallen apart, for I read from it the most of the events in it recorded on the very

Places Where they Occurred

Some of the leaves got wet as the waves dashed over our boat on Lake Galilee and the book was jostled in saddlebags for many weeks, but it is a new book to me, newer than any book that yesterday came out of any of our great printing-houses. All my life I have heard of Palestine and I had read about it, and talked about it, and preached about it, and sung about it, and prayed about it, and dreamed about it until my expectations were piled up into something like Himalayan proportions, and yet I have to cry out, as did the Queen of Sheba when she first visited the Holy Land: "The half was not told me."

In order to make the more accurate and vivid a book I have been writing—a life of Christ, entitled, "From Manger to Throne," I left home last October, and on the last night of November we were walking the decks of the *Senegal*, a Mediterranean steamer. It was a ship of immense proportions. There were but few passengers, for it is generally rough at that time of year, and pleasurists are not apt to be voyaging there and then. The stars were all out that night. Those armies of light seemed to have had their shields newly burnished. We walked the polished deck. Not much was said, for in all our hearts was the dominant word "to-morrow." Somehow the Acropolis, which a few days before had thrilled us at Athens, now in our minds lessened in the height of its columns and the glory of its temples. And the Egyptian pyramids in our memory lessened their wonders of obsolete masonry, and the Coliseum at Rome was not so vast a ruin as it a few weeks before had seemed to be. And all that we had seen and heard dwindled in importance, for to-morrow, *to-morrow* we shall see the Holy Land. "Captain, what time will we come

In Sight of Palestine?"

"Well," he said, courteously, "if the wind and sea remain as they are, about daybreak." Never was I so impatient for a night to pass. I could not see much for that night, anyhow. I pulled aside the curtain from the port-hole of my stateroom, so that the first hint of dawn would waken me. But it was a useless precaution. Sleep was among the impossibilities. Who could be so stupid as to slumber when any moment there might start out within sight of the ship, the land where the most stupendous scenes of all time and all eternity were enacted? Land of ruin and redemption, land where was fought the battle that made our heaven possible, land of Godfrey and Saladin, of Joshua and Jesus.

Will the night ever be gone? Yes, it is growing lighter, and along the horizon there is something like a bank of clouds, and as a watchman paces the deck, I say to him, "What is that out yonder?" "That is land, sir," said the sailor.

"The Land!" I Cried.

Soon all our friends were aroused from sleep and the shore began more clearly to reveal itself. With roar, and rattle, and bang, the anchor dropped in the roadstead a half mile from land, for though Joppa is the only harbor of Palestine, it is the worst harbor on all the coast. Sometimes for weeks no ships stop there. Between rocks about seventy-five feet apart a small boat must take the passengers ashore. The depths are strewn with the skeletons of those who have attempted to land or attempted to embark. Twenty-seven pilgrims perished with one crash of a boat against the rocks. Whole fleets of crusaders, of Romans, of Syrians, of Egyptians, have gone to splinters there. A writer eight-hundred years ago, said he stood on the beach in a storm at Joppa, and out of thirty ships, all but seven went to pieces on the rocks and a thousand of the dead were washed ashore.

A Rock-Bound Coast

Strange that with a few blasts of powder like that which shattered our American Hell Gate, those rocks have not been uprooted and the way cleared, so that great ships, instead of anchoring far out from land, might sweep up to the wharf for passengers and freight. But you must remember that land is under the Turk, and what the Turk touches, he withers. Mohammedanism is against easy wharves, against steamers, against rail-trains against printing-presses, against civilization. Darkness is always opposed to light. The owl hates the morn. "Leave those rocks where they are," practically cries the Turkish Government; "we want no people of other religions and other habits to land there; if the salt seas wash over them, let it be a warning to other invaders; away with your nineteenth century, with its free thought and its modern inventions." That Turkish Government ought to be blotted from the face of the earth, and it will be. Of many of the inhabitants of Palestine, I asked the question, "Has

The Sultan of Turkey

ever been here?" "No." "Why don't he come, when it belongs to his dominion?" And, after the man interrogated looked this way and that, so as to know he would not be reported, the answer would invariably be, "he dare not come." I believe it. If the Sultan of Turkey attempted to visit Jerusalem, he would never get back again. All Palestine hates him. I saw him go to the mosque for prayers in his own city of Constantinople and saw seven thousand armed men riding out to protect him. Expensive prayers! Of course that government wants no better harbor at Joppa. May God remove that curse of nations, that old hag of the centuries, the Turkish Government! For its everlasting insult to God and woman, let it perish! And so those rocks at the harbor remain the jaws of repeated destruction.

As we descended the narrow steps at the side of the ship, we heard the clamor, and quarrel, and swearing, of fifteen or sixteen different races of men of all features, and all colors and all vernaculars; all different in appearance, but all alike in desire to get our baggage and ourselves at exorbitant prices. Twenty boats and only ten passengers to go ashore. The man having charge of us pushes aside some, and strikes with a heavy stick others, and by violences that would not be tolerated in our country, but which seem to be the only manner of making any impression there, clears our way into one of the boats which heads for the shore. We are within fifteen minutes of the Christ-land. Now we hear shouting from the beach and in five minutes we are landed. The prow of the boat is caught by men who wade out to help us in. We are tremulous with suppressed excitement, our breath is quick, and from the side of the boat we spring to the shore, and Sunday morning, December 1, 1889, about eight o'clock, our feet touch Palestine. Forever to me and mine will that day and hour be commemorated, for that pre-eminent mercy. Let it be mentioned in prayer by my children and children's children after we are gone, that morning we were permitted to enter that land, and gaze upon those holy hills, and feel the emotions that rise, and fall, and weep, and laugh, and sing, and triumph at such a disembarkation.

On the back of hills one hundred and fifty feet high Joppa is lifted toward the skies. It is as picturesque as it is quaint, and as much unlike any city we have ever seen as though it were built in that star Mars, where a few nights ago this very September, astronomers through unparallelled telescopes saw a snow-storm raging. How glad we were to be in Joppa! Why this is the city where Dorcas, that queen of the needle, lived and died and was resurrected. You remember that the poor people came around the dead body of this benefactress and brought specimens of her kind needle-work, and said, "Dorcas made this;" "Dorcas sewed that;" "Dorcas cut and fitted this;" "Dorcas hemmed that." According to Lightfoot, the commentator, they laid her out in state in a public room and the poor wrung their hands and cried, and sent for Peter, who performed a miracle

by which, the good woman came back to life and resumed her benefactions. An especial resurrection day for one woman! She was the model by
which many of the women of our day have fashioned their lives, and at the
first blast of the horn of the wintry tempest, there appear ten thousand
Dorcases—Dorcases of Brooklyn, Dorcases of New York, Dorcases of
London, Dorcases of all the neighborhoods and towns and cities of
Christendom, just as good as the Dorcas of the Joppa which I visited.
Thank God for the ever-increasing skill and sharpness and speed and
generosity of Dorcas's needle.

"What is that man doing?" I said to the dragoman in the streets of
Joppa. "Oh, he is

Carrying his Bed."

Multitudes of the Eastern people sleep out-of-doors and that is the way
so many in those lands become blind. It is from the dew of the night falling
on the eyelids. As a result of this, in Egypt, every twentieth person is
totally blind. In Oriental lands the bed is made of a thin small mattress, a
blanket and a pillow, and when a man rises in the morning he just ties up
the three into a bundle and shoulders it and takes it away. It was to that the
Saviour referred when he said to the sick man, "Take up thy bed and
walk." An American couch or an English couch would require at least four
men to carry it, but one Oriental can easily manage his slumber
equipment. . . .

My Second Day in Palestine.
"I went up to Jerusalem." Galatians 1:18.

My second day in the Holy Land. We are in Joppa. It is six o'clock in the
morning, but we must start early, for by night we are to be in Jerusalem,
and that city is forty-one miles away. We may take camel or horse or
carriage. As to-day will be our last opportunity in Palestine for taking the
wheel, we choose that. The horses with harness tasselled and jingling, are
hitched, and with a dragoman in coat of many colors seated in front, we
start on a road which unveils within twelve hours enough to think of for all
time and all eternity. Farewell Mediterranean with such a blue as no one
but the divine Chemist could mix, and such a fire of morning glow, as only
the divine Illuminator could kindle! Hail! Mountains of Ephraim and Juda
whose ramparts of rock we shall mount in a few hours, for modern

engineers can make a road anywhere, and without piling Ossa upon Pelion, those giants can scale the heaven.

We start out of the city amid barricades of cactus on either side. Not cacti in boxes two or three feet high, but cactus higher than the top of the carriage—a plant that has more swords for defense, considering the amount of beauty it can exhibit, than anything created. We passed out amid about four hundred gardens, seven or eight acres to the garden, from which at the right seasons are plucked oranges, lemons, figs, olives, citron, and pomegranates, and which hold up their censers of perfume before the Lord in perpetual praise. We meet great processions of

Camels Loaded with Kegs

of oil and with fruits, and some wealthy Mohammedan with four wives— three too many. The camel is a proud, mysterious, solemn, ancient, ungainly, majestic, and ridiculous shape, stalking out of the past. The driver with his whip taps the camel on the fore-leg, and he kneels to take you as a rider. But when he rises, hold fast or you will fall off backward as he puts his fore-feet in standing posture, and then you will fall off in front as his back-legs take their place. But the inhabitants are used to his ways, although I find the riders often dismount and walk as though to rest themselves. Better stand out of the path of the camel; he stops for nothing and seems not to look down, and in the street I saw a child by the stroke of a camel's front foot hurled seven or eight feet along the ground.

Here we meet people with faces, and arms, and hands tattooed, as in all lands sailors tattoo their arms with some favorite ship or admired face. It was to this habit of tattooing among the Orientals that God refers in a figure, when He says of His church: "I have graven thee on the palms of my hands."

Many of these regions are naturally sandy, but by irrigation they are made fruitful and, as by this irrigation, the brooks and rivers are turned this way, and that, to water the gardens and farms, so the Bible says, "The king's heart is in the hands of the Lord, and he turneth it as the rivers of water are turned whithersoever he will."

As we pass out and on we find about eight hundred acres belonging to the Universal Israelitish Alliance. Montefiore, the Israelitish centenarian and philanthropist, and Rothschild the banker, and others of the large-hearted have paid the passage to Palestine, for

Many Israelites,

and they have also set apart lands for their culture; and it is only a beginning of the fulfilment of divine prophecy, when these people shall take possession of the Holy Land. The road from Joppa to Jerusalem, and all the roads leading to Nazareth and Galilee we saw lined with processions of Jews, going to the sacred places, either on a holy pilgrimage, or as settlers. All the fingers of Providence now-a-days are pointing to that resumption of Palestine by the Israelites. I do not take it that the prospered Israelites of other lands are to go there. They would be foolish to leave their prosperities in our American cities where they are among our best citizens, and cross two seas to begin life over again in a strange land. But the outrages heaped upon them in Russia, and the insults offered them in Germany, will soon quadruple and centuple the procession of Israelites from Russia to Palestine.

Facilities for Getting There

will be multiplied, not only in the railroad from Joppa to Jerusalem, to which I referred last Sabbath as being built, but permission for a road from Damascus to the Bay of Acre has been obtained, and that will connect with Joppa, and make one great ocean-shore railroad. So the railroad from Jerusalem to Joppa, and from Joppa to Damascus, will soon bring all the Holy Land within a few hours of connection. Jewish colonization societies in England and Russia, are gathering money for the transportation of the Israelites to Palestine and for the purchase for them of lands and farming implements, and so

Many Desire to Go,

that it is decided by lot as to which families shall go first. They were God's chosen people at the first, and He has promised to bring them back to their home, and there is no power in one thousand or five thousand years to make God forget His promises. Those who are prospered in other lands, will do well to stay where they are. But let the Israelites who are depreciated, and attacked and persecuted turn their faces towards the rising sun of their deliverance. God will gather in that distant land, those of that race who have been maltreated, and He will blast with the lightnings of His omnipotence those lands on either side of the Atlantic, which have been the instruments of annoyance and harm to that Jewish race, to which belonged Abraham, and David, and Joshua, and Baron Hirsch, and Montefiore, and Paul the Apostle, and Mary the Virgin, and Jesus Christ the Lord. . . .

The Sacred City.

Over another shoulder of the hill we go, and nothing in sight but rocks and mountains, and awful gulches between them, which make the head swim if you look down. On and up, on and up, until the lathered and smoking horses are reigned in, and the dragoman rises in front, and points eastward, crying, *"Jerusalem!"* It was mightier than an electric shock. We all rose. There it lay, the prize of nations, the terminus of famous pilgrimages, the object of Roman and crusading wars, and for it Assyrians had fought, and Egyptians had fought, and the world had fought; the place which the Queen of Sheba visited, and Richard Coeur de Lion had conquered. Home of Solomon. Home of Ezekiel. Home of Isaiah. Home of Saladin. Mount Zion of David's heart-break, and Mount Moriah, where the sacrifices smoked, Mount of Olives, where Jesus preached, and Gethsemane, where He agonized, and Golgotha, where He died, and the Holy Sepulchre, where He was buried. O Jerusalem! Jerusalem! Greatest city on earth, and type of the city celestial.

After I have been ten thousand years in heaven, the memory of that first view from the rocks on the afternoon of December 2d, will be as vivid as now. An Arab on a horse that was like a whirlwind, bitted and saddled and spurred, its mane and flanks jet as the night—and there are no such horsemen as Arab horsemen—had come far out to meet us, and invite us to his hotel inside the gates. But arrangements had been made for us to stay at a hotel outside the gates. In the dusk of the evening we halted in front of the place and entered, but I said "No thank you for your courteous reception, but I must sleep to-night

Inside the Gates of Jerusalem.

I would rather have the poorest place inside the gates than the best place outside." So we remounted our coach and moved on amid a clamor of voices, and between camels grunting with great beams and timbers on their back, brought in for building purposes—for it is amazing how much a camel can carry—until we came to what is called the Joppa Gate of

Jerusalem. It is about forty feet wide, twenty feet deep, and sixty feet high. There is a sharp turn just after you have entered, so planned as to made the entrance of armed enemies the more difficult. On the structure of these gates the safety of Jerusalem depended and all Bible writers used them for illustrations. Within five minutes' walk of the gate we entered, David wrote: "Enter into thy gates with thanksgiving," "Lift up your heads, O, ye gates!" "The Lord loveth the gates of Zion," "Open to me the gates of righteousness." And Isaiah wrote: "Go through, go through the gates." And the captive of Patmos wrote: "The city had twelve gates." Having passed the gate we went on through the narrow streets, dimly lighted, and passed to our halting-place, and sat down by the window from which we could see Mount Zion, and said: "Here we are at last, in the capital of the whole earth." And thoughts of the past and the future rushed through my soul in quick succession, and I thought of that old hymn, sung by so many ascending spirits:

> Jerusalem, my happy home,
>   Name ever dear to me!
> When shall my labors have an end,
>   In joy and peace and thee?
>
> When shall these eyes thy heav'n-built walls
>   And pearly gates behold?
> Thy bulwarks with salvation strong,
>   And streets of shining gold?

And so with our hearts full of gratitude to God for journeying mercies all the way from Joppa to Jerusalem, and with bright anticipation of our entrance into the shining gate of the heavenly city when our earthly journeys are over, my second day in Palestine is ended.

15. Out-of-Doors in the Holy Land

Author of many books, both fiction and nonfiction, Henry Van Dyke (1852–1933) was one of the most popular religious writers of his time. Educated at Princeton, both college and seminary, he served in several Presbyterian pulpits before returning to Princeton as professor of English literature.

Invited to journey through the Holy Land in exchange for his impressions in the form of magazine articles, he accepted, and the literary fruit of his early twentieth-century journey then appeared in book form. A poetic and nature-loving spirit, Van Dyke eschewed the Palestine of his time "to return into the long past, . . . to make acquaintance with the soul of that land where so much that is strange and memorable and for ever beautiful has come to pass." The picture that many of his readers received was a somewhat romanticized, quite poetic interpretation. The selections describe his first impressions of Jerusalem and his reflections at that place so important to Protestant piety, the Sea of Galilee.

Source: Henry Van Dyke, *Out-of-Doors in the Holy Land: Impressions of Travel in Body and Spirit* (New York: Charles Scribner's Sons, 1908; reprinted by Arno Press, 1977), pp. 47–52, 247–55.

A City That Is Set on a Hill

Out of the medley of our first impressions of Jerusalem one fact emerges like an island from the sea: it is a city that is lifted up. No river; no harbour; no encircling groves and gardens; a site so lonely and so lofty that it breathes the very spirit of isolation and proud self-reliance.

> "Beautiful in elevation, the joy of the whole earth
> Is Mount Zion, on the sides of the north
> The city of the great King."

Thus sang the Hebrew poet; and his song, like all true poetry, has the accuracy of the clearest vision. For this is precisely the one beauty that crowns Jerusalem: the beauty of a high place and all that belongs to it: clear sky, refreshing air, a fine outlook, and that indefinable sense of exultation that comes into the heart of man when he climbs a little nearer to the stars.

Twenty-five hundred feet above the level of the sea is not a great height; but I can think of no other ancient and world-famous city that stands as high. Along the mountainous plateau of Judea, between the sea-coast plain of Philistia and the sunken valley of the Jordan, there is a line of sacred sites,—Beërsheba, Hebron, Bethlehem, Bethel, Shiloh, Shechem.

Each of them marks the place where a town grew up around an altar. The central link in this chain of shrine-cities is Jerusalem. Her form and outline, her relation to the landscape and to the land, are unchanged from the days of her greatest glory. The splendours of her Temple and her palaces, the glitter of her armies, the rich colour and glow of her abounding wealth, have vanished. But though her garments are frayed and weather-worn, though she is an impoverished and dusty queen, she still keeps her proud position and bearing; and as you approach her by the ancient road along the ridges of Judea you see substantially what Sennacherib, and Nebuchadnezzar, and the Roman Titus must have seen.

"The sides of the north" slope gently down to the huge gray wall of the city, with its many towers and gates. Within those bulwarks, which are thirty-eight feet high and two and a half miles in circumference, "Jerusalem is builded as a city that is compact together," covering with her huddled houses and crooked, narrow streets, the two or three rounded hills and shallow depressions in which the northern plateau terminates. South and east and west, the valley of the Brook Kidron and the Valley of Himmon [Hinnom] surround the city wall with a dry moat three or four hundred feet deep.

Imagine the knuckles of a clenched fist, extended toward the south: that is the site of Jerusalem, impregnable, (at least in ancient warfare), from all sides except the north, where the wrist joins it to the higher tableland. This northern approach, open to Assyria, and Babylon, and Damascus, and Persia, and Greece, and Rome, has always been the weak point of Jerusalem. She was no unassailable fortress of natural strength, but a city lifted up, a lofty shrine, whose refuge and salvation were in Jehovah,—in the faith, the loyalty, the courage which flowed into the heart of her people from their religion. When these failed, she fell.

Jerusalem is no longer, and never again will be, the capital of an earthly kingdom. But she is still one of the high places of the world, exalted in the imagination and the memory of Jews and Christians and Mohammedans, a metropolis of infinite human hopes and longings and devotions. Hither come the innumerable companies of foot-weary pilgrims, climbing the steep roads from the sea-coast, from the Jordan, from Bethlehem,— pilgrims who seek the place of the Crucifixion, pilgrims who would weep beside the walls of their vanished Temple, pilgrims who desire to pray where Mohammed prayed. Century after century these human throngs have assembled from far countries and toiled upward to this open, lofty plateau, where the ancient city rests upon the top of the closed hand, and where the everchanging winds from the desert and the sea sweep and shift over the rocky hilltops, the mute, gray battlements, and the domes crowned with the cross, the crescent, and the star.

"The wind bloweth where it will, and thou hearest the voice thereof, but knowest not whence it cometh, nor whither it goeth; so is every one that is born of the Spirit."

The mystery of the heart of mankind, the spiritual airs that breathe through it, the desires and aspirations that impel men in their journeyings, the common hopes that bind them together in companies, the fears and hatreds that array them in warring hosts,—there is no place in the world to-day where you can feel all this so deeply, so inevitably, so overwhelmingly, as at the Gates of Zion.

It is a feeling of confusion, at first: a bewildering sense of something vast and old and secret, speaking many tongues, taking many forms, yet never fully revealing its source and its meaning. The Jews, Mohammedans, and Christians who flock to those gates are alike in their sincerity, in their devotion, in the spirit of sacrifice that leads them on their pilgrimage. Among them all there are hypocrites and bigots, doubtless, but there are also earnest and devout souls, seeking something that is higher than themselves, "a city set upon a hill." Why do they not understand one another? Why do they fight and curse one another? Do they not all come to humble themselves, to pray, to seek the light?

Dark walls that embrace so many tear-stained, blood-stained, holy and dishonoured shrines! And you, narrow and gloomy gates, through whose portals so many myriads of mankind have passed with their swords, their staves, their burdens and their palm-branches! What songs of triumph you have hard, what yells of battle-rage, what moanings of despair, what murmurs of hopes and gratitude, what cries of anguish, what bursts of careless, happy laughter,—all borne upon the wind that bloweth where it will across these bare and rugged heights. We will not seek to enter yet into the mysteries that you hide. We will tarry here for a while in the open sunlight, where the cool breeze of April stirs the olive-groves outside the Damascus Gate. We will tranquillize our thoughts,—perhaps we may even find them growing clearer and surer,—among the simple cares and pleasures that belong to the life of every day; the life which must have food when it is hungry, and rest when it is weary, and a shelter from the storm and the night; the life of those who are all strangers and sojourners upon the earth, and whose richest houses and strongest cities are, after all, but a little longer-lasting tents and camps. . . .

Galilee and the Lake.

Memories of the Lake.

A hundred little points of illumination flash into memory as I look back over the hours that we spent beside the Sea of Galilee. How should I write of them all without being tedious? How, indeed, should I hope to make them visible or significant in the bare words of description?

Never have I passed richer, fuller hours; but most of their wealth was in very little things: the personal look of a flower growing by the wayside; the intimate message of a bird's song falling through the sunny air; the expression of confidence and appeal on the face of a wounded man in the hospital, when the good physician stood beside his cot; the shadows of the mountains lengthening across the valleys at sunset; the laughter of a little child playing with a broken water pitcher; the bronzed profiles and bold, free ways of our sunburned rowers; the sad eyes of an old Hebrew lifted from the book that he was reading; the ruffling breezes and sudden squalls that changed the surface of the lake; the single palm-tree that waved over the mud hovels of Magdala; the millions of tiny shells that strewed the beach of Capernaum and Bethsaida; the fertile sweep of the Plain of Gennesaret rising from the lake; and the dark precipices of the "Robbers' Gorge" running back into the western mountains.

The written record of these hours is worth little; but in experience and in memory they have a mystical meaning and beauty, because they belong to the country where Jesus walked with His fishermen-disciples, and took the little children in His arms, and healed the sick, and opened blind eyes to behold ineffable things.

Every touch that brings that country nearer to us in our humanity and makes it more real, more simple, more vivid, is precious. For the one irreparable loss that could befall us in religion,—a loss that is often threatened by our abstract and theoretical ways of thinking and speaking about Him,—would be to lose Jesus out of the lowly and familiar ways of our mortal life. He entered these lowly ways as the Son of Man in order to make us sure that we are the children of God.

Therefore I am glad of every hour spent by the Lake of Galilee.

I remember, when we came across in our boat to Tell Hûm, where the ancient city of Capernaum stood, the sun was shining with a fervent heat and the air of the lake, six hundred and eighty feet below the level of the sea, was soft and languid. The gray-bearded German monk who came to meet us at the landing and admitted us to the inclosure of his little monastery where he was conducting the excavation of the ruins, wore a cork helmet and spectacles. He had been heated, even above the ninety degrees Fahrenheit which the thermometer marked, by the rudeness of a couple of tourists who had just tried to steal a photograph of his work. He had foiled them by opening their camera and blotting the film with sunlight, and had then sent them away with fervent words. But as he walked with us among his roses and Pride of India trees, his spirit cooled within him, and he showed himself a learned and accomplished man.

He told us how he had been working there for two or three years, keeping records and drawings and photographs of everything that was found; going back to the Franciscan convent at Jerusalem for his short vacation in the heat of mid-summer; putting his notes in order, reading and studying, making ready to write his book on Capernaum. He showed us the portable miniature railway which he had made; and the little iron cars to carry away the great piles of rubbish and earth; and the rich columns, carved lintels, marble steps and shell-niches of the splendid building which his workmen had uncovered. The outline was clear and perfect. We could see how the edifice of fine, white limestone had been erected upon an older foundation of basalt, and how an earthquake had twisted it and shaken down its pillars. It was undoubtedly a synagogue, perhaps the very same which the rich Roman centurion built for the Jews in Capernaum (Luke vii: 5), and where Jesus healed the man who had an unclean spirit. (Luke iv: 31-37.) Of all the splendours of that proud city of the lake, once spreading along a mile of the shore, nothing remained but these tumbled ruins in a lonely, fragrant garden, where the patient father was digging with his Arab workmen and getting ready to write his book.

"Weh dir, Capernaum" I quoted. The *padre* nodded his head gravely. *"Ja, ja,"* said he, *"es ist buchstäblich erfüllt!"*

I remember the cool bath in the lake, at a point between Bethsaida and Capernaum, where a tangle of briony and honeysuckle made a shelter around a shell-strewn beach, and the rosy oleanders bloomed beside an inflowing stream. I swam out a little way and floated, looking up into the deep sky, while the waves plashed gently and caressingly around my face.

I remember the old Arab fisherman, who was camped with his family in a black tent on a meadow where several lively brooks came in (one of them large enough to turn a mill). I persuaded him by gestures to wade out into the shallow part of the lake and cast his bell-net for fish. He gathered the net in his hand, and whirled it around his head. The leaden weights around the bottom spread out in a wide circle and splashed into the water. He drew the net toward him by the cord, the ring of sinkers sweeping the bottom, and lifted it slowly, carefully—but no fish!

Then I rigged up my pocket fly-rod with a gossamer leader and two tiny trout-flies, a Royal Coachman and a Queen of the Water, and began to cast along the crystal pools and rapids of the larger stream. How merrily the fish rose there, and in the ripples where the brooks ran out into the lake. There were half a dozen different kinds of fish, but I did not know the name of any of them. There was one that looked like a black bass, and others like white perch and sunfish; and one kind was very much like a grayling. But they were not really of the *salmo* family, I knew, for none of them had the soft fin in front of the tail. How surprised the old fisherman was when he saw the fish jumping at those tiny hooks with feathers; and how round the eyes of his children were as they looked on; and how pleased they were with the *bakhshish* which they received, including a couple of baithooks for the eldest boy!

I remember the place where we ate our lunch in a small grove of eucalyptus-trees, with sweet-smelling yellow acacias blossoming around us. It was near the site which some identify with the ancient Bethsaida, but others say that it was farther to the east, and others again say that Capernaum was really located here. The whole problem of these lake cities, where they stood, how they supported such large populations (not less than fifteen thousand people in each), is difficult and may never be solved. But it did not trouble us deeply. We were content to be beside the same waters, among the same hills, that Jesus knew and loved.

It was here, along this shore, that He found Simon and his brother Andrew casting their net, and James and his brother John mending theirs, and called them to come with Him. These fishermen, with their frank and free hearts unspoiled by the sophistries of the Pharisees, with their minds unhampered by social and political ambitions, followers of a vocation which kept them out of doors and reminded them daily of their dependence on the bounty of God,—these children of nature, and others like them, were the men whom He chose for His disciples, the listeners who had ears to hear His marvellous gospel.

It was here, on these pale, green waves, that He sat in a little boat, near the shore, and spoke to the multitude who had gathered to hear Him.

He spoke of the deep and tranquil confidence that man may learn from nature, from the birds and the flowers.

He spoke of the infinite peace of the heart that knows the true meaning of love, which is giving and blessing, and the true secret of courage, which is loyalty to the truth.

He spoke of the God whom we can trust as a child trusts its father, and of the Heaven which waits for all who do good to their fellowmen.

He spoke of the wisdom whose fruit is not pride but humility, of the honour whose crown is not authority but service, of the purity which is not outward but inward, and of the joy which lasts forever.

He spoke of forgiveness for the guilty, of compassion for the weak, of hope for the desperate.

He told these poor and lowly folk that their souls were unspeakably precious, and that He had come to save them and make them inheritors of an eternal kingdom. He told them that He had brought this message from God, their Father and His Father.

He spoke with the simplicity of one who knows, with the assurance of one who has seen, with the certainty and clearness of one for whom doubt does not exist.

He offered Himself, in His stainless purity, in His supreme love, as the proof and evidence of His gospel, the bread of Heaven, the water of life, the Saviour of sinners, the light of the world. "Come unto Me," He said, "and I will give you rest."

This was the heavenly music that came into the world by the Lake of Galilee. And its voice has spread through the centuries, comforting the sorrowful, restoring the penitent, cheering the despondent, and telling all who will believe it, that our human life is worth living, because it gives each one of us the opportunity to share in the Love which is sovereign and immortal.

16. Reflections of a Black Pastor

Adam Clayton Powell, Sr. (1865-1953) graduated from Virginia Union University and then attended the Yale Divinity School. After serving a congregation in New Haven, he was called to New York's Abyssinian Baptist Church, where he led his growing congregation into many avenues of outreach and into a new location in Harlem. For a time, it was believed to be the largest Protestant congregation in the country.

On his retirement, Powell toured the Holy Land and devoted a good portion of his next book to the experience. As described in the preface, his aim was to give a human story of Palestine and "to help stem the world's rising tide of fierce, ungodly anti-Semitism," for his trip came on the eve of World War II. He believed his was the first such effort by a black person. His chapters had a double focus: on the Palestine of the past and the present, on the land of the Bible and the land of contemporary struggle, and he allowed the two perspectives to illumine each other.

Source: Adam Clayton Powell, Sr., *Palestine and Saints in Caesar's Household* (New York: Richard R. Smith, 1939), pp. 24-33.

Chapter Two.
The Jaffa-Jerusalem Road.

You can see the Holy Land through the window of a railroad coach, on the back of a camel, or from an automobile seat. The last is by far the most comfortable, and it guarantees the most satisfactory results, so at Jaffa we took our seat in a Buick car with an Arab guide at our side and an Armenian at the wheel.

Jerusalem was our final objective. The Jaffa-Jerusalem Road is forty miles long, and every mile of it is crowded with sacred memories and interesting history. Just outside Jaffa, we passed Tel-Aviv, the only one hundred percent Jewish town in the world. This town was founded by the Jews who believe in the Zion Movement. Its population is rapidly approaching 100,000, thus making it the second largest city in Palestine.

The Zion Movement, one of the most significant in the world today, is made up of Jews in all parts of the world, some of whom are moving back to Palestine to live the remainder of their lives. These settlers, who have met with such bitter antagonism, are more prosperous in the Jaffa section than in any other part of Palestine.

We were fortunate in traveling with David Sternberg, Mayor of the Zicron David [Zichron Yaakov] Colony in the northern part of Palestine, near Haifa. We had the pleasure of his company from Alexandria, Egypt, to Paris. When we finally got him to talking, he gave us more information about the Jewish point of view of the Zionist Movement than we were able to get from any other source. We learned from him that the Jews who are coming from all parts of the world to Palestine are not studying religion, that none of them believes in Christianity, that they are not going back to Palestine to build synagogues and churches. It is in no sense a religious movement, as many people seem to think, especially those who are using this as a proof of the Second Coming of Christ. It is a commercial and political movement pure and simple.

As a commercial venture, it has been a signal success. With the aid of the British, who administer the territory under the mandate of the League of Nations, more than 5,400 factories and workshops are being operated. These employ nearly 40,000 persons.

One is surprised to find such excellent transportation facilities. More than 2,000 ships enter the ports of Palestine annually, with average yearly cargo of five and one half million tons. It has 620 miles of railroads, and the automobile highway from Jaffa to Haifa compares favorably with the American rural highways before they were improved by the Works Progress Administration. The whirr of the airplane is common over the town where the angels sang two thousand years ago.

Despite all interpretations and statements to the contrary, the declared policy of the British Government, as set forth in a letter by Lord Balfour in 1917 is to turn the Holy Land into a Jewish state, finally to be owned and ruled by the Jews. The Jews and all other civilized people throughout the world still place this interpretation upon the now-famous Balfour declaration.

This policy has stirred up the most vitriolic animosity of the Arabs. The Jews and many Englishmen argue that Palestine belongs to the Jews because the Hebrew race was born there. The Arabs answer this argument by saying that Ishmael, from whom their race descended, was not only born in Palestine but that he was born before his half-brother Isaac, who is the progenitor of the Jewish race; and that by virtue of this priority of birth, Palestine belongs to the Arabs.

Palestine today has a population of 1,200,000, two-thirds of whom are Arabs, and they say that the majority should rule. At the rate the anti-Semitic campaigns in Europe drove the Jews back to Palestine, this majority-rule argument would have lost its force in a few years. During 1935, before the immigration restrictions were imposed by the British Government to satisfy the Arabs who were twisting the lion's tail, more than 61,000 Jews entered Palestine. Plans were pushed to have the restrictions removed so that at least 100,000 German-Jewish refugees could have been settled there during the next year.

All the world knows that on May 17, 1939, the British Government issued a white paper which made "confusion worse confounded" in Palestine. The policy set forth in this paper is to establish, within ten years, an independent Palestine state dominated by the Arabs. To make this domination certain and permanent, the paper limits the Jewish emigration to one-third of the Arab population.

Viscount Samuel declares that the white paper cannot be the last word. He concludes his masterly opposition by saying, "As the policy stands it can bring no settlement." As to the future of war-weary Palestine, one man's guess is as good as another's.

It can be said, however, that as these lines are being written, 179 members of the House of Commons and the majority of people under democratic governments throughout the world, feel that the British have betrayed the Jews and failed at a most tragic time to keep the promise made during the World War to give them a home in Palestine if not an independent Jewish state. Can the British Government follow its announced policy in Palestine, despite the strong minority opposition at home and the rising tide of public sentiment abroad, while ships loaded with Jewish refugees are sailing the seven seas with no place to land? If so, let us admit that universal brotherhood is a cruel myth and that the milk of human kindness has become a Dead Sea.

The Arabs further make this sentimental point: When the Jews had Palestine, they persecuted and killed all their good men. They crucified Christ, who came to save them; and now they should not be allowed to return to rule the land which they soaked with the blood of all the prophets, until they have repented in sackcloth and ashes.

One must go to Palestine to understand the terrific force of this argument among the Arabs. The feeling against the Jews now, for crucifying Jesus, is just as bitter among the Arabs as if it had happened ten days ago. When a Jew attempts to enter any holy place, he is ordered away. If he doesn't move in a hurry, he is roughly handled. While our Arab guide was showing us the empty tomb of Mary, we noticed that he kept his hand on his revolver and his eye on a group of Jews who were standing near. When we asked why he seemed so agitated, he replied, "If those dirty Jews had attempted to enter the tomb of Mary, after killing her son in the most brutal way, I would have shot them full of holes."

Despite the fact that the Jewish colonies are guarded night and day by British soldiers, there are weekly riots, with arson, bombings and snipings. Within six months, hundreds of lives were snuffed out and more than $15,000,000 worth of property destroyed. Remove the British soldiers from the land and the English gunboats from the Mediterranean Sea, and in less than two weeks the Holy Land would run red with the blood of that race, which before Pilate's Judgment Hall 1,900 years ago, cried, "Let His blood be upon us and our children."

Arab after Arab said to me, "Before we will let the Jews come back here and rule the Holy Land they desecrated, every one of us will die with our shoes on." They say this with a look of cruel murder on their faces and the hiss of a serpent in their voices.

How much of the foregoing argument is sincere and how much is manufactured by the mischievous propaganda of the Italians, is a question this observer cannot answer. This much, however, is commonly known— that before the covetous eyes of the Italian dictator looked upon the Suez Canal and certain parts of the Mediterranean, the Jews and Arabs lived side by side, in Palestine and other countries, without experiencing any serious trouble. Whatever the cause of the Jew's trials in the Holy Land and many other lands, they are confronted by a fact and not a theory—to use the words of former President Grover Cleveland.

No one can remember the picture of 4,000 Jews trudging across the snow-clad Alps on March 12, 1939, the day on which Pope Pius XII was publicly recognized as the Christian leader of Italy and the Catholic leader of the world, without tears in his heart for the sad plight of the Jews and their senseless Italian persecutors. Why were they driven out of Italy? Because they were Jews. Why were they not wanted where they were going? Because they were Jews.

The Negroes in America who are complaining about race prejudice have scarcely had a taste of it compared to the Jews. Everywhere I went abroad, I saw Negroes living peacefully and many of them prosperously. At the hotel in Rome where we stayed, a black man who could speak seventeen languages was the interpreter at the telephone. On the Island of Crete where our ship unloaded eighteen Ford cars, a jet-black man bossed the job. At our hotel in Jerusalem, a colored man from the Abyssinian country had charge of the dining room. In France, black men are members of the Chamber of Deputies and everywhere enjoy the same rights and privileges that the white Frenchmen enjoy. In Egypt, colored men practically run everything.

Colored people can live in any state in the United States, despite the fact that you may read in some states signs like these: "Niggers and dogs not admitted"; "Nigger, don't let the sun go down on you in this town." Thank God, these signs are growing beautifully fewer; but even in states where such signs still disgrace civilization, the Negro has made commendable advancement and can count some of his warmest and most valuable friends among white people.

Not long ago I visited a good-sized town in the deep south, where the most cultured and wealthy colored person cannot ride in a taxi driven by a white man. Before leaving that town, I learned upon the best authority that a Negro had contributed $6,000 to the campaign fund which elected the mayor, and that whatever this colored man says in that town, goes. That colored man cannot ride behind a white taxi driver, but he can request the town's commissioner of motor vehicles not to grant that same driver a license and his request will more than likely be granted.

I was in a large southern city three years ago, where a colored chauffeur from Chicago was not permitted to drive his white employer's car down a certain famous boulevard. Yet, I vividly recall that during the migration of the southern Negro to the North, that city united with other cities in the state to prevent the Negroes from leaving. Leading white people of the south, during that nervous period, hired colored men to tell Negroes that they loved them and wanted them to stay in the south, which offered them their best opportunity for living, and that they would continue to be their best friends. Even when a southern senator talks about colonizing the American Negroes in Africa, he is ridiculed by his white colleagues. I doubt seriously whether you could get 5,000 white people in any southern state to vote in favor of sending Negroes to Africa. On the other hand, who would object to the Jews going to Africa?

To the recent suggestion made to colonize the Jewish refugees in Africa, the only group that made a serious objection was the Africans living in that territory. These Jews are not wanted in Africa, America, England, France, Russia, Italy, Germany or Rumania. Last and most tragic of all, they are not even wanted in Palestine, which was given them 4,000 years ago by Almighty God.

The Negroes ought to be glad that they are colored and that they live in America.

On our way to Lydda, twelve miles from Jaffa, we passed through the famous Plain of Sharon, which produces the rose of Sharon, known the world over for its beauty and fragrance. It is so beautiful that it is used to try to express the matchless beauty of the Son of God—"I am the Rose of Sharon." Lydda was founded millenniums ago, in the dateless past. Three thousand years ago, Lydda was called the valley of the smiths because at that time it possessed the only blacksmith shop in the land of Canaan, and every Jew from Dan to Beersheba was forced to bring his farming implements here to be sharpened.

Christianity got an early foothold in Lydda, and it became very popular because here Peter healed Aeneas, who had been paralyzed for eight years. This fact still gives the town a Christian atmosphere.

We next reached the town of Ramallah. Ramallah deserves to be mentioned, because the best authorities believe this was the ancient Arimathaea where lived Joseph, who presented his own tomb to the family of Jesus to prevent Him from being buried in the potter's field. At the west end of this town is a convent named after Joseph. It is said that this building stands on the spot where stood the home of the man who was the best friend to Jesus in the hour of His shameful death.

We passed on to Ekron, an old city of the Philistines. It was the chief seat of Beelzebub, who was the ruler of all evil spirits and the king of all devils. It was here that the Ark of the Covenant was captured and carried through the Vale of Sorek to Beckshemesh [Beth Shemesh], where it remained for twenty years and was then taken by David to Jerusalem. After being placed in the temple by Solomon, it mysteriously disappeared from the Hebrew religious life. No place on our sight-seeing tour between Jaffa and Jerusalem captured my imagination like the Vale of Sorek because it was the scene of the mighty exploits of Samson.

IV

American Protestant Residents In The Holy Land

17. Selah Merrill: Archaeologist and Consul

It did not seem unusual in the late nineteenth and early twentieth centuries, when Protestantism exerted an unofficial but strong influence in American life, for a series of ministers to be appointed to the office of consul in Jerusalem. Conspicuous among them was Selah Merrill (1837–1909). Educated at Yale and ordained to the Congregational ministry in 1864, he served as an army chaplain, underwent further study in Germany, and taught Hebrew at Andover Seminary. He went to the Holy Land as archaeologist for the short-lived American Palestine Exploration Society, and then was appointed three times as American consul at Jerusalem, 1882–85, 1891–93, and 1898–1907. He continued to devote much attention to archaeological work, insisting on a scientific, fact-finding approach, as outlined in the introduction of one of his best-known books. He was widely known as a lecturer on antiquarian and archaeological topics; among his other well-known books were Exploration East of the Jordan (1881) *and* Galilee in the Time of Christ (1881).

Source: Selah Merrill, *Ancient Jerusalem* (New York: Fleming H. Revell Co., n.d. [1908]; reprinted by Arno Press, 1977), pp. 13–23.

As in a court of justice not every person is considered a competent witness although he may know something of the matter in question, so not every person who writes or speaks on Palestine is entitled to equal consideration. A lack of proper discrimination as to authorities has been and is a great obstacle in the way of successful investigation. Under what conditions was this or that book produced; how has this person or that one qualified himself to write; are questions that should be asked in every case when the matter of authority arises. Moreover, it is not enough to have been a resident of a country to qualify one to speak on that country with authority. Although this principle may be generally accepted, it is often violated.

On the matter of discriminating between so-called "authorities" the writer is well aware that it is a delicate subject, especially if names were to be mentioned, which it is not now proposed to do; but several examples may make tolerably clear what is meant, the examples being drawn from personal experience.

An intelligent person arrives in Jerusalem and spends there two or three days. At last he approaches me and says, "I hear that you have studied Jerusalem thoroughly, and may I ask your opinion on such and such a point?" I reply, "The question is difficult, but considering all the archaeological and historical evidence I have come to such and such a conclusion." The stranger looks pleased and responds, "That is exactly my view." Such an incident is not of infrequent occurrence, and such minds

147

are to me a perfect marvel. In twenty-four hours' observation they accomplish as much as I have done in twenty-five years of study. Later I find such persons quoted as "authorities" on the topography of Palestine and the archaeology of Jerusalem.

Another example.—There comes to Jerusalem a clergyman who has received the usual education afforded by a theological seminary and who has enjoyed the usual reading of an intelligent but busy pastor. His letters to his people at home are bright, interesting, highly appreciated, and are soon made up into book form. This is perfectly proper. It is when this writer begins to be quoted as an "authority" that harm is done.

Far more common and more harmful are the instances of which the following is a sample.—A man is eminent in the scholarly and literary world, widely known and highly respected. He has never given any special study to Palestine or Jerusalem, but the opportunity comes and he visits the Holy Land. He travels hastily through the country like any ordinary tourist. After he reaches home he is persuaded to write a book, his friends knowing that his name will make it a financial success. Thus far no possible criticism can be made.

But this man's opinions and utterances are sure to be estimated by the high regard in which he is held in the circle to which he belongs. If he makes remarks about disputed sites, about any of the peculiarities of the country, about geological or archaeological questions, he is certain to be held up to the world as an "authority" on these points. But being an eminent man in his own department of study or learning does not make him an authority upon a subject which he knows little about. Behind this supposition are prominent men, some of them eminent Biblical scholars, whose names, were they to be mentioned, would occasion great surprise. It is certain that here a clear distinction ought to be made; but it is no doubt true that the great majority of those who have to do with Palestine do not make it. The failure to discriminate between so-called authorities can be illustrated and verified by reference to any Dictionary of the Bible now extant, including the two most scholarly Dictionaries that have recently appeared in England.

A Mommsen makes the history of Rome a life-study. Another person studies Roman history in school and college, perhaps later in life he reads a history of Rome, and, it may be, visits Rome as a traveller. All this does not qualify him to be regarded as an authority on special matters pertaining to that city. In this case the distinction that should be made between this man and Mommsen is likely to be made. Why should it not be made between writers on Palestine? It is made by a very few experts; but it is not generally made, and this is the ground of objection.

In the form of published letters, magazine articles, and books a vast amount of literature on Jerusalem and Palestine is put forth every year, and the crude statements, to say nothing of statements that are untrue and absurd, thus given to the public are surprising. Palestine has been particularly unfortunate in this respect, and the amount of injustice that has been done her cannot be estimated. Were London and England, or Paris and France, to be treated in a similar manner there would be a loud outcry against it.

Another important matter is the advantage one has in studying the topography and archaeology of a place on the ground itself. Two men equally careful and studious write upon such a topic as San Francisco, California. One of them has lived in that city ever since gold was discovered in 1849. He knew the ground before it was built upon and is intelligently conversant with all the changes that have taken place in the last half-century. The other may have made a brief visit to that city, and has studied the place chiefly from plans, maps, and such books as he could command. There is no question which of these men should be regarded as the higher authority.

One of the clearest and most significant lessons of history, certainly to those who believe in God and in an overruling Providence, is the small regard God has for places. A place, a temple, a country, a people appear, accomplish their mission, and then disappear. Their work remains and helps the world in its onward movement.

Directly opposite to this is another fact, namely, that in the two great churches of the centuries one of the most conspicuous features is the importance attached to places. This feeling still exists and amounts in some cases to idolatry. To disbelieve in these alleged sites is to disbelieve in religion—to disbelieve in God.

To believe in the infallibility of tradition in this enlightened age is more common than is ordinarily supposed. From many examples I will select one and give the circumstances and conversation exactly as they occurred. I went about with this man, showed him bits of wall still in position belonging to a certain period, called his attention to hills and valleys which must be taken into account, and pointed out other facts which made a certain conclusion inevitable. He listened attentively although far from sympathetically, but was courteous enough to thank me. He then said, "I have the fullest belief in the traditions of the church, and the stones, walls, and other archaeological evidence which you have brought forward are nothing to me. Whatever amount of evidence of this sort you may bring forward, I believe in the tradition every time." Nothing could be more definite. I was glad to draw his fire because it showed me exactly where he stood. Not all of this class show equal frankness, hence his testimony is valuable. It is not asserted that every traditionalist holds such extreme views, still this man's position indicates the general attitude of this class towards investigation.

One of the greatest obstacles in the search after truth is a preconceived theory. For example, a certain problem arises which has a certain and definite solution, although not yet known. A person tries one method, then another, and even a third and a fourth before the proper solution is reached. This is quite different from the method of one who approaches the problem with a fixed notion of what the solution must be. For a concrete illustration the site of Calvary may be taken. One person tries this way, that way, and still another way in his effort to arrive at the most probable location of the site, which can never, we believe, be determined with absolute certainty. Another person starts with a theory, a preconceived idea which has to him the force of indisputable truth. The one person is an investigator; the other is a dogmatist. The one can argue and reason, the other cannot. If he pretends to argue or reason it is breath wasted, for he would sooner lose his right hand than come out at any other point than the one where he started. Of this class there are many writers who, perhaps unintentionally, do much harm. In the list are the names of some prominent persons who are sure to have a following. David and Solomon collected materials before the Temple was built. The class now referred to are bound that their Temple shall be built whether they have any materials or not. The only person worthy of respect is the one who collects slowly, and who is satisfied with collecting slowly fact after fact, leaving the work of reconstruction till the last, or it may be to those who come after him.

I must be allowed to make the personal statement that in my study of Jerusalem I did not start with a theory. I have for a long period of years collected facts and tried to see whither they would lead or point. I know that Christ came to this world and lived and died for sinners, and that the place of his death and burial was Jerusalem. But to me the particular spot here or there is not essential. This does not affect in any way Christ's great work. This is the position which I occupy with regard to the crucifixion and burial of our Lord. Then follows the specific question as to the claims of the Holy Sepulchre, which I am ready to accept as valid the moment the proof is furnished; but thus far the proof has not been furnished nor have even the probabilities been furnished. What I sincerely wish is that Christians of every denomination felt as ready and willing as I am to accept any place the moment its claims are substantiated. In modern times we build what we call "memorial churches"; had Christians of another creed than mine and another age been willing to say "We erect here a memorial church," without saying "This is the exact spot," what years of bitter controversy would have been spared!

I think I have made it clear that I not only disclaim any preconceived theory for myself, but I strongly disapprove the method of those who begin the investigation of important subjects with a decided partisan bias towards one theory or another. For such a course there is to my mind no justification whatever.

In such a work as the present no progress whatever could be made without the writings of Josephus, who deserves a brief mention at least. The treatment he has in general received from scholars and writers is well known. Probably no scholar rejects him entirely, but many receive his statements with doubt and mistrust, and many of his statements they absolutely reject. If a passage is difficult "it has been interpolated"; if a statement cannot be explained "it is the romancing," or "the usual exaggeration, of Josephus." A writer has a theory, and if Josephus does not confirm it he is cast aside. It is not too much to say that Josephus is the most defamed and maligned Jew that has lived during the past two thousand years. What harm is there in accepting him as a reliable historian and trying to give to his writings a reasonable explanation? A reasonable explanation has been sought for the writings of Shakespeare,—every play and every individual paragraph. So far as the writer is aware, Josephus has never been accorded the same fair and honest treatment. Competent scholars have devoted their energies to the text of Josephus and have published it in what they consider a reliable form; and after very careful study the present writer considers that the historian has given us a connected and in the main a correct account of the events which he records.

In studying the topography of ancient Jerusalem the point of time at which the subject is approached is of great importance.

Some writers begin with the first mention of the place in history and try to follow its development through many centuries till its capture by Titus in the year 70 of our era.

Others begin somewhere in the middle, say with Nehemiah, and make him a sort of pre-Christian Baedeker, accepting his statements as final without considering the historical reasons behind them.

Others still, who without offence are to be designated as "traditionalists," begin with A.D. 330, when the Basilica-Market which Constantine granted to Jerusalem was being erected. The preceding as well as the subsequent history of the city they care little for; but when pressed for an opinion on any earlier or later point their reply is always shaped by what they have been taught was "miraculously discovered" three centuries after the death of Christ.

The first and second of these methods the present writer has during the past thirty years tried repeatedly, only to find them beset with difficulties so great that no satisfactory results could be obtained. In the present work he has made the arrival of Titus before Jerusalem in A.D. 70 his point of departure, and from that date has worked backwards as far as it has seemed possible to go.

Every minaret in the city, many of the housetops, the city wall, the Castle, the churches, the synagogues, and every elevated point that affords a new view or any help in understanding the contour of the city has been visited repeatedly. Some special points have been visited scores of times. The plan has been to make a visit to such or such a point and make notes. Then to go home and re-examine Josephus, the references in the Bible, and the map of Levels, and as soon as possible make another visit to the same point. As Jerusalem comprised hills and valleys it is certain that the hills cannot all have been levelled nor all the valleys filled. The variations of surface as they originally existed are still apparent to the eye, in spite of all the changes that have taken place in twenty or more centuries. Here and there a rise, here and there a depression, all are significant. The study of the Levels of Jerusalem as they have been ascertained and recorded is most important; but almost of equal importance is the study of the contour of the city from its elevated points. The Levels give the information sought in the abstract; the views give the same information to a degree in the concrete. This is not so perfect or striking as it would be were the débris removed; still the views illustrate, confirm, and make real to the mind what the Levels teach. Both these methods are equally necessary, and the views are of such importance in enabling one to accept or reject certain theories that it is impossible for a person who has never tried it to appreciate what is now said.

During the past thirty years I have paid a great deal of attention to the

Ancient Topography of Jerusalem and have studied the subject from every conceivable point of view. I have tried to state my conclusions with dignity and fairness, but it has been no part of my work to give the precise date of this or that discovery, nor have I stopped to ascribe this or that discovery to any particular person. It is a very delicate matter to speak of priority of claim to any particular view. As an illustration I will mention that certain important things have been attributed to others which in fairness should be attributed to myself. The discovery of the one hundred and twenty feet of the Second Wall which runs northward from the Castle of David, is due to myself. If in all the investigations made in Jerusalem anything is certain, this is certain, and yet it has been assigned to others. When I took Mr. Schick (it was in 1885) to see it he was sure it was the wall of a castle, and I had the greatest difficulty in persuading him that it was not the wall of a castle but a city wall. He seemed determined to publish it as the wall of a castle, but eventually did not do so. In regard to the remains of Acra near or just east of the Holy Sepulchre, I spent hours with Mr. Schick trying to persuade him of the existence there of that ancient fortress, and at last he was convinced. In the German *Zeitschrift* he has reproduced it; but if there was any borrowing he borrowed from me and not I from him. My intercourse with him was always friendly, and what I have said now is not said in any spirit of complaint or contention. There are other matters in regard to which I can rightly claim priority of discovery; but as this is not a controversial work, I trust that the reader will not make the question of priority in any case a matter of contention. I will also remind the reader of the length of time that I have been engaged in this study, and views which he thinks were new five or ten years ago may have been ascertained and published by me twenty-five or thirty years ago.—I have conversed freely with many persons, compared notes with different investigators, discussed views and theories with those who appeared to be competent to judge in these matters, and I have lived to put my notes and observations into definite form, hoping they may be of service.

18. Edwin Wallace: Consul and Interpreter of the Holy City

Edwin Sherman Wallace, a graduate of Washington and Jefferson College and Princeton Theological Seminary, interrupted a series of Presybterian pastorates to fill the post of U.S. consul to Jerusalem between two of Merrill's terms, 1893–98. As consul, he sought to awaken a deeper interest in the city's sacred memories and sites, and "to prepare visitors for an intelligent comprehension of what they shall see when they arrive in the Holy City." In a book on the city in which he studied and worked for five years, he combined a survey of its history with a careful description of the place and its peoples. His picture was a rather drab and realistic one, but, as the excerpts show, he predicted that the land would be brought back to productivity by the Jewish people.

Source: Edwin S. Wallace, *Jerusalem the Holy: A Brief History of Ancient Jerusalem, with an Account of the Modern City and Its Conditions, Political, Religious and Social* (New York: Fleming H. Revell Co., 1898; reprinted by Arno Press, 1977), pp. 84–88, 351–59.

The spirit of modern progress has not touched the city yet. It has come from the west, swept across the Mediterranean, left its impress on Alexandria and Cairo, but has passed through the Suez Canal and on to the Far East. Jerusalem has been passed by and, were it not for its popularity as a stopping-place for tourists from Europe and America, would be as Oriental as any one could wish. These visitors are leaving some of their customs and costumes. Some of the rising generation of natives affect the European dress. The combination of the man and the habit is not a success; each detracts from the other.

When the railway from Jaffa to Jerusalem was completed in 1893 it was the wonder of the year, not only of the day. The great majority of the people had never seen such a thing as a locomotive. It frightened them so that when some of them saw it coming they could not get out of the way. It might reasonably have been expected that other improvements would follow rapidly. There has not been a single one.

Some of the letters of inquiry from our enterprising American firms which are sent to the consulate are laughable in the light of present conditions. Electric engineers and manufacturers of electric goods want to know all about the system of street railway now employed and what is the likelihood of introducing their special improved appliances for rapid transit. If they could only see what system is in use! To go from one part of the city within the walls to another, one must walk or mount a donkey. A line of carriages runs from the Jaffa Gate a mile west along the road. But such carriages! He who enters some of them does so at the expense of comfort and safety.

Street illumination is still in its infancy. In the entire city there are twenty-eight small oil lamps stuck up here and there on the sides of the houses. They are uncared for and on a dark night do nothing more than indicate that they are lighted. To believe that they do anything in the way of lessening the gloom is a freak of imagination. American companies wish to put in electric lights if the way is clear. But it is not; several insurmountable barriers intervene. In the first place the Turkish authorities do not desire so much light; it would reveal too much. They would not permit the introduction of electricity for illuminating purposes if some company should agree to furnish it gratis. Another reason is it would never pay. With the great scarcity of fuel the expense of operating the electric plant would be enormous. Another reason is that the Turk fears electricity in any form. He only admits the telegraph because he is compelled to. In Bergheim's flouring mill, however, and in the French Pilgrim's Building, both in the New City, there are some incandescent lights.

There are no telephones and not likely soon to be any. An American missionary who had charge of some schools several miles away and with which it was necessary for him to have frequent converse had a telephone sent to him. When he proceeded to put it in condition for service a Turkish officer was sent to make inquiries. The affair and the benefit of it was explained to him and he went away and reported it to his superiors. Word soon came to the progressive missionary that he must desist in its operations. Such an innovation could not be allowed unless he had an order from the sultan. He had no such order and was in no mood to pay the sum necessary to obtain it. The telephone has been lying unused for several years.

This is the kind of people who have control of the city. As long as they retain it Jerusalem will be mediaeval in appearance. The native and Jewish inhabitants do not care; the visitor prefers to see a city untouched by the hand of modern improvement. The former are indifferent in the matter; the latter have a sentiment. The one will not be roused from their indifference so long as the Turk is governor; the other is in no danger of having his sentiment destroyed.

The population numbers fifty-five thousand. This is a conservative estimate and yet only an estimate; nothing more satisfactory can be had under present conditions. The Turks never take a census. Certain individuals or societies have attempted a systematic canvass, but have had too many difficulties to meet in the way of overcoming fears and prejudices. The people look with suspicion upon any one who comes to their houses and asks questions about the inmates. They fear some new tax list is about to be prepared, and if they must answer are sure to minimize their numbers. With these difficulties to contend against it is not to be wondered that estimators differ somewhat in their calculations and their differences must not be charged to intentional error.

The estimate here given includes the permanent residents of both the old and the new city, and is based upon careful observation after a continuous residence of nearly five years and upon the opinions of the various civil and religious authorities. It was taken for granted in making the estimate that the patriarchs and bishops of the various Christian bodies would be in positions to know the exact number of their adherents and would be honest in stating that number. On the other hand great dissatisfaction resulted from efforts to learn the real number of the Jewish population. The leading rabbis know, but soon convince an inquirer that they wish to preserve their knowledge. The inference from this desire to conceal the number is that there are many more than the Jews wish the Turkish authorities to believe. They have an object in decreasing the number, or the report of the number of their people, and I have no doubt that they do so, by from ten to fifteen thousand.

The most careful estimate yet made was in 1892, by the missionary workers of the London Jews' Society. The result was as nearly exact as has yet been made and may safely be depended upon. According to this there are just about forty-two thousand Jews in the city and contiguous colonies, whose inhabitants are justly classed among Jerusalem residents. Since that partial census there has been little variation in the number, for it was made just about the time restrictions were placed upon Jewish immigration. Some have come since, but about an equal number have left. Should the restrictions against the immigration of the Jew be removed they would come in ever increasing numbers, until the Christian and Moslem dwellers in the Holy City would be so few as to be conspicuous. As it is, nearly three-fourths of the entire population are descendants of Jacob.

Next in numerical strength are the Christians, including all sects who so call themselves. Of this part of the population nearly a half are adherents of the Greek orthodox body. In wealth as well as in numbers this is the leading sect. The entire number of Christians is about 8,630, divided as follows:

Greek Orthodox	4,000
Roman Catholic	3,200
Armenian	600
Protestant (all branches)	500
Coptic	120
Greek Catholic	100
Abyssinian	60
Syriac	50
Total	8,630

The Moslems number about 6,500 and though the smallest numerically, are the strongest officially. They look with a measure of scorn upon Jews and Christians, and, were it not for the financial benefit to them resulting from the presence of these representatives of despised religions, would gladly be rid of them.

There is less friction between members of these three great religions than is generally supposed. In fact there is very little. The worst exhibitions of intolerance are between certain of the Christian sects. Each devotee of religion enjoys full freedom to worship God as he wishes so long as he respects the rights of the others. There are in the city Jews, orthodox and reformed—though the latter are few. There are Ashkenazim, or Jargon-speaking, Sephardim, or Spanish, and Caraites, or repudiators of the Talmud. There are Christians of every shade of faith, orthodox, unorthodox and peculiar. There are representatives of the various sects of Islam. So in every respect, civil and religious, physical and political, Jerusalem is unique among the cities of the world. . . .

Chapter Nineteen.
The Future of Jerusalem.

In the preceding pages an endeavor has been made to tell something of the Sacred City's past and present. The facts brought forth must have convinced the reader that Jerusalem, like the Jews, is—as it ever was—peculiar. Its location away from any adequate water supply, on rugged, almost barren hills, is unusual. Its nearly four thousand years of strange, many times destructive, experiences give it an unique place in history. Its religious preeminence is undoubted. Its present material prosperity is a fact in spite of the great and ill-reconciled variety of its people.

What reasons governed the choice of its site is a question neither so difficult nor so interesting as how it has been preserved. Founded it was and it was preserved; there was a Divine purpose in the founding and in the preservation; nor is it rash to go further and say that there was a *special* Divine purpose in both.

Judged by the ordinary standards on which human judgments are framed Jerusalem ought never to have been anything more than a mountain hamlet where a few hardy villagers could live, because their wants were few and their courage great. The land of which it became the capital was much greater in area than in value. On the east and south was the desert, on the west the sea, and on the north the rival kingdom of Syria. The central range, running from north to south, on which the city stands, does not, and probably never did, present a pleasing view to the husbandman. Its hills are rugged, its valleys deep gorges where cultivation can only be affected with great labor. That labor has been available, however, and patient industry, when labor cost almost nothing, has succeeded where to-day it would surely fail.

The land of Palestine does not now alone support the city of Jerusalem as it is; Jerusalem is not self-supporting. By this it is not meant that it differs from other cities, for it is true in one sense that no city is self-supporting; no city is independent in the sense that it produces all that is necessary for the sustenance and comfort of its residents. The people of London and New York would soon starve were they shut off from outside communications. But London and New York are self-supporting in that they produce that which they can exchange for the products of other places. Jerusalem produces nothing, and therefore has nothing to exchange. The land of which the city is the capital now produces little more than its villagers require. The formerly terraced hills are sadly denuded of soil and stand, naked limestone mountains, on which but little vegetation can find room to live.

This barren appearance at first sight puts a damper on any belief in the country's future, and many visitors immediately jump to the conclusion that it has no future. Centuries of negligence, and governmental oppression that encourages negligence, have made a sorry spectacle of a land that once flourished with every form of vegetation that pleased the eye and delighted the taste. But I am satisfied that what once was produced here will, or may be, again produced, and by similar methods of industry and skill. Fifteen years ago the hills near Bethlehem were as void of fields, vineyards and orchards as any in the land; the soil upon them was thin and the rocky ledges very prominent. Now all around this little city are fields of grain, abundant vineyards and grand orchards of fig and olive trees. Industry has wrought the transformation. The terraces have been rebuilt, the earth brought from the valleys into which it had been washed and the result is all that could be desired. There are similar spots all over Palestine, as, for example the grounds of the American Friends' Mission, in Ramallah, the precincts, the numerous Jewish colonies, and the lands of the Latin Convents. All these improvements, accomplished in a few years, indicate that the land that once supported a population of at least two millions could again do so. The divine conditions of soil and climate are the same as ever, only the human conditions of industry in the individual and encouragement in the government are sadly lacking.

Supposing the latter two conditions to be met, there is no doubt that Jerusalem would become the centre of an agricultural district that could compete with other countries in the great world markets. This may seem a strange statement to those who have depended upon the accounts of casual visitors, or professional writers, who presume to know all about it after a few days' stay, for their information. The Jordan valley is now desert. It has in it the possibilities of a Paradise. East of the Jordan, the land of the homeless Bedouin, is an unknown country to most people. I venture to state that there is no finer wheat land on earth than this. The methods of agriculture are of the crudest, but the harvest that results would abundantly remunerate a more skillful husbandman. The Jewish committee that presented a memorial to Lord Salisbury in 1891 did not prophesy the unlikely when they said: "If at this moment the ground is barren in parts and refuses to yield its increase, we know that it is the hand of man that has wrought the evil. The hand of man shall remedy it."

Certain it is that when the country contiguous is properly cared for, the city will thrive. Temporal prosperity is in sight. Societies of colonization have been formed in recent years in Roumania, Southern Russia, Germany, England, and, quite lately, in America. Agents have been sent to purchase lands and have succeeded in acquiring possession of desirable tracts along the maritime plain in the neighborhood of Jaffa and near the base of Carmel. The majority of the colonists thus far have been Jews, and when they have had some previous knowledge of agricultural life have been reasonably prosperous. It has been learned at the same time that the attempt to make tillers of the soil out of shopkeepers and petty artisans is a waste of money. The German colonists have been uniformly successful, because of their ability and willingness to work. One cannot help admiring their neat villages and comfortable looking homes at Haifa, Jaffa and

Jerusalem; they are like little bits of the prettiest of German rural life.

It is impossible to foretell the future of colonization plans, because of the uncertainty of the political horizon. Naturally the present rulers do not wish to see these foreigners coming and settling here, bringing their foreign ideas, habits, and religions, and retaining their allegiance to their governments in Europe and America. They are small foreign states in the land of the Turk, and the Turk is aware that the longer they remain the more determined and intelligent will be their opposition to him. Thus it will be readily understood that intending colonists will hesitate to come, not wishing to risk their all in the face of present opposition and future uncertainty.

Conditions are changing. Even the unprogressive Turk is submitting gradually to modern improvements. If a prophet twenty years ago had predicted as many changes for the better as have been made in Palestine during that time he would have been treated as a dreamer. There are now some good carriage roads, where then there were only miserable paths threading the land. Now there is a railroad from Jaffa to Jerusalem, and another is building from Haifa to Damascus, passing through the rich valley of Jezreel, by Lake Galilee and across the fertile Haúran. These improvements, continued as they surely will be, are the presages of a future for that city which is destined to be the capital of the land. It needs no prophet to foretell this now, but the majority may need some one to recall to them the fact that present conditions and future improvements were foretold centuries ago.

My own belief is that the time is not far distant when Palestine will be in the hands of a people who will restore it to its former condition of productiveness. The land is waiting, the people are ready to come and will come as soon as protection to life and property is assured. I am ready to go further and say that the coming inhabitants will be Jews. This must be accepted or the numerous prophecies that assert it so positively must be thrown out as worthless. The subject of Israel's restoration I freely admit is not a popular one now; but the unpopular of to-day is the universally accepted of to-morrow.

It certainly will not be considered out of place to introduce in this connection a few of the many prophetic passages that assert this return of the dispersed of Israel: "He that scattered Israel will gather him" (Jer. xxxi. 10). "He shall assemble the outcasts of Israel and gather together the dispersed of Judah" (Isaiah xi. 12). "Like as I have watched over them to pluck up and to break down and to destroy and to afflict, so will I watch over them to build and to plant, saith the Lord" (Jer. xxxi. 28). "For I will take you from among the heathen and gather you out of all countries and will bring you into your own land" (Ezekiel xxxvi. 24). Now this gathering has not yet taken place; it must be made or prophecy counts for nothing. The present movements among Jews in many parts of the world indicate their belief in the prophetic assertions. Their eyes are turning toward the land that once was theirs, and their hearts are longing for the day when they as a people can dwell securely in it. With every improvement of the country the city must improve. It will always be the centre of Palestine. Should an independent nation arise and occupy the land as it once did we should see history being repeated and Jerusalem a city of prominence. There are physical obstacles that would have to be overcome, but they are not so great as has been often assumed and asserted. There is room for a large city. The Plain of Rephaim as far south as the Convent of Saint Elias—half way to Bethlehem—is admirably adapted to city construction. The broad plateau on the north, now being rapidly built over, is all that could be desired for residence sites. There is ample room for a large city.

There is something more needed than room, however; there must be means of support for the people. These means are at hand, but, as already mentioned, they are undeveloped. Rich mineral deposits have been discovered, but work upon them has been abandoned because of the paralyzing policy of the government. Copper and tin have been found; coal exists in paying quantities in the Lebanon and near Sidon; at the former mines the coal is of good quality and 12,000 tons were at one time mined, then the works were abandoned. With the introduction of railways these fields would all be worked and made to pay. There are large mineral deposits in Gilead and Moab and along the shores of the Dead Sea. Petroleum is said by experts to exist in abundance in the southern part of the Jordan valley. There are salt deposits in and near the Dead Sea sufficient to supply the world's demands. All this wealth of minerals is of no value now, but once capital is assured of safe investment the present death will give place to activity. In such an event Jerusalem would be the natural manufacturing centre and could not only supply her own demands, but be able to compete with other manufacturing cities in the markets of the world.

The greatest difficulty in the way is the lack of water. No doubt this was always a difficulty, but one which in the former days of prosperity was met by great skill and great labor, which were applied in devising and building the great aqueducts that led from distant fountains into the city. Many of the early kings made the providing of water for their capital their chief concern. Large pools—as Upper and Lower Gihon, Hezekiah, Bethesda, Siloam—collected and preserved for public use large quantities. Cisterns were then much more numerous than now. And it is more than probable that the Virgin's Fountain was a much more copious stream. Whether added to these was another natural source springing up in the midst of the city or in the temple area is a question on which the authorities differ. The inhabitants of the modern city do not enjoy the blessing of an abundance of water, but they have omitted the efforts to obtain it and preserve it put forth by their predecessors. It really is not so much a question of lack of water as lack of energy and public spirit; an honest capable city government would soon have it. The money necessary for the work was once offered by an English company, but as the capitalists stipulated that an English superintendent was to oversee expenditures, the local authorities declined the offer.

But in the city that the prophets beheld in moments of inspired vision this great lack was to be supplied by natural means. There will be an abundant supply in the very midst of the city. Perennial streams shall issue. Zechariah (xiv. 8) tells us, "And it shall be in that day that living waters shall go out from Jerusalem, half of them toward the former sea and half of them toward the hinder sea; in summer and in winter shall it be." That this great change is to occur in the millennial age is generally conceded. To speculate any further about it, to attempt any description of the changes physical and spiritual that must attend it would be going too far for this work. At the same time it may be said, and repeatedly, that the city of prophetic assertion must be realized or prophecy be relegated to a position on a par with fictitious literature.

Any one desiring to know the millennial future of Jerusalem can find it described on many pages of the Inspired Word. The only legitimate method for the interpretation of the various allusions to that future city is the natural one, *i.e.,* to take just what is there said as it is said and attempt neither to add to nor detract from the statements.

Forgetfulness, or rather, disregard, of this has led to many fanciful and some foolish conclusions. The result has been that serious-minded people have come to believe that there is no interpretation of these passages that can lead to any certainty. There may be some grounds for the belief, they are due however to fault, not in the prophetic narrative, but in our methods of treating that narrative. Better take the narrative as it stands and believe that what is there said of the future of Jerusalem will come to pass, or believe, as many do, that the city can have no future that will make it sufficiently important to command the attention of the modern world. For my part I see no reason to question the Bible statements about the future of Jerusalem and believe there are many signs in the present pointing to the fulfillment of what the Scriptures say about it.

It is very certain that Mohammedanism will have nothing to do with the city's future. Its six hundred years of possession and its present deplorable condition warrant the assertion. Jerusalem has been ground under the heel of Moslem oppressors, in spite of the fact that as a holy city it is with them second only to Mecca. It would still be in the same deplorable condition were the Christian nations and their many Jewish subjects not becoming so much interested in it. Quietly the Jew and Christian have been getting possession of desirable building sites and erecting substantial structures. Less than half of the city within the walls is owned by Moslems, while hardly any of the new city outside the walls is now in their hands. This desire to acquire Jerusalem real estate, a desire that animates Christians and Jews, gives a strong indication of what the city of the future is to be. Its destiny is bound up with religion. For similar reasons Christian and Jew love it; to each it is holy for what it has been; it will become holier and greater still.

It has already been said in this chapter that the coming inhabitants of Palestine will be Jews. The fact that Christians now hold a goodly portion of the city and land counts for nothing against this. The time has come when Jew and Christian can live together without persecution on either side. The "wall of partition" still stands. It is higher and stronger in Jerusalem than any place else on earth. But even here it is crumbling. There is at least tolerance for the narrowest Christianity in this capital of the severest Judaism; and this tolerance must grow into something more friendly. Christianity and Judaism are radically the same religion. We believe that Christianity has the real life—the life of the Spirit—a stage of development to which Judaism has not attained, but Judaism will advance; that when it has reached the spiritual stage, the "wall of partition" will be broken down and a union will be effected in a religion nearer the divine ideal than this world has yet witnessed, whose adherents shall be "Israelites indeed."

19. The American Colony

In 1881, a unique group of Americans settled in Jerusalem. Horatio and Anna Spafford, devout Presbyterian lay persons, lost four daughters in an accident at sea in 1873 and a few years later lost their only son of scarlet fever. The religious pilgrimage that arose in part out of these tragic experiences led the Spaffords to found the American Colony. They also wanted to follow the pattern of groups of early Christians who held all things in common. The colony prospered, eventually growing to include about 150 persons, who carried out ministries of welfare, teaching, and nursing. But some, especially Selah Merrill and Edwin Wallace, American consuls at Jerusalem, regarded the group as a heretical and socialistic sect. A long struggle broke out between the colony and the consulate. The problem was at last overcome when Alexander Hume Ford, an American journalist, visited the colony in 1906 and published an article that, with the help of Merrill's successor in the consulate, completely cleared the colony. The informative article is here reprinted in part.

Source: Alexander Hume Ford, "Our American Colony at Jerusalem," *Appleton's Magazine* 8 (1906): 643–55. For a full story of the colony, written by the daughter of the founders, consult Bertha Spafford Vester, *Our Jerusalem: an American Family in the Holy City, 1881–1949* (Garden City, N. Y.: Doubleday & Co., 1950; reprinted by Arno Press, 1977).

I have returned from the Holy Land, where I was shown the Mount of Calvary, the tomb of Christ, and the manger in which the Savior of mankind was cradled. Near by these most sacred spots in the universe I fell upon a God-fearing colony of American-born citizens, who for more than a quarter of a century, while enjoying the respect and friendship of an "infidel" Turkish Government, have been subject to renewed controversy with one of their own creed and country; one who should, of all others in the wide world, be their best and truest friend, counselor, and protector. For not only is this man a duly ordained minister of the Gospel, but he is America's consul at Jerusalem, with far-reaching power to help or harm his fellow-citizens in the Holy City.

A slight difference in the interpretation of a verse of Scripture, and once more, at the very sepulcher, the father is turned against his children, and they against him. Perhaps it is in the air, these religious feuds on sacred soil, where Mohammedan soldiers still patrol the Church of the Nativity, so that Christians of differing sects may not cut each other's throats at the very manger where their God became man.

I had heard of the American Colony years before in Chicago, from which city it had migrated to Jerusalem; but its affairs had passed almost completely from my memory until now I met its people again at the goal of their ambitions. They had patterned their life at Jerusalem upon that of the early church there; lived together in brotherly love, more than a hundred and twenty of them; owned everything in common, and after twenty-five years of such an experiment still held fast to the belief of the early Christians at Jerusalem, that it was Christ's teaching that those calling themselves Christians should give all their accumulated earnings to the poor, and no one member of the great brotherhood be content if he could find anyone poorer than himself. They had carried absolute unselfishness to its extreme, and, truth to tell, seemed a most contented and industrious household, speaking lightly even of the persecutions that had all but made them beggars in the desert, a lot from which they were saved only by the kindness of the Turkish Government.

Whatever may be my religious differences with the American Colony—and they are many—I shall hereafter speak with reverence of any movement toward Christian socialism, the actual practical possibility of which, in one instance, has been demonstrated here at the birthplace of Christ by an undaunted body of American citizens; a body that, with the hand of its own Government repeatedly and inexplicably raised against it, has persevered to the end.

The American Colony, for a quarter of a century, has had one uncompromising accuser—and only one that I could find in Jerusalem or elsewhere—and the accuser has not crossed the threshold of the little band he condemns, for more than a score of years. Yet he ever stoutly maintains to all who will hear him that the American Colony is the home of midnight orgies in which its founders, now white-haired men and women who have passed their sixtieth and seventieth birthdays, still take an active part. It is perhaps comforting to Americans to know that no one in Jerusalem takes these charges of our consul seriously, but, unfortunately, strangers, visitors, and foreigners are sadly influenced against a community that has won the respect of every nationality in the Holy Land, and is visited on terms of equality and friendship by every consul in Jerusalem but our own. These women of America, whom he so bitterly denounces in his reports to Washington, belong to some of the oldest and most respected families of New England and Illinois; they have dear ones at home who still love them, believe in them, and trust them as do the people of Jerusalem, including our own vice consul.

In vain these discredited Americans and their friends at home have appealed to the State Department either to prove or forbid the circulation of the horrible charges. The State Department keeps these on file, but refused to permit any member of the American Colony to learn the particulars of any specified charge. It is chiefly for this reason that from every part of the country protests and appeals have been forwarded to Washington demanding "fair play," while the thousands returning from the now popular annual cruises to the Holy Land are becoming more and more an advance guard, making friends everywhere for our little Colony in Jerusalem and creating a desire on the part of the people to know something of this strange community that has triumphed over so many obstacles in a far-off land.

The Origin of the Colony

The American Colony had its inception in Chicago, when, in 1880, a number of religious enthusiasts broke away from the famous "fighting" Fullerton Avenue Presbyterian Church. At the head of the movement was a man of intellect, wealth, and refinement, Horatio Spafford, one of the most prominent lawyers and church workers of his time in the city of Chicago. He was the author of several world-wide-known hymns that are still sung in the churches of two continents. It was Mr. Spafford's belief that the desire of sin could be overcome by a return to the early practices of the Christian church—for this reason he and his co-workers were termed in contemptuous ridicule "overcomers," a name that long stuck to them.

The Fullerton Avenue congregation is, and always has been, comprised largely of wealthy members, so that Mr. Spafford's declaration that no one had a right to call himself a Christian who was content to do what Christ would not have done, and own property while others around him were in dire need, met with little response. But fourteen members of the church were ready to give up all and follow him to Jerusalem, to take up there the work organized by the early church, and carry it on until the second coming of Christ, which many of the little band believed to be near at hand. Mr. Spafford and his wife were probably then the only wealthy ones to give up their all. There were fourteen adults and five children who arrived in Jerusalem in September, 1881, and this was the nucleus of the American Colony.

Unfortunately for the little band, its religious beliefs had been heralded far and near, and about the same time it set out for the Holy Land a clergyman of a kindred denomination to that from which the "overcomers" had seceded, also turned his eyes toward Jerusalem. The Rev. Selah

Merrill, of Andover, Mass., early in the administration of President Arthur, was appointed to the office of the American consul at Jerusalem. An enthusiastic antiquarian, he made no secret that his desire for the office lay in the fact that it enabled him to carry on such research in the Holy Land, but, unfortunately, early in his career as consul, he selected the American cemetery at Jerusalem as a place to dig for relics, and as he turned up the bones of the dead in doing so—including sometimes freshly interred bodies—the most bitter religious warfare Jerusalem has known in a century was engendered. Unpleasant friction began within the American Colony, which finally resulted in the loss to that body of all its dead, who still lie in a jumbled heap in an out-of-the-way pit. It is not surprising, therefore, that it required skilled generalship on the part of the leader of the American Colony to postpone the precipitation of the "War of the Graveyard," and that after the death of Mr. Spafford, in 1887, hostilities did begin and on one side at least have never ceased.

From the very start, however, the American Colony made powerful friends. Its members learned Arabic, and went forth to instruct the children of the land. They passed their word, and kept it, that they would attempt no proselyting. Inadvertently, however, they accomplished the impossible, for in Turkey, while many conversions are made by the Protestant missionaries among Greek and Roman Catholics, or *vice versa*, the conversion of an adult Mohammedan, does not happen. A young Mohammedan, however, took up his home in the Colony and became a servant. No attempt was made to convert him, but at the end of three years he asked to be baptized and expressed the desire to join the Colony as a firm believer in Christ and his teachings. . . .

[Ford then traced in detail the difficulties the young man faced in the Turkish Army, but eventually he returned to Jerusalem with honor and joined the Colony.]

Next, the Turkish officials saw that the Colony was doing good work, and began to observe the educational classes there. In time, when it was decided by the Government to establish a girls' school in Jerusalem, the ladies of the American Colony were asked to take entire charge, which they did. Thus the education of Syrian womanhood fell into the hands of Yankee citizens, there being at times more than one thousand children under the charge of the Americans. The school was located in the mosque of Omar, the most sacred spot in all Jerusalem, to Jew and Mohammedan alike, although to this day no Hebrew may enter this sacred enclosure where the Temple of Solomon once stood, and the only persons in all

Christendom who may enter at will, without special permit and a guard, are the members of the American Colony.

By the Jews of Jerusalem, the American Colony is also held in reverence. Unknown to the world, for thousands of years, even before the Babylonian captivity, there has been a remnant of the tribe of Gad in the province of Yemen. Some years ago they received a revelation that they should return to Jerusalem. Three hundred set out, and arrived at the Holy City totally destitute. No one would receive the strange wanderers, who spoke an ancient dialect of Hebrew, so the American Colony mortgaged all that it had and shared with the strangers. To the credit of the Gadites, be it said that they at once sought work and soon came to their patrons to announce that they would support themselves; but the tax of supporting 300 even for a short time left the Colony in destitute circumstances, and it was only through the friendship of the Mohammedan officials that they were not then turned out in the desert to starve.

It was Mr. Spafford's genius that organized the work. Each man was taught a trade. One became Colony carpenter, another turned tailor and made Colony clothing. A botanist in the little band turned his attention to the *flora* of the Holy Land, collecting specimens of the flowers mentioned in the Bible, which the young people of the Colony pressed and pasted on cards to be sold to pilgrims. Each members of the Colony had to work and each received all that he actually needed. The Colony grew and prospered; others in America became willing to sell all they had and give to the poor. They joined the Colony; as did a little body of workers organized along the same lines in Sweden; but never at any time did the proportion of American-born of the Colony fall below fifty per cent of the entire number, although the latchstring has always been out to the poor and needy of all nations, races, and creeds. When, after seven years of faithful work in Jerusalem, Mr. Spafford died, the Colony was well organized and had begun to prosper.

"The War of the Graveyard"

The bitter feeling between the American consul and the American Colony began to develop soon after this time. In October, 1892, word came to the Colony that workmen had been seen digging in the cemetery on Mount Zion, under the direction of Consul Merrill; and a prompt investigation revealed excavations, evidently in the interest of antiquarian research. Graves had been dug into and coffins broken, even to the point of the exposure of the dead.

Just after this, another member of the Colony died, and by the time of the funeral the excavations had been partly filled up, but there were still deep holes visible, while fragments of bones, coffins, hair, and clothing were lying on the surface of the ground. In one place, the coffin of Mr. Spafford was still exposed, and was seen by his daughter, who was present at the funeral, and who was taken home in a fainting condition as a result.

From that day to this has lingered "The War of the Graveyard," waged bitterly between two successive clergyman consuls and a missionary on the one side, and on the other, the members of the American Colony, who have never asked more—and asked that in vain—than that the remains of their dead should be left to rest in peace.

Consul Merrill's successor, under President Cleveland's first administration, was another clergyman, the Rev. Edwin S. Wallace, in whose term the controversy became even more acute.

It will seem incredible to any American reader that our consul, a Christian clergyman, should have any part in the removal, at the dead of night, of the bodies of his fellow-citizens, from a cemetery under his charge, to be dumped unceremoniously into a common pit, concealing its very whereabouts from the knowledge of the friends and relatives of the dead. Not only is this true, as documents on file in Washington will prove, but it was only through the British bishop and British consul at Jerusalem that the members of the American Colony forced their consul to reveal to them where their dead lay hidden, and prevented him, again at the dead of night, from removing them to still another spot. The story of the American graveyard at Jerusalem is grewsome [sic] in the extreme, but it so fully illustrates the undue power wielded by our consuls in Turkish countries, and the bitterness of religious warfare in the Holy Land, that I give it as the documents in my possession—from both sides—set it forth.

About seventy years ago the American Board of Commissioners for Foreign Missions purchased a burying ground on Mount Zion, for the Americans who died in Jerusalem. On their withdrawing from active work in that field, the graveyard was turned over to the Presbyterian Board of Foreign Missions, and the key to the inclosure was sent to the American consulate at Jerusalem, to be called for by any American wishing to inter their dead in such a Christian cemetery.

This identical spot finally coming to be identified by the antiquaries as the veritable site of the "Dormition de la Sainte Vierge," the Roman Catholic Church, through the Spanish consul, made most tempting offers in the earnest effort to secure the holy ground. In the course of years, ten of their dead had been buried in the American cemetery, when once again the colonists applied for the key, only to be informed by the consul that the cemetery had been sold and the dead removed by the Rev. William K. Eddy, of Sidon, representing the Presbyterian Board. In vain the members of the American Colony appealed to the consul at Jerusalem and our ambassador at Constantinople. They were compelled at last to turn to the British consul, who officially demanded of the American consul the whereabouts of the body of Captain Sylvester, a British subject, who had been a member of the Colony.

It was found that the bodies had been moved at the dead of night by native workmen, who had been paid a shilling apiece. They had dismembered the bodies and forced them into packing cases, the largest thirty by sixteen inches, and some of these containing the bones of more than one body. There were no names, and few of those boxes were numbered; all had been dumped unceremoniously in a pit fifteen by fifteen feet. . . .

[Here Ford quoted in full a letter by Ismail El Hussani, Superintendent of Public Instruction at Jerusalem, to the President of the United States, dated September 27, 1897, confirming the above account. The President ordered Consul General Dickinson at Constantinople to investigate, but it led to a cover-up on a technicality.]

In 1905 the Rev. William K. Eddy returned quietly to Jerusalem. The American Colony by this time was on the watch. Immediately the Colony appealed—not to the American but to the British consul—for protection of their dead from still further desecration. Their representatives, with proper documents, arrived at the pit in time to discover Mr. Eddy in the act of ordering his porters to remove the boxes he had redug, from the pit, the object being to remove them to a new American cemetery. He was working under authority from Consul Merrill and without the supposed knowledge or consent of the friends and relatives of the dead, whose only request to the American consul was that at last, and forever, they be permitted to rest.

Pictures were taken to show how impossible it was to discriminate as to the contents of the boxes, and the Swedish and other consuls joined in the protest against the further desecration of the American dead. . . .

[At this point, Ford provided other instances of Merrill's dislike of the American Colony, including the stopping of funds for the American Colony, and imprisoning a member. He then described meeting the consul with a witness:] I have since seen Vesuvius in eruption, her most magnificent display in thirty-four years, but the memory palls before the recollection of that half-hour with the American consul in Jerusalem.

Almost my first remark was a request for information concerning the American Colony. The Rev. Mr. Merrill arose from his chair, demanding to know if we were friends of the Colony stating that if we were he could not receive us. He insisted that the Colony did not exist, and that if it did, there were no Americans connected with it, and in the next breath denounced every member of the Colony as immoral, declaring that the stench of their "goings on" was the most putrid odor in the nostrils of Jerusalem.

I tried to ask questions, but it was impossible to break into the bitter storm of vituperation. The consul insisted that he had not degraded himself by crossing the threshold of the home of the American Colony in more than a score of years, yet his knowledge of its inner workings was little short of marvelous.

The women were one and all immoral, the children were trained to become immoral; they could neither read nor write, and idleness was rampant. As for the "American Colony store" that flourished within a hundred paces of the room in which we were discussing the iniquities of the "non-existents," the consul proclaimed loudly that it was a fraud and denied that any article therein was manufactured at the Colony, and, moreover, he insisted that I should not visit the store, but make my purchases in that of a native friend.

The final explosion of pyrotechnics occurred when I asked the consul for some specified charge against the members of the Colony. He arose to his feet and denounced me as a friend of the Colony, ordering me out of his presence, if such were the case. When I still insisted upon some reason for his denying the Colony the protection of the United States flag, Mr. Merrill declared that they were cranks and heretics. I tried to ask if cranks and heretics were barred by our constitution from the rights of citizenship, but the flow of verbal lava was too strong to breast—I was swept away, carried off my feet in a torrent of molten vituperation at the crimes of the heretical Colony, and took my departure under orders never again to appear in the presence of the American consul in Jerusalem if I dared disobey his mandate and visit the American Colony. . . .

[But of course, Ford did:]

A Visit to the Colony

To the best of my ability I investigated the charges of the American consul, and it must be borne in mind that I visited the Colony day after day, that I met scores of Americans from conducted tours, who stopped for days and weeks at the Colony; that I secured the opinions of the members of the other consulates in Jerusalem, and of leading citizens, Christian and non-Christian. The universal comment was that the American Colony was an industrial organization, self-supporting and highly respected; that no breath of scandal had ever been breathed against the women of the organization save by the American consul and the natives—so claim the colonists and their friends—whom he cajoled into making defamatory statements against them, but who denied these statements the moment they were out of his presence.

I rode out with Dr. [C. C.] Higgins to the buildings of the American Colony, for in their prosperity the 120 members of the community have left their cramped quarters within the city walls for very spacious grounds, a mile beyond the Damascus gate. Here we were welcomed, although perfect strangers, and invited to partake of refreshments. Many American ladies were present from the *Moltke* and the *Arabic*, both cruising steamers from New York. Some of these women were in tears over the cruel charges they had heard.

At last I sat in a little circle of women whom the consul had denounced to me as free lovers and worse. The youngest of these women was that day celebrating her sixty-fourth birthday. Her hair was white, but her form proud and erect, her face kindly but firm, for she had been dubbed "leader" by the outsiders since the death of her husband, Horatio Spafford, a score of years ago. . . .

Everything in the American community is owned in common. All fare alike. The single men have a building to themselves, the boys have their building, and the families their separate apartments. Those who wish to stop with the Colony are taken care of, and if they cannot afford to pay for accommodation, there is no charge made. Everything is free and open to inspection. . . .

[The article continues with a description of some of the Colony's departments: weaving, butter-making, grain-grinding, baking, pressing flowers, photography, and concludes with criticism of Merrill.]

20. "The Most Beautiful Y in the World"

*The Young Men's Christian Association in Jerusalem was founded in 1878, largely under
British auspices. Following World War I the leadership was assumed by an American, A. C.
Harte, who expanded its interracial and interreligious work among the youth of Jerusalem and its
environs, under the direction of the International Committee of the YMCA of North America.
He had the vision of a large and beautiful building for the varied program and was instrumental,
along with John R. Mott of the International Committee, in raising funds for it. At the time of
its dedication in 1933 the new building was often called "the most beautiful Y in the world." It
had been decided that this institution directed by laymen would not be a missionary endeavor, but
would serve all races and religions. Through decades of tension it continued to be a meeting place
for Muslims, Jews, and Christians, and the staff included Arab, Jewish, and American workers,
the latter residing in Jerusalem during periods of service.*

*At the time of the dedication of the new building, a brief history was circulated in a brochure
prepared for the event, from which this excerpt is drawn.*

Source: "History of the Jerusalem Young Men's Christian Association," *The
Jerusalem Young Men's Christian Association* (Jerusalem: YMCA, 1933), pp.
19-24.

The Jerusalem Young Men's Christian Association has had an interesting
and varied career. The Rev. Canon J. E. Hanauer tells us of early attempts
to organize in 1876. This is similar to the organizations which preceded the
founding of the Y.M.C.A. in London before 1844. The oldest available
record of the organization of a Y.M.C.A. in Jerusalem was recently
presented to the Jerusalem Association by Dr. T. Canaan, a member of the
Board of Directors. This document is the first constitution, handwritten in
Arabic by his father, the Rev. B. Canaan, dated January 8, 1878. It states
that: "The aim of this Association and its principles shall be exactly the
same as those of the Young Men's Christian Association of London and it
shall be the duty of this Association to adopt fully the rules and regulations
of the London Association."

For some ten years, the organization met in the C.M.S. bookshop, and
its activities were divided into sections according to nationalities, Anglo-
Hebrew, Arabic, German, and others. On November 7, 1890, at a meeting
in the Grand Hotel, Wm. Hind Smith, Organizing and Visiting Secretary
of the National Council of the Y.M.C.A.'s of England, called for a more
general meeting for Monday, November 10, in the Assembly Room of the
Grand Hotel. At that meeting Mr. Hind Smith addressed the members on,
"The purpose, principles, work, agencies, and progress of the Young
Men's Christian Association." His proposals for organization were

adopted and comprised virtually the second constitution on record. A Central Committee was appointed at this time, and George Williams, Esq., founder of the first Y.M.C.A. in the world (London, 1844) was elected President, and personally subscribed funds for the support of the Jerusalem Association.

Appeals for a Secretary were then made, but other calls on the Foreign Committee in England made it impossible to grant the request at that time.

On May 20, 1891, Mr. Luther D. Wishard, of the Foreign Division, International Committee, New York, addressed the members and told them of his world tour and of the organization of Young Men's Christian Associations in forty different countries.

The early meetings were held in the C.M.S. bookshop on Jaffa Road, now a drapery shop. The next home of the Association was behind the third balcony in the adjacent building to the south, now used as a lawyer's office. Later the members moved to quarters on the south side of Mamillah Road, now used as a grocery shop. At this time, the Arabic section of the Association, dissatisfied with the Central Committee, wrote to England and secured a separate charter for their organization, in 1892, and drew up a separate constitution in Arabic, which is also on record. New quarters were secured in following years on Jaffa Road directly opposite the new buildings of Barclay's bank, where the Association met until 1908.

In 1909, Mr. Stuart Donnithorne was sent by the English National Council as the first employed Secretary of the Jerusalem Association. He took quarters for the Association behind the covered balcony on the north side of Mamillah Road, now used by the Arab Sports Club. He resided above the Association rooms. During his secretaryship, a site for a building near the Damascus Gate was secured through the generosity of people in Jerusalem, of friends in England, and particularly of Sir Robert Laidlaw, who contributed five hundred pounds. The premises which were taken in 1909 had the effect of increasing the membership from 40 to 200, but the building was altogether inadequate for a membership of this size. During the year 1911, Dr. John R. Mott, General Secretary of the International Committee of Young Men's Christian Association, first visited the Jerusalem Association. Mr. Donnithorne was the General Secretary during this period and until the outbreak of war in 1914, and many still speak of the good influence of the Association in the city under his leadership. During the war, the Association had to close its doors because of suspicion on the part of the Turkish Government, and the work suffered a temporary eclipse.

In 1917, the moment came for the Egyptian Expeditionary Force to march across the Desert of Sinai to the Gaza front. Soon a military railway, regarded as a magnificent feat of engineering, was opened along the whole route from Kantara, East of the Suez Canal, to Deir-el-Belah, in Palestine, so that the distance could be covered in thirteen hours. As the E.E.F. proceeded from Romani into Palestine, troops were massed along the railway from Kantara. Large Y.M.C.A. centers were established at Kantara, Romani, Bir-el-Abd, Mazar, El-Arish, Rafa, Khan Yunis, and Deir-el-Belah, and an improvised service rendered which will never be forgotten by those who took an active part in that remarkable campaign.

Following the occupation of Jerusalem by General Allenby, fresh openings for service presented themselves to the Association. Probably the most conspicuous service was the free guidance provided daily for the men on leave from every part of the Empire to the sacred sights of the Holy City. Fifty thousand men, most of whom would not otherwise have known where to go or what to see, were guided to the historic sites, and listened to "sermons in stones" retelling their immortal stories in simple and reverent language. Army Y.M.C.A. huts, tents, and marquees were provided for the troops on the area west of the Russian church compound.

In May, 1920, Dr. A. C. Harte, a secretary of the International Committee of the Young Men's Christian Association of North America, was called to the General Secretaryship of the Association at Jerusalem. The coming of Dr. Harte was the fulfillment of his dream of many years, to serve the youth of the Holy Land. Possessing unusual gifts of leadership and great personal magnetism, he had previously rendered distinguished service with the Young Men's Christian Association in the United States, in India and Ceylon, endearing himself to an ever widening circle of friends on each succeeding field of service. Dr. Harte came to the work in Jerusalem fresh from what was probably the greatest service of his career. Throughout the period of the Great War he had directed that most Christlike service which the Association rendered during those tragic years to the prisoners of war in the various countries of Europe. An interesting record of this service in the form of a valuable collection of the handiwork of war prisoners assembled by Dr. Harte will be found in the Directors' Room of the new building. Under Dr. Harte's wise administration the work grew apace. Foreseeing large possibilities for the Association service to the youth of Jerusalem, he took up at once the task of providing better housing for the constantly enlarging work. Progressively the quarters . . . were acquired for the expanding work. They include an old army hut which saw service in the war, until recently utilized as a hall for meetings.

Here in these limited and necessarily temporary quarters Dr. Harte and his associates carried on a wonderful fellowship with young men of all nationalities, built up a splendid library and reading-room equipment, organized the Association membership for service to each other and for the advancement of their physical, mental, social and spiritual lives. The developments under Dr. Harte were so promising as to convince his friend, the late James Newbegin Jarvie, of Montclair, New Jersey, that an enlargement of the work was fully justified by the opportunity to serve youth in and about the Holy City.

On Christmas eve, 1924, Mr. Jarvie advised Dr. Harte of his resolution to provide the required funds. Mr. Jarvie did not live to see the fulfillment of his plans, but before his death made ample provision for their consummation. The property now to be dedicated for the high use for which the funds were provided stands as a memorial to him and as a tribute to his Lord in whose Name and for whose glory the gift was made. The buildings constitute the most beautiful and complete Association property in the world.

The well-chosen site was secured through the good offices of the Holy Orthodox Patriarchate of Jerusalem and is the gift of the International Committee of the Young Men's Christian Association of North America, in which the British National Council and a group of Jewish friends of Manchester, England, have generously shared.

On August 23, 1926, the work of excavation began and on July 23, 1928, Lord Plumer, then High Commissioner for Palestine, laid the cornerstone.

The four-manual Austin organ installed in the auditorium is the gift of the Juilliard Musical Foundation of New York. The beautiful carillon of 35 bells assembled in the bell chamber of the tower is the gift of Miss Amelia F. G. Jarvie, of Gloucester, Mass. Other friends provided, through Dr. John R. Mott, endowments to assist in the maintenance of the work at Jerusalem. The gift of the library of the life of Jesus was given in January, 1932, by Miss Margaret Hopper, of Honolulu, Hawaii. It provides one of the most complete collections on this subject in the world. Similar libraries on Judaism and Islam are needed for research students and residents.

The Camp Peniel at Galilee, with its stone house is the gift of Mrs. Charles F. MacLean, and the near-by athletic field—Hakl-Eldridge-el-Riadi—is the gift of Mr. Fred I. Eldridge, both large-hearted American friends of this Association. Tel-Boaz camp, the gift of Mr. James Turner and Mr. George W. Davison, of New York, in the Field of the Shepherds, at Bethlehem, is used annually for the Christmas Eve celebrations, a unique feature of our activities. Both camps have an endowment for maintenance given by Mr. Isaac C. Jenkins. The Robert Maiben Fondè Fund amounting to £P.66, is given for the help of boys of the Holy Land and is in memory of the son of Dr. and Mrs. George Heustis Fondè, of Mobile, Alabama. The gift of Mr. James Bunce, of Middletown, Connecticut, amounting to £P.50, is for general endowment purposes. The A. C. Harte Scholarship Fund is accruing until it reaches £P.100, when the interest may be used for a scholarship to aid boys in pursuit of further education in the Jerusalem Y.M.C.A. A fund of £P.23, known as the Hoover Fund, is used for the purchase of trees for our camp sites. These trees have been planted and give promise of greatly adding to the attractiveness of the camps in a few years. These gifts have fulfilled our greatest dreams and afford not only an opportunity for unparalleled service, but impose as well a great responsibility.

In the year 1925 Arthur Loomis Harmon, eminent architect of New York, was commissioned by the International Committee as architect for the buildings made possible by Mr. Jarvie's gift. The impressively beautiful religious and spiritual symbolism now revealed in the finished structure was the concept of Dr. A. C. Harte. It was the architect's task to blend in the design all this symbolism and meaning with the practical service values so requisite in a modern Association building. The result transcends our fondest hopes. The finished buildings stand as an eloquent witness to the high qualities of skill, understanding and devotion Mr. Harmon brought to the project. The Architectural Bureau of the National Council of the Young Men's Christian Associations in the United States collaborated in the planning processes and is responsible for designing the furnishings and interior decoration.

The Board of Directors and the Building Committee at Jerusalem have given invaluable support to the project from the beginning, exercising the most competent supervision and control of the project throughout the long period of construction.

To Mr. A. Q. Adamson, who had already built more than a score of Association buildings in the Orient, was committed the task of coordinating and directing the building operations in Jerusalem. The successful completion of the work is largely due to his extraordinary executive and engineering ability, his patient thoroughness and unswerving devotion to the Association cause. He was ably assisted by Mr. Herman Glunker,

formerly architect for the Indian National Council of Y.M.C.A.'s.
The general contractors, Awad, Dounie and Katinke and J. L. Maude &
Co., have labored devotedly to make this building their outstanding
achievement. To these and all others who have labored with heart and
hand and mind we express our grateful thanks.

Upon the retirement of Dr. A. C. Harte in May, 1930, one of his
associates, Mr. Nicholas M. Lattof, was appointed Acting General Secretary, and carried most faithfully the responsibility for the work, until the
arrival in May, 1932, of the present General Secretary, Mr. Waldo H.
Heinrichs, who was appointed on December 8, 1930. Like his predecessor,
he had much of his Association experience in India, serving there from
1915 until this appointment, with the exception of two and one-half years'
service in the American Flying Corps in France. In the battle of Saint
Mihiel he was shot down, near Metz, severely wounded, and as a prisoner
of war received the benefits of the Y.M.C.A. service for prisoners, which
was at that time directed by Dr. A. C. Harte. Mr. Frederick Auburn has
been allocated by the International Committee as Physical Director in the
Jerusalem Association since November 11, 1929, and has had the best of
technical training and experience in the work.

Many friends seem to think that because of the above-mentioned
generous gifts, no further financial help is needed by the Jerusalem
Y.M.C.A. There could be no greater mistake. The present equipment and
work have increased the recurring expenses, and funds are needed to carry out the programme of service in Jerusalem and other communities of
Palestine.

V

Restoration: Pro and Con

21. Prophetic Traditions

The expectation that the Jews would eventually be restored to the Holy Land, one rooted in biblical prophecies, has been a persistent motif in Christian history. It has surfaced many times, in varying forms. In early American history, it was sometimes coupled with the tradition, since refuted, that the Indians were descendants of the lost tribes of Israel. An exponent of this perspective was Elias Boudinot (1740–1821), who had been a member of the Continental Congress, commissary-general of prisoners during the Revolution, thrice a congressman from New Jersey, and president of the American Bible Society. His book, A Star in the West, showed great knowledge of biblical history and of Indian languages and customs, and looked toward the restoration of the Jews to Jerusalem.

Later in the nineteenth century, the expectation of the restoration was intensified by dispensationalist teaching. This strain of millenarianism was defended by John Nelson Darby (1800–82) an itinerant British evangelical who traveled frequently in the United States. A later dispensationalist was William E. Blackstone (1841–1935), a successful businessman of Methodist background. His book, Jesus is Coming, was first published in the 1880s; a special "presentation edition," from which the second passage was chosen, was published in 1908. Approximately 700,000 copies of the book were printed, and it was translated into 31 languages. Among the most popular of the many millenarian writings of the time, it contributed significantly to the interest in Zionism among conservative Protestants.

Sources: A. Elias Boudinot, *A Star in the West; or, A Humble Attempt to Discover the Long Lost Ten Tribes of Israel, Preparatory to their Return to their Beloved City, Jerusalem* (Trenton, N.J.: D. Fenton, S. Hutchinson, and J. Dunham, 1816), pp. 43–52.

B. W. E. B. [William E. Blackstone], *Jesus is Coming* (Chicago: Fleming H. Revell Co., 1908), pp. 234–41.

A. Boudinot

By this representation [of biblical passages] it plainly appears—

1st. That the people of the Jews, however scattered and lost on the face of the earth, are in the latter day to be recovered by the mighty power of God, and restored to their beloved city Jerusalem in the land of Palestine.

2nd. That a clear distinction is made between the tribes of Judah, in which Benjamin is included, and the ten tribes of Israel, agreeably to their particular states. The first is described as dispersed among the nations in the four quarters of the world—The second as *outcasts from the nations of the earth.*

3d. Thus they shall pass through a long and dreary wilderness from the north country, and finally enter into Assyria, (it may possibly be) by the way of some narrow strait, where they will meet together in a body and proceed to Jerusalem.

4th. That this restoration is said to be accomplished a second time. The first was from Egypt—the second is to be similar to it, in several of its remarkable circumstances.

5th. The places from whence they are to come, are expressly designated. They are to come first from Assyria and Egypt, where it is well known, many of the tribes of Judah and Benjamin were carried captive, and are now to be found in considerable numbers, and from Pathros bordering on *Egypt*— and from Cush and from Elam, different parts of Persia, where the present Jews are undoubtedly of the same tribes, and perhaps mixed with a few of the ten tribes who remained in Jerusalem and were carried away by Nebuchadnezzar. And from Shinar still more east and where some of the same tribes are now found. And from Hamah near the Caspian sea, where some of the ten tribes have remained ever since the time of Salmanazar; and from the *western regions.**

6th. Thus we have the two tribes of Judah and Benjamin well known to be dispersed throughout the three quarters of the world—But as to the majority of the ten tribes, although every believer in divine revelation has no doubt of their being preserved by the sovereign power of God in some unknown region; yet as the whole globe has been traversed by one adventurer or another, it is a little astonishing that they have not hitherto been discovered. By the representation above, it is clear that we must look for them, and they will undoubtedly, at last be found, in the *western regions*, or some place answering this description as the place of their banishment.

God proceeds in his encouraging prospects, in language of the greatest affection. "But now saith the Lord, who created thee O Jacob, and he who formed thee O Israel. Fear not, for I have redeemed thee; I have called thee by thy name; thou art mine. When thou passest *through the waters*, I will be with thee, and *through the rivers*, they shall not overflow thee; when thou walkest through the fire, thou shalt not be burned, neither shall the flame kindle upon thee. For I am the Lord thy God, the holy one of Israel, thy saviour. I gave Egypt for thy ransom, Ethiopa and Seba for thee. Since thou was precious in my sight, thou hast been honourable, and I have loved thee, therefore will I give men for thee and people for thy life. Fear not, for I am with thee, I will bring thy seed from the *east* and gather thee from the *west*; I will say to the *north* give up, and to the *south* keep not back;

---

* See Lowth.

bring my *sons from afar* and my daughters *from the ends of the earth.*" Isaiah xliii. 1-6.

Again, "Thus saith the Lord, in an acceptable time I have heard thee, and in a day of salvation helped thee, and I will preserve thee, and give thee for a covenant of the people to establish the earth, to cause them to inherit the desolate heritages. That thou mayest say to the prisoners go forth: to them who are in darkness, show yourselves.* They shall feed in the ways, and their pastures shall be in all high places. They shall not hunger nor thirst; neither shall the heat or sun smite them; for he who shall have mercy on them shall lead them, even by the springs of water shall he guide them. And I will make all my mountains a way, and my high ways shall be exalted. Behold *these* shall come *from far:* and lo, these from the *north* and from the *west;* and these from the land of *Sinim.*" Isaiah xlix. 8-13.

Here again they are described as passing mountains *from far,* or a great distance, and that from the *north* and *west,* or *north-west;* and others are to come from the land of Sinim, or the eastern country. "Moreover, thou son of man, take thee a stick and write upon it, *for Judah and for the children of Israel his companions.* And then another stick, and write upon it, for Joseph, the stick of Ephraim, and *for all the house of Israel, his companions.*" Ezekiel xxxvii, 16.

It appears by this chapter, that there are some few of the Israelites still with Judah; but all are again to become one people at a future day. It also appears that the body of the house of Israel are remote from Judah, and are to be brought from distant countries to Jerusalem, when they are to become one nation again.

Their approach to their own land, is so joyous an event, that Isaiah breaks forth in language of exultation. "Sing O heavens! and be joyful O earth, and break forth into singing O mountains, for the Lord hath comforted his people, and will have mercy upon his afflicted."

"Thus saith the Lord of Hosts, behold! I will save my people from the east country (the tribes of Judah and Benjamin) and from the west country (the ten tribes;) and I will bring them, and they shall dwell in the midst of Jerusalem, and they shall be my people and I will be their God in truth and in righteousness." Zech. viii, 7-8. Ezekiel, also refers to the same event: "As I live saith the Lord, with a mighty hand and astretched-out arm, and

---

*Mr. Paber translates this "to them who are in darkness," "Be ye discovered." This is peculiarly applicable to the present state of the Israelites, as we herein after suppose them to be.

with fury poured out I will rule over you. And I will bring you out from the people, and will gather you out of the countries wherein ye are scattered, with a mighty hand, and with a stretched out arm, and with fury poured out. And I will bring you into the wilderness of the land of Egypt, so will I plead with you saith the Lord. And I will cause you to pass under the rod; and I will purge out from among you *the rebels and them who transgress against me.* I will bring them forth out of the country where they sojourn, and *they shall not enter into the land of Israel,* and ye shall know that I am the Lord." Ezekiel xx. 35–43.

Here we see that they are distinguished again, by those of the east country and those of the west country, and that they are finally to be united under one government again, when they shall be restored to Jerusalem, yet they must suffer greatly by the way, for their sins and continued obstinacy, which would require God's fury to be poured out upon them, for the reluctance with which they will attempt the journey back to Jerusalem. In short their restoration again to the city of God, will in many things be similar to their Exodus from Egypt to Canaan. They will be obstinate and perverse in their opposition to the journey: and on the way will show much of the same spirit as their fathers did in the wilderness, as they will be attached to the land of their banishment, as their fathers were to that of Egypt. Many of them will have a wilderness to pass through, as Israel of old had. God will also have a controversy with them by the way, and will destroy many of them, so that they shall never see Jerusalem, the beloved city. But those who hold out to the end, in their obedience to the heavenly call and submission to the divine will, shall be accepted, and *these* shall sincerely repent of their past transgressions. Again "I will accept you with your sweet savour, when I bring you out from the people, and gather you out of the countries wherein ye have been scattered, and I will be sanctified in you before the heathen. And ye shall know that I am the Lord, when I shall bring you into the land of Israel, into the country, for the which I lifted up my hand, to give it to your fathers. And there shall ye remember your ways, and all your doings, wherein ye have been defiled, and ye shall loath yourselves in your own sight for all the evils that you have committed." Bishop Warburton's observations on this passage are worthy of notice.—He says, "It is here we see denounced, that the extraordinary providence under which the Israelites had always been preserved, should be withdrawn, or in scripture phrase, that God would not be enquired of by them. That they should remain in the condition of *their fathers in the wilderness*, when the extraordinary providence of God, for their signal disobedience, was, for sometime, suspended. And yet that though they strove to disperse themselves among the people round about, and projected in their minds to be as the heathen and the families of countries, to serve wood and stone, they should still be under the government of *a theocracy* which when administered without an extraordinary providence, the blessing naturally attendant upon it, was, and justly, called *the rod and bond of the covenant.*"

Every serious reader, who takes the divine scriptures for his rule of conduct, must believe that these people of God are yet in being in our world, however unknown at present to the nations—and as God once had seven thousand men, who had not bowed the knee to Baal in the days of Elijah, when he thought that he was the only servant of God, left in Israel, so God has preserved a majority of his people of Israel in some unknown part of the world, for the advancement of his own glory. And we plainly see in the quotations above, that they are distinguished again, by those of the east country, and those of the west country, and that though they were finally to be united into one government, when they shall be restored to Jerusalem, yet they must suffer greatly by the way, for their sins and continued obstinate provocations of the divine majesty, who was their king and governor, which would require his fury to be poured out upon them and particularly for the reluctance with which they should be prevailed on to attempt a return to Jerusalem, when God should set up his standard to the nations for that purpose. In short, their sufferings and perverse conduct in their Exodus from Egypt to the land of Canaan, seems to be a type of their final return to Jerusalem. They will be obstinate and perverse in their setting off and in their way, as they will be greatly attached to the land of their banishment—They, at least a great part of them, will have a wilderness to pass through, as their fathers had. God will have a controversy with them by the way, on account of their unbelief and the customs and habits indulged among them contrary to the divine commandments, as he had with their fathers, and will destroy them in like manner, so that they shall never arrive at the beloved city, as was done to the rebels in the camp of Moses and Joshua. They are to pass through waters and rivers and be baptized therein as their fathers were in the red sea, and will receive the same divine protection.—Those who shall hold out to the end in a line of obedience and submission to the divine will, shall be accepted and safely returned to the land promised by Abraham, Isaac and Jacob, and their seed after them, where they shall sincerely repent and mourn for all their former transgressions.*

We are not left to the prediction and encouraging declaration of one or two prophets of God; but Ezekiel also confirms and continues the divine interference in their favour, for he says, "Thus saith the Lord, behold! I will take the children of Israel from among the heathen, whither they be gone, and will gather them on every side, and bring them into their own land; and I will make them one nation in the land upon the mountains of Israel: and one king shall be king to them all, and they shall no more be two nations, neither shall they be divided into two kingdoms any more at all. Neither shall they defile themselves any more with their idols, nor with their detestable things, nor with any of their transgressions. But I will save them out of all their dwelling places, wherein they have sinned, and will cleanse them, so they shall be my people, and I will be their God. And David my servant shall be king over them; and they all shall have one shepherd, they shall also walk in my judgments and observe my statutes to do them. And they shall dwell in the land that I have given unto my servant Jacob, wherein your fathers have dwelt, and they shall dwell therein, even they and their children, and their children's children forever. And my servant David, shall be their prince forever.

"Moreover I will make a covenant of peace with them; it shall be an everlasting covenant with them. And I will place them and multiply them, and will set my sanctuary in the midst of them for evermore. My tabernacle shall also be with them, yea, I will be their God and they shall be my people. And the heathen shall know, that I the Lord, do sanctify Israel, when my sanctuary shall be in the midst of them foreever more."

From this representation it appears, that the posterity of Abraham, Isaac and Jacob, are still God's peculiar people—That he brought them with a mighty arm from Egypt, by the way of the wilderness and through the red sea. That he gave them laws and ordinances to which he commanded the most strict obedience. And in case of failure and wilful disobedience, the severest curses were denounced upon them. They were to be divided into two nations—to be scattered among the gentiles, to the north and the south, to the east and the west. They were to be driven by the hand of God, to the utmost parts of the earth—Into Assyria—Egypt—Pathros—Cush—

*Some of them are to be carried in ships, by seafaring nations, as a present to the Lord at Jerusalem.

Elam—Shinar—Hama—and into the western regions and the land of Sinim. They were to serve gods, the workmanship of men's hands, of wood and of stone. Israel is heavily charged with stubborn disobedience, and is threatened with being cut off suddenly, as in one day, and with great and accumulated distress and anguish. They are expressly charged with the sin of *drunkenness*, as adding *drunkenness to thirst*, as their prevailing sin.

On the other hand, the promises to them are very great, in case of obedience, or on sincere repentance in case of failure. After great sufferings, in the latter days, that is about the end of the Roman government, if they shall seek the Lord their God, they shall not be entirely forsaken, or totally destroyed . . .

B. Blackstone.   *Israel.*

God's sun-dial.

If we want to know our place in chronology, our position in the march of events, look at Israel.

God says of Israel: "I will make a full end of all the nations whither I have scattered thee, but I will not make a full end of thee." Jer. 30:11, R.V.

Like Tennyson's brook they can sing, nations come and nations go, but I go on forever. They are the generation which pass not away.

Israel shall be restored to Palestine and no more be pulled up out of their land.[1]

Hundreds of prophecies affirm this dispensational truth. Like the red thread in the British rigging, it runs through the whole Bible. Prophecies to the people like Ezek. 37, and prophecies to the land like Ezek. 36.

The title deed to Palestine is recorded, not in the Mohammedan Serai of Jerusalem nor the Serglio of Constantinople, but in hundreds of millions of Bibles now extant in more than three hundred languages of the earth.

The restoration was summed up at the first council of the apostles in Jerusalem, as their conclusion based upon the words of the prophets.[2]

---

[1]Amos 9:15. And I will plant them upon their land, and they shall no more be pulled up out of their land which I have given them, saith the Lord thy God.

[2]Acts 15:13. And after they had held their peace, James answered, saying, Men *and* brethren, hearken unto me:

14. Simeon hath declared how God at the first did visit the Gentiles, to take out of them a people for his name.

As the fig-tree which Jesus found bearing nothing but leaves, Israel hath been set aside for a whole (aion) dispensation.[3]

Jerusalem was to be trodden down until the times of the Gentiles be fulfilled.[4]

But note carefully that a little later Jesus said, "Now learn a parable of the fig-tree (and all the trees): when her branch is yet tender, and putteth forth leaves, ye know that summer is near. So likewise, ye, in like manner, when ye shall see these things come to pass, know that it is nigh, even at the doors." Mark 13:28; Luke 21:29.

In Ezek. 31 the trees are used as symbols of the nations.

"The fig-tree was THE JEWISH PEOPLE full of the leaves of an useless profession, but without fruit."—*Dean Alford.*

Now if Israel is beginning to show signs of national life and is actually returning to Palestine, then surely the end of this dispensation "is nigh, even at the doors."

This brings us to speak of

Zionism,

the present movement of the Jews to return to the land of their fathers.

Zionism is a modern term expressing the national hopes and sentiments of the Jews.

These sentiments, however, are based upon widely different views, as held by the most extreme sections of the parties into which the Jews are divided.

As is well known the Jews have, in the past fifty years, become divided into three great sections, viz.: the orthodox, the status quo, and the reformed.

---

15. And to this agree the words of the prophets; as it is written,

16. After this I will return, and will build again the tabernacle of David, which is fallen down; and I will build again the ruins thereof, and I will set it up:

17. That the residue of men might seek after the Lord, and all the Gentiles, upon whom my name is called, saith the Lord, who doeth all these things.

18. Known unto God are all his works from the beginning of the world.

[3]Mark 11:13. And seeing a fig-tree afar off having leaves, he came, if haply he might find any thing thereon: and when he came to it, he found nothing but leaves; for the time of figs was not *yet*.

14. And Jesus answered and said unto it, No man eat fruit of thee hereafter for ever (an aion). And his disciples heard *it*.

[4]Lu. 21:24. And they shall fall by the edge of the sword, and shall be led away captive into all nations: and Jerusalem shall be trodden down of the Gentiles, until the times of the Gentiles be fulfilled.

The orthodox hold to the Old Testament Scriptures, as interpreted by the Talmud, as the literal Word of God, and also to the hopes and heritage of their ancestors founded thereon. They believe in the oft repeated utterances of the prophets, that some day they shall return to Palestine and become permanently settled as a holy and happy nation, under the sovereignty of their coming Messiah.

These hopes are the very core of their intensely religious life, and are embedded in the most solemn devotions of their prayer-book.

Every morning, throughout every nation and clime, whither they are scattered over this whole world, the orthodox Jew lifts up his prayer:

"Save us, O God of our salvation, and gather us together and deliver us from the nations."

"May it be acceptable unto thee, Eternal; our God and the God of our Fathers, that the sanctuary may be rebuilt speedily in our days and our portion assigned us in thy law. There will we serve thee in reverence as of old, in days of yore."

In that solemn service of the Passover they cry out,

"At present we celebrate it here, but the next year we hope to celebrate it in the land of Israel," and again,

"O build Jerusalem the holy city speedily in our days. Blessed art Thou, O Lord!"

With such faithful and earnest prayers have these orthodox Jews kept alive the fires of devotion and the glorious hopes of restoration, while being driven up and down the earth with the rods of enmity, ostracism and banishment. But for over seventeen centuries, while they have thus fervently prayed, they have made no effort to return to Palestine, believing that they should wait until God Himself, brought about their restoration by supernatural means.

About 200 years ago the persecutions began to abate, and in the eighteenth century they were gradually emancipated from these various disabilities. With this coming of liberty, there was a noise and a shaking and the dry bones of Ezek. 37 began to come together.[5]

---

[5]Ezek. 37:1. The hand of the Lord was upon me, and carried me out in the Spirit of the LORD, and set me down in the midst of the valley which *was* full of bones,

2. And caused me to pass by them round about: and, behold, *there* were very many in the open valley; and, lo, *they were* very dry.

3. And he said unto me, Son of man, can these bones live? And I answered, O Lord GOD, thou knowest.

4. Again he said unto me, Prophesy upon these bones, and say unto them, O ye dry bones, hear the word of the LORD.

The Universelle Israelite Alliance was organized in Paris in 1860, and later the Anglo-Jewish Association in England. Through these powerful organizations the Jews can make themselves felt throughout the world. And now, within a few years, there have been organized Chovevi (lovers of) Zion and Shova (colonizers of) Zion societies, mostly among the orthodox Jews of Russia, Roumania, Germany, and even in England and the United States. This is really the first practical effort they have made to regain their home in Palestine.

In a few words, followers of the status quo are striving to reconcile the genius of Judaism with the requirements of modern times, and in Western Europe are in a great majority.

The Reformed Jews or Neologists have rapidly thrown away their faith in the inspiration of the Scriptures. They have flung to the wind all national and Messianic hopes. Their Rabbis preach rapturously about the mission of Judaism, while joining with the most radical higher critics in the destruction of its very basis, the inspiration of the Word of God. Some have gone clear over into agnosticism.

Strange to say, from these agnostics now comes the other wing of the Zionist party. And not only have they joined this party, but they furnished the leaders, viz.: Dr. Max Nordau of Paris, and Dr. Theodore Herzl of Vienna.

The orthodox Jews who have enlisted under the Zionist banner, are animated by the most devout religious motives. But the agnostics aver that this is not a religious movement at all. It is purely economic and nationalistic. Dr. Herzl, its founder and principal leader, espoused it as a *dernier resort,* to escape the persecutions of anti-semitism, which has taken such a firm hold of the masses of the Austrian people. He conceived the idea that if the Jews could regain Palestine and establish a government, even under the suzerainty of the Sultan, it would give them a national standing which would expunge anti-semitism from the other nations of the world, and make it possible for all Jews to live comfortably in any nation they may desire.

---

5. Thus saith the Lord GOD unto these bones, Behold, I will cause breath to enter into you, and ye shall live:

6. And I will lay sinews upon you, and will bring up flesh upon you, and cover you with skin, and put breath in you, and ye shall live; and ye shall know that I *am* the Lord.

7. So I prophesied as I was commanded: and I prophesied, there was a noise, and behold a shaking and the bones came together, bone to his bone.

See also verses 8 to 14.

Not all the orthodox Jews have joined this movement. Indeed, the leaders of the Chovevi Zion Societies hold aloof.

The call, issued by Dr. Herzl, for the Zionist Congress, held in Basle, Switzerland in 1897 met with severe opposition from the German Rabbis and also a large portion of the Jewish press, as well as the mass of rich reformed Jews. Nevertheless, over 200 delegates, from all over Europe and the Orient and some from the United States, met and carried through the program of the congress with tremendous enthusiasm.

Memorials, approving the object of the congress, came in from all sections, signed by tens of thousands of Jews.

The congress elected a central committee and authorized the raising of $50,000,000 capital.

It has certainly marked a wonderful innovation in the attitude of the Jews and a closer gathering of the dry bones of Ezekiel.

And now, after ten years of wonderful growth and progress it remains to be seen what the providential openings in the Ottoman Empire may be that shall give opportunity to realize its object.

Zionism is now the subject of the most acrimonious debate among the Jews. Many of the orthodox criticise it as an attempt to seize the prerogatives of their God.

While others say that God will not work miracles to accomplish that which they can do themselves.

Most of the reformed Jews, now that they can no longer ridicule the movement, decry it, as an egregious blunder that will increase instead of [diminish] anti-semitism.

They have no desire to return to Palestine. They are like the man in Kansas, who, in a revival meeting said he did not want to go to heaven, nor did he wish to go to hell but he said he wanted to stay right there in Kansas.

Just so these reformed Jews are content to renounce all the prophesied glory of a Messianic kingdom in the land of their ancestors, preferring the palatial homes and gathered riches which they have acquired in Western Europe and the United States. They coolly advise their persecuted brethren, in Russia, Roumania, Persia and North Africa, to patiently endure their grievous persecutions until anti-semitism shall die out.

But these brethren retort that their prudent advisers would think very differently if they lived in Morocco or Russia, and that even in Western Europe anti-semitism instead of dying out, is rather on the increase.

In the midst of these disputes, the Zionists have seized the reins and eschewing the help of Abraham's God they have accepted agnostics as leaders and are plunging madly into this scheme for the erection of a Godless state.

But the Bible student will surely say, this godless national gathering of Israel is not the fulfilment of the glorious divine restoration, so glowingly described by the prophets.

No, indeed! Let it be carefully noted that while God has repeatedly promised to gather Israel, with such a magnificent display of *His* miraculous power, that it shall no more be said, "The Lord liveth that brought up the children of Israel out of the land of Egypt; but the Lord liveth, that brought up the children of Israel from the land of the north and from all the lands whither he had driven them," Jer. 16:14; yet has He also said, "Gather yourselves together, yea, gather together, O nation that hath no longing, before the decree bring forth, before the day pass as the chaff, before the fierce anger of the Lord come upon you." Zeph. 2:1, 2. Could this prophecy be more literally fulfilled than by this present Zionist movement?

One of the speakers at the first congress said of the Sultan, "If His majesty will now receive us, we will accept Him as our Messiah."

God says, "Ye have sold yourselves for nought and ye shall be redeemed without money." Isa. 52:3.

But Dr. Herzl is reported to have said, "We must buy our way back to Palestine, salvation is to be by money."

What a sign is this that the end of this dispensation is near.

If it stood alone we might well give heed to it. But when we find it supported by all these other signs, set forth in the Word, how can we refuse to believe it?

Shall we Christians condemn the Jews for not accepting the cumulative evidence that Jesus is the Messiah; and ourselves refuse this other cumulative evidence that His second coming is near?

It is significant that this first Zionist congress assembled just 1,260 years after the capture of Jerusalem by the Mohammedans in A.D. 637. Dan. 12:7.

It is probable that "the times of the Gentiles" are nearing their end, and that the nations are soon to plunge into the mighty whirl of events connected with Israel's godless gathering, "Jacob's trouble" (Jer. 30:6, 7), that awful time of tribulation, like which there has been none in the past, nor shall be in the future. Mat. 24:21.

But we, brethren, are not of the night. We are to watch and pray always that we may escape all these things that shall come to pass and stand before the Son of Man. Lu. 21:36.

Oh! glorious Hope. No wonder the Spirit and the Bride say come. No wonder the Bridegroom saith, "Surely I come quickly," and shall not we all join with the enraptured apostle,

"Even so come, Lord Jesus"?

22. The Blackstone Memorial

The dispensationalist background of Blackstone's thought did not appear in the famous "Memorial" on behalf of Russian Jews sent to President Benjamin Harrison, though some overtones of that position can be glimpsed in his accompanying letter. The appeal of the Memorial was made largely in humanitarian terms. It was signed by more than 400 leaders in American life, including publishers, figures of government and business, and clergymen, both Christian and Jewish, including occupants of many of the nation's leading pulpits. Persons of many shades of religious and theological opinion signed the document. The ten pages of names with brief identifications are omitted in the selection, but Blackstone's accompanying letter is included.

Source: Palestine for the Jews: A Copy of the Memorial Presented to President Harrison, March 5, 1891 (n.p., n.d. [1891]; reprinted in Arno Press anthology, Christian Protagonists for Jewish Restoration, 1977), pp. 1–2, 12–15.

What shall be done for the Russian Jews? It is both unwise and useless to undertake to dictate to Russia concerning her internal affairs. The Jews have lived as foreigners in her dominions for centuries, and she fully believes that they are a burden upon her resources and prejudicial to the welfare of her peasant population, and will not allow them to remain. She is determined that they must go. Hence, like the Sephardim of Spain, these Ashkenazim must emigrate. But where shall 2,000,000 of such poor people go? Europe is crowded and has no room for more peasant population. Shall they come to America? This will be a tremendous expense, and require years.

Why not give Palestine back to them again? According to God's distribution of nations it is their home—an inalienable possession from which they were expelled by force. Under their cultivation it was a remarkably fruitful land, sustaining millions of Israelites, who industriously tilled its hillsides and valleys. They were agriculturists and producers as well as a nation of great commercial importance—the center of civilization and religion.

Why shall not the powers which under the treaty of Berlin, in 1878, gave Bulgaria to the Bulgarians and Servia to the Servians now give Palestine back to the Jews? These provinces, as well as Roumania, Montenegro, and Greece, were wrested from the Turks and given to their natural owners. Does not Palestine as rightfully belong to the Jews? It is said that rains are increasing, and there are many evidences that the land is recovering its ancient fertility. If they could have autonomy in government, the Jews of the world would rally to transport and establish their suffering brethren in their time-honored habitation. For over seventeen centuries they have patiently waited for such a privileged opportunity. They have not become agriculturists elsewhere because they believed they were mere sojourners in the various nations, and were yet to return to Palestine and till their own land. Whatever vested rights, by possession, may have accrued to Turkey can be easily compensated, possibly by the Jews assuming an equitable portion of the national debt.

We believe this is an appropriate time for all nations, and especially the Christian nations of Europe, to show kindness to Israel. A million of exiles, by their terrible sufferings, are piteously appealing to our sympathy, justice, and humanity. Let us now restore to them the land of which they were so cruelly despoiled by our Roman ancestors.

To this end we respectfully petition His Excellency Benjamin Harrison, President of the United States, and the Honorable James G. Blaine, Secretary of State, to use their good offices and influence with the Governments of their Imperial Majesties—

Alexander III, Czar of Russia;

Victoria, Queen of Great Britain and Empress of India;

William II, Emperor of Germany;

Francis Joseph, Emperor of Austro-Hungary;

Abdul Hamid II, Sultan of Turkey;

His Royal Majesty Humbert, King of Italy;

Her Royal Majesty Marie Christiana, Queen Regent of Spain; and with the Government of the Republic of France and with the Governments of Belgium, Holland, Denmark, Sweden, Portugal, Roumania, Servia, Bulgaria, and Greece, to secure the holding, at an early date, of an international conference to consider the condition of the Israelites and their claims to Palestine as their ancient home, and to promote, in all other just and proper ways, the alleviation of their suffering condition. . . .

Respectfully presented by Wm. E. Blackstone, chairman of the Conference of Christians and Jews lately held in Chicago.

Washington, D.C., March 5, 1891

To His Excellency BENJAMIN HARRISON, President of the United States,

and HON. JAMES G. BLAINE, Secretary of State.

In presenting the Memorial asking your good offices with the Governments of Europe for an international Conference in behalf of the Russian

Jews, the undersigned begs to state that he has not sought for a multitude of signatures, but only representative names, and the cordial endorsement which the Memorial has received, gives assurance that the signatures could be indefinitely multiplied.

That the Memorial is really an outgrowth of the Conference between Christians and Jews recently held in Chicago.

That it was not deemed wise to hold further public meetings, or in any way, protest against the course being pursued by the Russian Government, and that therefore he undertook the task of presenting the Memorial personally to the signers.

That he is peculiarly gratified to find the plan proposed, commended by most eminent Jewish and Christian individuals, after carefully scrutinizing it in all its bearings.

That he spent several weeks in Palestine and Syria in 1889 and has somewhat carefully studied the conditions of the Jews there and in Europe and in America, and that he believes the project of restoring the autonomy of government of Palestine to them to be both feasible and politic.

That while a very few, of what are termed ultra radical, reformed, Jewish Rabbis have renounced their belief in ancient Scriptures, and openly proclaim that the Jews should amalgamate with the various nations, wherein they are scattered, the great body of the Jews, both clergy and laity, still cling to their time honored hopes of national restoration and will quickly respond to any such opportunity with abundant energy, means, and enthusiasm.

That the land of Palestine is capable of remarkable development, both agriculturally and commercially. Its geographical situation, as the half way house between Europe and Asia, is unequaled. That the Railroad now building from Joppa to Jerusalem, if extended via Damascus, Tadmor and the Euphrates valley, could not fail to become an international highway.

That while the Turkish government has lately shown some improvement, and has fostered the building of excellent common roads and given greater freedom for the activity of foreigners, still it is marvelously behind the times in which we live, and no great development can be expected under it.

That in support of this statement he would mention the unreasonable tax upon olive trees, and also the fanaticism which, because of a little cemetery on the shore at Joppa, prevents the excavating and dredging out of the ancient remarkable harbor, so greatly needed for commercial purposes.

That all the great European powers are jealous of each other's influence in, or possible occupation of, Palestine, and that this favors the giving of it to such an energetic small nation as the Jews under international guarantees and protection.

That the powers have already taken somewhat similar action by the appointment of a Christian governor over the Lebanon district of Syria.

That the poverty of the Turkish Government, makes the possible funding of a portion of the National debt by rich Jewish bankers, an important factor in the case.

That the unsettled indemnity claimed by Russia against Turkey is another significant item, which may be favorably used to promote the accomplishment of this plan.

That all the European nations sympathizing with the sad condition of the Jews in Russia, and yet not wishing them to be crowded into their own countries, will, he believes, cheerfully assent to this restoration to Palestine as the most natural alternative.

That he has special reasons for believing such sentiment already prevails, to a large extent, in Great Britain, and it seems to appeal to all classes of Christians as a magnificent humanitarian movement.

That only peaceable diplomatic negotiation is necessary, he believes, to accomplish the object, and that all private ownership of land and property should be carefully respected and protected.

That being on such friendly terms with Russia and having no complications in the Orient, it is most fitting and hopeful that our government should initiate this movement.

That there seem to be many evidences to show that we have reached the period in the great roll of the centuries, when the everliving God of Abraham, Isaac and Jacob, is lifting up His hand to the Gentiles, (Isa. 49:22) to bring His sons and His daughters from far, that he may plant them again in their own land, Ezk. 34, &c. Not for twenty-four centuries, since the days of Cyrus, King of Persia, has there been offered to any mortal such a priviledged opportunity to further the purposes of God concerning His ancient people.

May it be the high privilege of your Excellency, and the Honorable Secretary, to take a personal interest in this great matter, and secure through the Conference, a home for these wandering millions of Israel, and thereby receive to yourselves the promise of Him, who said to Abraham, "I will bless them that bless thee," Gen. 12:3.

Most Respectfully,

Your humble servant,

WM. E. BLACKSTONE

23. Pastor Russell and Zionism

Certain conservatively oriented Protestants of various denominations who had been schooled in the literalistic prophetic interpretation of the Bible came to believe that Zionism was a fulfillment of prophecy, and hence was of God. One of the most outspoken was Charles Taze Russell (1852–1916). Raised in a Congregationalist family, he undertook an independent ministry in the 1870s. In 1881 he founded the Watch Tower Bible and Tract Society, which in time grew into the movement known as Jehovah's Witnesses. In 1910, Russell was invited to speak of "Zionism in Prophecy" at New York's Hippodrome by a Jewish Mass Meeting Invitation Committee, and addressed a capacity audience of about 5,000 on October 9. He later gave similar addresses in Europe and America.

Source: [Charles Taze Russell] "Zionism in Prophecy," *Pastor Russell's Sermons: A Choice Collection of his most Important Discourses on all Phases of Christian Doctrine and Practice* (Brooklyn: International Bible Students Association, 1917), pp. 476–82. For extended treatment of Russell and Zionism, see Yona Malachy, *American Fundamentalism and Israel: The Relation of Fundamentalist Churches to Zionism and the State of Israel* (Jerusalem: Institute of Contemporary Jewry, 1978), Part 2.

While once I had been inclined to discard the Bible as unreliable along the lines of Higher Criticism, I subsequently have given it very earnest study, entirely apart from all creeds and theories of men. This study has greatly enlightened my mind and has given me a very different view of the sacred Book. I now have absolute confidence in it. I now realize, not only that there is a great Creator, but that He is definite, orderly, in His dealings with humanity, in His shaping of earth's affairs. For instance, Psalm 102 mentions the time, yea, the set time, for the return of Divine favor to Zion. So we find matters all through the Scriptures. In due time David, Solomon and others represented Jehovah in the kingdom of Israel and "sat upon the throne of the kingdom of the Lord." Later the kingdom was taken from Zedekiah, the last of the line of David to sit upon the throne of God's typical Kingdom. When the dominion was taken from him the Gentile governments were recognized, but not in the same manner as was Israel. None of them was designated the Kingdom of God. None of them was given perpetuity of rule.

Zedekiah Rejected—Nebuchadnezzar Acknowledged

But Gentile governments were promised a lease of power during the period when Israel would be cast off from God's favor. Then at the end of the appointed time the Gentile lease of earthly power in turn, and God's original provision for Israel to represent His Kingdom in the world, would return. These are the set times referred to by the Psalmist. God's promise to David—"The sure mercies of David"—were that of the fruit of his loins one should sit on the Throne of the Lord forever. The real purport of this promise was that Messiah, the long-promised King of Israel, would be the root and off-shoot of the Davidic line and blessed of the Lord; His Kingdom should be an everlasting one and fully competent to fulfil all of the Divine promises made to Abraham—"In thy Seed shall all the families of the earth be blessed."—Gen. 12:3.

So long as God acknowledged the nation of Israel as His Kingdom their kings were His representatives; but when Zedekiah was rejected it was not inconsistent on the Lord's part to recognize the Gentile governments, as above suggested. Of King Zedekiah we read, "O thou profane and wicked Prince, whose time has come that iniquity should have an end. Remove the diadem. Take off the crown. This shall not be the same. I will overturn, overturn, overturn it until He come whose right it is [Messiah], and I will give it unto Him." (Ezek. 21:25-27.) It was at this very time that God gave the lease of earthly power to Nebuchadnezzar and his successors, as is related in Daniel's prophecy. Nebuchadnezzar dreamed, but forgot his vision. Daniel the Prophet, made prisoner at an earlier date, was by Divine providence introduced to the king as the one person in all the world able to rehearse the king's dream and to give its interpretation, and his power so to do is declared to have been of the Lord.

Nebuchadnezzar's Vision of Gentile Dominion

The vision was of a stupendous image. Its head of gold represented Nebuchadnezzar's Empire—Babylon. Its breasts and arms of silver represented the Medo-Persian Empire. Its belly and thighs of brass represented the Grecian Empire. Its strong legs of iron represented the Roman Empire, East and West. Its feet of iron and clay represented Papal Rome. The iron continues to represent civil governments; and the miry clay, making them appear like stone, represented ecclesiasticism as it is now mixed up with the politics of the ten kingdoms of Europe. The whole period of time in which these various Gentile governments would dominate the world would last until Messiah's promised Kingdom. And this period is symbolically stated to have been "seven times"; that is, seven years—evidently not literal years, but symbolical.—Dan. 2:28-45; Lev. 26:18, 24, 28.

At their end the lease of earthly power of Gentile governments will terminate in the great Time of Trouble foretold by Daniel (12:1). Then Messiah shall stand up in the sense of assuming control of earth's affairs and Gentile governments will cease; for all nations shall serve and obey Messiah. Then God's Chosen People, Israel, will come to the front in the world's affairs; for they will become the representatives and instruments amongst men of Messiah's Kingdom, which will be spiritual and invisible, as is that of the Prince of this world, the Prince of Darkness, whom Messiah will bind or restrain during the thousand years of His Reign of Righteousness and destroy at the conclusion, when He shall deliver over the Kingdom of earth to the Father. Mankind will then be perfect; for all wilful sinners will be destroyed in the Second Death. Meantime, not only will Messiah's Reign bless and uplift Israel, but through Israel the blessing will extend to every nation, people, kindred and tongue in full accord with the Divine promise and oath made to Abraham more than thirty centuries ago.

All this is briefly and beautifully represented in Nebuchadnezzar's dream, as explained by Daniel. He saw a stone taken from the mountain without human aid. He watched and saw the stone smite the image on its feet and beheld, as the result, complete demolishment of the Gentile systems. This smiting of the image in the feet symbolically represents that it will be by Divine Power that present institutions will all come to naught preparatory to the establishment of the Kingdom of God in their stead.

Messiah's Kingdom in the Vision

Then Messiah's Kingdom, symbolized by the stone, not only will fill the place where the image stood, but gradually increasing, will fill the whole earth. From this standpoint it is not difficult for us to believe the words of the Psalmist that there is a time for God's gathering Zion, yea, a set time—fixed and unalterable. I do not pretend to say the day or month or year in which these things would be accomplished, in which the Gentile lease of earth's dominion would expire and Messiah's Kingdom assume control. I do, however, offer a suggestion: So far as I can discern, the time for these stupendous events is very much closer than many of us had supposed. The seven Times, or years, of Gentile domination, reckoned on the basis suggested in the Scriptures themselves, should be interpreted a day for a year, lunar time. Seven years in lunar time would represent 2520 days; and these symbolically interpreted, would mean 2520 years—from the time Nebuchadnezzar, the head of the image, was recognized down to the time of the expiration of the lease of Gentile power, when the stone shall smite the image in the feet. So far as I have been able to determine, the year of Zedekiah's dethronement was 606 B. C. Thus calculated the 2520 years of Gentile lease of power will expire in October, 1914. There are some who claim that Zedekiah's dethronement should be dated B. C. 588. If this be true it could make a difference of but eighteen years and give the date 1932. My convictions, however, favor 1914.

Zionism's Future Assured

For more than thirty years I have been presenting to Christian people the views I am today presenting specially to Jews, at the invitation of your Committee. Thirty years ago I attempted to tell to Israel the good tidings that God's set time to remember Zion had come. But that seemingly was too early. God's set time for Israel to hear was still future. I am still waiting for God's own time and way for the fulfilment of Isaiah 40:1, 2, and other Scriptures relating to Israel.

About twenty years ago Providence raised up for your people a great leader, Dr. Herzl, whose name is now a household word with your race. While your people were unready for any message that I could give them they were ready for what God sent them through Dr. Herzl—a message of hope, a message of national aspiration which quickened the pulse of your people into new hope respecting the future of the Jews. Dr. Herzl's endeavor was to have all loyal sons of Israel rise from the dust and aspire to be a nation amongst nations and to provide a home for the persecuted of their race in Russia and Eastern Europe. Dr. Herzl struck the popular chord in the hearts of the people. At first it was purely political, and the name of Zion meant little or anything religious; but gradually Dr. Herzl and all the leaders of the counsels of your people began to see that the religious element of the movement was the most powerful.

Dr. Herzl has been succeeded by Dr. Nordau, also evidently a man of great talent and great patriotism; but Zionism languishes. I am disclosing no secret when I tell you that amongst the leaders as well as amongst the rank and file, Zionism is trembling in the balances and fearful of coming to naught. It has spent its force along the lines originally inaugurated; but it will not fail, as many fear. Without assuming the role of a seer I answer you that Zionism is about to take on fresh vigor; that its most prosperous days are yet to come. According to my understanding of the Hebrew Prophets the time of "Jacob's trouble" is not yet ended. Further *pogroms* of Russia may be expected, and further atrocities in Roumania and elsewhere.

202 *The Holy Land in American Protestant Life*

It is sad indeed to be obliged to admit that these tribulations will probably come to you from professed Christians. How ashamed I feel of those who thus dishonor the name and the teachings of my Master, I cannot find words to express! They are deluded. They have misunderstood the Teacher whom they profess to follow. Their thought is that God will torment eternally all who do not profess the name of Christ. Controlled by delusion they are serving the god Adversary and dishonoring Jesus. But as the trials and difficulties of the patriarch Joseph were God's providences to lead him on to influence and power and honor, so will all these experiences and persecutions work blessings for your race and tend to drive them out of their present satisfaction and make them long for home—for Palestine. These experiences, in connection with the voice of the Prophets, which will henceforth more and more ring in your ears, will be the providences of God to accomplish for you more along the lines of Zionism than personal pride and national patriotism.

It is not my thought that the eight millions of Jews in the world will all go to Palestine, even though it has been estimated that, under most favorable conditions, the land could support more than twice that many. It is my thought that some of your most earnest and saintly people will go to Palestine quickly, that the rejuvenation there will be astonishing to the world. Further, it is my thought that Jews in every part of the world, in proportion as they come under the holy influences of God's promises through the Prophets, will go to Palestine sympathetically—by encouraging those who can better go than themselves and by financial assistance and the establishment there of great enterprises. Permit me to suggest that in the Time of Trouble, incidental to the transfer of Gentile rule to the power of Messiah, all financial interests will be jeopardized. Many of your race, growing wealthy, will surely take pleasure in forwarding the work of Zionism, as soon as they shall realize that it is of God, foretold through the Prophets. And those of your people of insufficient faith to use their means in forwarding the Lord's work at this important juncture will, before very long, find themselves in the condition pictured by the Prophet Ezekiel, who declares (7:19) that in this great Day of Trouble—"They shall cast their silver in the streets and their gold shall be removed; their silver and their gold shall not be able to deliver them in the day of the wrath of the Lord." The great Messenger of the Covenant whom ye delight in (Mal. 3:1-3) will test and prove you as a people. Those who worship idols of gold and silver, stocks and bonds, will receive severe chastisement at His hand before He will grant them a share in the coming blessings.

24. A Christian Assessment of Zionism, 1928

Harry Emerson Fosdick's widely read book, A Pilgrimage to Palestine, has already been introduced in Part I. The last chapter of his influential work, "Palestine Tomorrow," was an attempt to give a balanced assessment of Zionism as he encountered it in the Holy Land in 1926, and to note its impact on the Arab inhabitants. A convinced opponent of anti-Semitism and a pacifist who hoped that war and violence could be avoided, Fosdick's own hopes rested with the moderate rather than the "political" Zionists.

Source: Harry Emerson Fosdick, *A Pilgrimage to Palestine* (New York: Macmillan Co., 1928), pp. 271-83, 288-90, 292-4.

Chapter Twelve.

Palestine Tomorrow.
I.

No observant traveler can visit Palestine today without being sure that the country has a future. The days of its living importance to humanity are far from ended and in it movements are afoot which may either contribute signally to man's welfare or land the world in fresh confusions and alarms. When the archeologists, the historians, and the Biblical scholars have seen in Palestine all that their specialties reveal, the student of contemporary affairs has a large and lively residue to handle.

For weal or woe the new day was launched in the Holy Land by the famous Balfour Declaration:

His Majesty's Government view with favor the establishment in Palestine of a national home for the Jewish people, and will use their best endeavours to facilitate the achievement of this object, it being clearly understood that nothing shall be done which may prejudice the civil and religious rights of existing non-Jewish communities in Palestine or the rights and political status enjoyed by Jews in any other country.

The reading of that is brief and easy, its purport seems generous and laudable, but its results are visibly exciting, offering alike spectacles of heroic adventure and possibilities of tragic failure.

Come down, for example, to Dilb [now Kiryat Anavim] in the Shephelah hills, a few miles below Jerusalem, where a hardy band of Jewish colonists is establishing its homes and farms. The story of folk like this is one of the romances of modern times and one hopes that, whether they win or lose in their venture, they may sometime find a historian worthy to record their exploits. The tale of this group begins in Odessa in the Ukraine in 1917. There local Zionists founded an agricultural school and for two years the future colonists attended it. Like most Jews, they knew nothing of agriculture. Ten university graduates, a printer, a druggist, a bookstore keeper, a carpenter, small merchants—such was the constitution of the group. After two years of preparation an advance section came to Palestine and were assigned this rough, rocky, untilled valley, treeless and largely soilless, where from the ground up they had to create the very elements on which agriculture depends. They cleared the land, terraced the hillsides to make soil, constructed a water system in an arid and hitherto unwatered land, built barns, houses, a school, and when I was there had 160 acres under cultivation. This is pioneering with a vengeance. Almost any Western country would reward such toil with far greater returns, but these Jews have come from patriotic motives to help rebuild Zion.

The meagerness of living in a colony like Dilb, the grim struggle against a niggardly land, the paucity of the results, and the terrific cost of work and money to achieve them, add glamour to the courageous idealism of the colonists. The £22,500 required to purchase the land, prepare it for cultivation, build barns, houses, and waterworks, buy farming instruments and animals, came from the Zionist central funds. In 1926, with one-third of their vineyards just coming to fruitage, they paid sixty per cent of their running expenses; they hoped two years later to pay all; but only in 1929 do they expect to start paying a small interest on the capital which they have borrowed. The adventure is not only moral but economic. One wonders how it will turn out.

Meanwhile, at the time of our visit, a hardy group of seventy-five men and women were endeavoring here to make their ancient land bloom again. Already they had a flourishing forest nursery with sixty different kinds of eucalyptus trees. Granted the colony's success, in a few years these hills will be wooded and green once more. The oldest colonist was aged forty. Fifteen young children were in a school which the colony maintains. The manner of life is communistic; no private property is held; and the moving ideal which has brought the settlers here combines the love of Palestine with the desire to create a cooperative fellowship where each shall give according to his strength and receive according to his need.

This is Zionism in the concrete. This is its cutting edge and crucial exhibition. Here its enthusiasm meets the test of barren, unwatered land and poor soil, costing immense expenditure of toil and means to transform into fertility. And here, too, are the lure and thrill of Zionism, where pioneers dedicate life to the rebuilding of the Holy Land.

II

The motives which have made this new movement toward the homeland so kindling to Jewish imagination are not difficult even for a non-Jew to understand. The patriotism of Jews for Palestine has a long tradition. In the days when Nineveh and Babylon practised the cruel policy of exile, many peoples were absorbed and lost in the populations among which they forcibly were settled, but the Jews survived. Out of the midst of that supreme temptation to assimilation in Babylon came the passionate cry,

> If I forget thee, O Jerusalem,
> Let my right hand forget her skill.
> Let my tongue cleave to the roof of my mouth,
> If I remember thee not;
> If I prefer not Jerusalem
> Above my chief joy.[1]

We ate the Passover supper in Jerusalem with a Jewish family of the humbler sort. They came from forefathers who had fled out of Spain when the Jews there were persecuted in the sixteenth century. Three generations were at the table, from an aged grandsire past ninety to a brisk youth who had come down from the American University in Beirut to keep Passover with his family. It was a rememberable occasion for a Christian, both because one cannot often eat Passover in Jerusalem, where the Master kept it with his disciples, and because this fine-spirited and friendly family of the Master's race made us feel anew the depth and warmth of Hebrew loyalty to Zion. In particular I recall the old man's commenting on those words of the ritual which Jews have used for centuries when keeping Passover in any other country: "This year we celebrate it here; but we hope next year to celebrate it in the land of Israel; this year we are bondsmen, but next year we hope to be freemen."

This long-cherished dream of restoration to their ancient land has become the more alluring to Jewish people as the hardships of their life

[1] Psalm 137:5-6.

elsewhere, their confinement in European ghettos, their persecutions and pogroms, have shut against them other doors of hope. The treatment of Jews in Christendom makes one of the most appalling stories of truculence and bigotry that history knows. Even now for millions of Jews in eastern Europe life is hardly tolerable. A weak folk long since would have collapsed but the Jews, vigorous, persistent, imperturbable, with physical and intellectual vitality which nothing can dampen, much less extinguish, have not collapsed. Hated, ostracized, hemmed in, fretting for an outlet, a great people without a national home—no wonder their aspirations have turned increasingly to their ancient land.

Multitudes of Jews today, even in countries where they are not persecuted, feel continually that they are aliens; their natural loyalties are outraged and their sensitiveness is hurt. As one put it to me: if in Belgium a Jew rises to great distinction he is heralded as an eminent Belgian; if he falls into disgrace he is called an accursed Jew. Can this be God's intention for his people? the religious Jew asks. I have sat in the chambers of one of the eminent members of the Supreme Court of the United States and in the home of the leading British jurist in Palestine, and from these two eminent Jewish lawyers have heard stirring pleas for Zionism, based on the argument that Providence could not mean to leave a nation so able to contribute spiritual gifts to humankind without a land and a culture of its own through which to channel the contribution.

Such motives lie behind Zionism, mingled with pity on the part of prosperous Jews for their unfortunate fellows and with desire to open in Palestine a place of refuge from the pogroms of eastern Europe. The United States sent only 166 Jewish immigrants to Palestine in 1922 and only 125 in 1923. From such a land there is no lure for Jews in the exhausting toil and small reward of Zionist colonies in Palestine. But America furnishes from two-thirds to three-quarters of the funds which bring Jews from Poland, the Ukraine, and Russia as fast as the immigration authorities will allow.

III

What, then, is the truth about Zionism as it appears to a non-Jew who, neither Zionist nor anti-Zionist, is interested without prejudice to observe the facts? For myself, I found my mind swaying like a pendulum between two positions: first, sympathy with the ideals of the moderate Zionists, mingled with profound admiration for their devotion to their cause, their daring confidence in its success, and many of their practical achievements up to date; second, clear perception that before this courageous venture can succeed it must face serious problems whose solutions are not easy to see. The economic problem is colossal. Everything hinges upon that. Here is a people famous for its financial shrewdness and yet plunging, on the basis of emotional loyalties, sacred memories, patriotic sentiment, and racial altruism, into an enterprise which obviously flies in the face of economic fact. The rehabilitation of Palestine is not a task that any one would dream of undertaking for economic reasons. Dr. Weizmann, the supremely influential figure in Zionism, said to me in Jerusalem that for the movement to succeed it was necessary both to remake the people and to remake the land. That is the succinct truth. To make Jews into farmers, which is alien to all their history, and to make Palestine profitably arable—these two colossal tasks the Zionists have undertaken. The costs are inevitably tremendous. In 1925, according to official Zionist figures, it was averaging about $3500 a family to settle colonists upon the land, and while a few of the colonies have become self-supporting, and others hope to be so in a few years, the phrase "self-supporting" is generally used to mean the covering of running expenses without payment of any substantial interest on the original outlay. No colony founded since the war has yet become self-supporting in the fuller sense of handling on a financial basis the capital investment. The head of the Zionist Executive in Palestine told me that in half a century he expected two and a half million Jews to be settled there. Personally, I cannot see where he is going to put them. Moreover, that would mean, if present averages should obtain, an initial capital expenditure running into an immense sum. It is no kindness to minimize the crucial nature of this problem. Even a ten-year program of settling two hundred thousand colonists upon the land would mean a capital expenditure of many millions. The success of Zionism depends, in the last analysis, on the willingness of American Jews over a period of at least a quarter of a century to pour out a steady stream of lavish gifts, annually amounting to millions, to finance the colonies in Palestine.

Meanwhile, the struggle to make this naturally unfertile land a competitive success in modern markets is going bravely but hazardously on. A Jew in Jerusalem can buy finished flour from Australia or the United States more cheaply than he can buy raw grain upon the threshing-floors of his own colonies in the environs of the city, and the best wines of Italy cost no more in Jerusalem than the wines of Rishon le-Zion, a colony over forty years old near Jaffa.

I confess to profound admiration for the courage with which these facts are faced by the leaders of Zionism. They are sure that Palestine can be reclaimed and made economically prosperous. They are encouraged by the example of Switzerland, a land without natural economic advantages, which, for all that, thrives. They point to the exports from Palestine of £468,000 worth of oranges annually; to the immense mineral deposits of the Dead Sea; to the sacredness of the land, which can be capitalized alike in exports such as Passover bread, and in attractiveness to tourists who will leave money there; to the harnessing of Jordan for electric power, which is about to be undertaken; to the multiplication of small manufactures for local consumption; and to large export businesses like the cement works at Haifa already afoot and flourishing. Meanwhile, week by week, the movement as a whole survives only by virtue of contributions from abroad. One month while we were there the income fell below the average and teachers in Jewish schools in Jerusalem went unpaid.

IV

Another crucial problem is presented by racial relationships. In the early stages of its development Zionism was advertised as the movement of a people without a land to a land without a people. Nothing could be more dangerously false than such simplification of the issue. Palestine is not without a people and no one understands the situation who does not see that over half a million Moslem Arabs, who easily constitute seventy-three per cent of the population, naturally regard with suspicion, if not with rage, the deliberate endeavor to make a "national home for the Jewish people" in their country.

The Zionists themselves have contributed largely to make this bad matter worse. One of the most prominent Jews in the world, in his exuberance over the new hopes of Zionism, told the Arabs to "trek along," and the repercussions of that phrase are heard wherever Arabs live today. Zionism to the Jew is an idealistic movement; seen from the Arab side it is predatory, and one who gains entrée to the Arabs' confidence will hear bitter words expressing their desire to convert the Jewish national home into the Jewish national cemetery.

One who is neither Jew nor Arab can readily sympathize with both. It is a difficult and teasing impasse into which Zionism has thrust these races. The Arab is not a fit competitor of the Jew and he knows it. Whether the Arab be a Bedouin living in a tent, or a small tenant farmer, or a rich landlord living in the city and established in his pride of race and culture, he is not now prepared to make Palestine live again. The Jew, however, can do that. He comes with the very qualities which the Arab notoriously lacks—energy, vitality, aggressiveness, knowledge of the methods of modern science—and the Arab has not the faintest chance in competition. He knows that and the Jew knows that too. The knowledge makes the Arab afraid and angry and the Jew confident and aggressive.

Slowly but steadily the proportion of Jewish population has been creeping up. The latest estimate which I can obtain puts the matter thus: in 1920, 66,600 Jews to 606,600 Moslems and Christians; in 1922, 83,794 Jews to 673,388 Moslems and Christians; in 1926, 147,000 Jews to 721,000 Moslems and Christians. And now come estimates from prominent Zionists that some two million and a half Jews are the goal. Naturally, the Arabs are anxious. The fact that the British government is officially committed to Zionism deepens the anxiety. In many Arabs anxiety is intensified into anger so that one of the most prominent Arab leaders in the land recently said to a friend of mine that if it were not for American dollars and British airplanes there would not be a Jew in Palestine.

Meanwhile the Zionists themselves are displaying two attitudes, one tending to mollify the Arabs and the other to infuriate them. On one side stands the unwisdom and arrogance of Dr. Eder, former acting-chairman of the Zionist Commission in Palestine. Publicly before a court of inquiry on Jewish-Arab disturbances in Jaffa, he said in 1921, as the report of the commission reads: There can be only "one National Home in Palestine, and that a Jewish one, and no equality in the partnership between Jews and Arabs, but a Jewish predominance as soon as the numbers of that race are sufficiently increased." That is typical of the madness with which some Zionists have rushed into trouble. They have professed their determination that "Palestine should be just as Jewish as America is American and England is English." Even in the Palestine Weekly, published in Jerusalem itself, they have insisted that as between the two portions of the Balfour Declaration, the first promising a national home for the Jews and the second promising that the rights of previous inhabitants shall not be invaded, "the principle of the British policy for Palestine lies not in the second but the first." The upshot of all this has been disastrous. The Anglican bishop of Jerusalem has summed it up: "Zionists by their statements and by their demands, by their intolerance and by their lack of sympathy with the people of the country, have alienated them to such a degree that it will take years of patient effort to counteract the effect."

On the other hand, the moderate Zionists have tried sensibly to save the situation. Sir Herbert Samuel, first High Commissioner of Palestine under British rule and himself an ardent Zionist, was a sincere friend to the Arabs. His principle was ethical and sane: "If the growth of Jewish influence were accompanied by Arab degradation, or even by a neglect to promote Arab advancement, it would fail in one of its essential purposes." Despite reiterated statements of this kind, however, made by British officials, Zionist congresses, and individual Jews, the racial situation, while less openly violent than it was, still is dangerous, and I know no point on which Zionists seem to me to be indulging so obviously in wishful thinking as in their self-persuasion that all is well. . . .

VI

Meanwhile, no one does justice to the situation who does not fairly estimate the positive achievements already won in the first few, experimental years of this venture. One who knows the apparently exhaustless vitality of the Jewish race would expect its energies, released by the ardent hope of a national home, to flow into Palestine in multiplying streams. That such is the case any one who stays here long enough to see must testify.

Wherever the Jews go, education goes, and schools are flourishing in all the Zionist colonies, with higher schools of advanced standing in Jerusalem already crowned by a university. Illuminating statistics make plain the superior standards which the Jews are introducing into Palestine and show how difficult will be the competition of the Arabs, whether Christian or Moslem, with the education-loving Zionists. According to official figures in 1923, of the children of Palestine from five through fourteen years of age, seventeen per cent of the Moslems, eighty-one per cent of the Christians, and ninety-six per cent of the Jews were in school. Of children from fifteen through eighteen years of age, three per cent of the Moslems were still proceeding with their education, thirty-seven per cent of the Christians, and forty-two per cent of the Jews.

As they bring with them their passion for education, so they bring their Western ideas of medicine and philanthropy, and one sees in Jerusalem the beginnings of hospital service, public clinics, child welfare work, under the direction of thoroughly trained British and American Hebrews who are putting expert knowledge at the disposal of their people. Typical of this fine spirit of philanthropy which is transferring the best Western ideals and methods to the Holy Land is the children's village on the slope of Little

Hermon, overlooking the Esdraelon plain. This is an agricultural community of children, admirably housed, with trained care in home and school. When we visited it in 1926, eighty boys and thirty-five girls, war orphans from the Ukraine, were growing up there supported by Jewish funds from South Africa. The colony was only two and one-half years old and it seemed to me an extraordinary achievement to have been wrought out in so short a time. Well-conditioned children the little villagers were, well cared for, well educated, and happy. And they obviously reveled in their practical training for the work of the Zionist colonies. Already, as recreation in their free time, these children had set out over ten thousand new trees from their own nurseries.

It is the Zionist colonies themselves, however, that present the ultimate test of the movement. Picture after picture rises in memory as I recall these little settlements newly founded, still struggling, like all pioneers, with the preliminary difficulties of land and water, sometimes fairly hopeful, sometimes obviously in straits. . . .

Most visitors do not see these little settlements which are the real evidence of Zionism's vitality and the ultimate test of its success. Most travelers visit Tel-Aviv, an amazing town near Jaffa which since the war has grown from nothing to sixty thousand folk. Tel-Aviv, however, is rather an excrescence on Zionism than its normal fruit. It looks like a boom town in the Middle West with its raw newness, its paved streets, modern buildings, electric light plant, Western stores. Like the Zionism which it represents, it stands for the aggressive invasion of a new civilization. The contrast is vivid as one turns to Jaffa's neighboring bazaars and streets so Orientally picturesque. Not here in Tel-Aviv, but out in the colonies where pioneers invest life itself in the reclamation of the Holy Land, are alike the lure and hardship, the test and the possible tragedy of Zionism.

While tragedy is obviously possible, I personally hope that Zionism may succeed. What other fortunate outlook there is for Palestine I do not see. The Arabs, in the present stage of their development, would doubtless leave it as it is. Under their sway it has been stripped and impoverished, and they lack, at least at present, the ability swiftly to change either themselves or their environment. In time, these Arabs, who are a great race, will be compelled to achieve a synthesis of their ancient culture and modern life, but the time for that seems distant. Meanwhile, the present hope of a rejuvenated Palestine lies in Zionism under British guidance.

The hope of Zionism, however, lies in its own moderation and wisdom.

If it would be successful it must be unselfish. It must count Arab welfare as precious as its own. It must center its efforts on creating in the Holy Land a cultural expression of world-wide Judaism. It must forego grasping ambition for political dominance and turn its back on chauvinistic nationalism. It must cease its absurd pretense that into this poor land as a place of refuge millions of persecuted Jews from southeastern Europe can be poured when the plain fact is that the country can do no more than absorb with difficulty a few thousand each year. If Zionism will thus clean house of wild extravagances and lay hold on a few immediate and obtainable objectives that can be reached with profit to all Palestinians and with wrong to none, then success may come. But if the partisans of political Zionism, as now seems probable, are allowed to force the issue, I am willing to risk my reputation on prophecy: Zionism will end in tragedy.

A Christian who, like a Jew, loves the Holy Land as the homestead of his faith, will regard the progress of events with eager, sympathetic interest. This is not the first time the Jews have undertaken a desperate venture in Palestine. Going north one day from Haifa, along the Mediterranean shore, we saw a great field of cucumber vines and in the midst of it a torn and tattered booth where, before the fruit was gathered, a guard had watched. The booth, made of a few bare poles and interlaced with faded vines, was now deserted—a perfect picture of lonely desolation. We recalled as we saw it Isaiah's description of Jerusalem in his day left "as a lodge in a garden of cucumbers."[2] More than once the Jews have thus seen their sacred land desolate or have lost it altogether and yet have rewon it by the very power of their passionate loyalty.

One who knows what happened when the little band of returning exiles from Babylonia long ago refounded on Zion their struggling commonwealth amid the ruins of their sacred city and the scornful antagonism of their neighbors will not be so much impressed by difficulties now as to be certain that the Jews cannot win again. Perhaps they can. The whole world is debtor to them for having won before. By that victory they set the stage for all that followed of tremendous import alike to them and to mankind. One hopes, although sometimes against hope, that they may so handle their present penetration of their ancient land that future generations with good cause may be grateful for another contribution to mankind's enrichment.

[2]Isaiah 1:8.

25. A Gentile's Survey of Zionism, 1929

John Haynes Holmes (1879–1964), a graduate of Harvard College and Divinity School, served several Unitarian pulpits before undertaking his long ministry at the Church of the Messiah, later to become The Community Church of New York. A prolific author, a pacifist who was a cofounder of the American branch of the Fellowship of Reconciliation, and an outspoken reformer, Holmes was widely known in his day.

Early in 1929 he visited Palestine, talking with many persons representing many points of view in that troubled land, soon to be torn by serious disturbances. His own great hopes for Zionism were boldly expressed in the last chapter of the book that grew out of his journey. The concluding pages of that chapter, entitled "The Promise," follow.

Source: John Haynes Holmes, *Palestine To-Day and To-Morrow: A Gentile's Survey of Zionism* (New York: Macmillan Co., 1929; reprinted by Arno Press, 1977), pp. 262–71.

The spirit of Zionism, like the valor of the Zionists, has never been doubted. Only its success! Now that success is achieved, or being achieved by labor that grows not tired nor afraid, the nature of this success is doubted. Yesterday the skeptic cried, It can't be done! To-day he complains, It isn't worth doing!

If the Jews are doing in Palestine under difficulties only what others have done, or they themselves may do, in other places, under more favorable conditions, then men may well have doubt as to whether the enterprise is necessary, or worthwhile. But there is a spirit in Zion which is unique. This spirit has been generated and preserved through the centuries by the weakness of an heroic people in the face of outrages and persecutions they had not the strength to end but only to endure. This spirit is now in its fulfillment preserved anew by the weakness of this same people in the face of difficulties and dangers they have not the strength to overcome but only to use. If these difficulties and dangers persist, this unique spirit will endure, even as it has endured through death and agony until this day. If they are lifted, or pass away, then this spirit may die for lack of sustenance upon which to feed. But Palestine is itself the perpetual guarantee that such conditions, while they may be tempered, cannot be changed. The land serves the genius of the people it has bred. The task sustains the ideals of the workers it has called. The mission of the Jew remains still what it has always been—to find strength in weakness, and victory in suffering.

What Such Success Means

The establishment of Zion, as thus defined, means great things for the world.

First of all, it means the preservation of the Jews. This is important to the Jews themselves, but more important to the world. There is tragedy in the loss of any people. Governments may come and go, be merged in one another and happily disappear, but people should endure. For each people brings to humanity, as each child brings to a family, a unique character, a special genius, which enriches the human spirit and its achievement upon the earth. Especially is this true of the Jews, who, like the ancient Greeks, developed a type of culture and enlightenment unrivaled in the history of mankind. Unlike the Greeks, the Jews were saved from degeneracy and ultimate disappearance as a people. They survive to-day not in the relics and ruins of the civilization which they produced, but as a vital force in the life of contemporary society. This force must be preserved for the intellectual power it embodies, the spiritual values it conserves, the vast influence of prophetic insight and vision it can contribute to mankind. Yet it was never in such peril of extinction as it is to-day. For the Jews are still a scattered people. If they are to survive as something more than a memory and tradition, they must have some rallying center to which to cling, and from which to draw the peculiar nurture of their tribe. For ages this rallying center was the ghetto, in the darkness of which burned the unquenchable flame of the Messianic hope. But to-day the ghetto walls are down—the flame is in danger of being lost in the bright light of outer day. What now shall hold the Jews to one another, and to Israel?

The answer to this question is Zion. It is the new rallying center which shall "bind all Jews together," to quote again the words of Achad Ha-Am, by holding them fast to the recovered ideals of their race. In Zion the far-flung sons of Jacob have a common work to do, and a common hope to cherish. To this new homeland, the Jews of Russia, Poland, Roumania, Czecho-Slovakia, Austria, Germany, England, America, Bokhara, Tur-kestan, Morocco, turn with a common affection and desire and thus feel kinship with one another. And it is kinship on the highest level of racial experience! For amid these ancient hills, upon this sacred soil of Palestine, they see Israel reborn and thus redeemed. Here the Jew is become himself again. He stands upon his own ground, and feels within the quickening of his own spirit. This spirit he obeys. For he need no longer now be obsequious, or imitative, or submissive. The hour is past when he need bow his head and "wash his hands" before his betters, and thus by his debasement buy the favor wherewith to live. In Zion he has achieved his independence, recovered his self-respect, and thus may be true to his essential genius. "If you wish to see the genuine type of Jew," writes Achad Ha-Am, "where [sic] it be a rabbi, or a scholar, or a writer, a farmer or an artist, or a business man—then go to Palestine and you will see it."

It is this vision, this achievement, not only in Palestine but throughout the world, which is remaking the Jew into the likeness of his own spirit, and thus saving him, in the hour of his emancipation, from disintegration and decay, and thus from ultimate dispersal and disappearance as a people. To many an ardent Zionist, the vindication of the great adventure lies not so much in what it is doing for the pioneers in Palestine as in what it is doing for the great host of Jewry outside the borders of the national homeland. Two perils beset the Jews in this modern age. The one is the peril of atrophy in the traditions and ceremonialisms of an ancient faith. The other is the peril of corruption from the gross materialism of a machine-made civilization. In the one case, the Jews would wither away into a sect, and perish. In the other case, they would become absorbed into the substance of a worldly society, and disappear. That in either case they would vanish as a racial entity is as unlikely as that the Negroes will be so lost in any time that can now be foreseen by the mind of man. But that in both cases they would vanish as a spiritual force which can redeem mankind, is certain. To save the Jews from such a fate, and humanity from such a loss, nothing can serve but the emergence within the life of Israel of that which Israel was born to serve—a task, a mission, an ideal. The religion of Israel must be made real again. The visions of the prophets must become not words but deeds. And it is this, precisely this, which Zion brings! In the hope of the homeland Jewry lives again, and therewith brings light and leading not merely to itself but to the world.

A second thing implicit in the establishment of Zion was pointed out by George Eliot as long ago as 1876, in the flaming speech of Mordecai, the Jew, in "Daniel Deronda," who saw in Palestine "a new Judaea, poised between East and West, a covenant of reconciliation."

This reconciliation between East and West has been long delayed. For centuries the struggle between the two halves of the human family has waxed and waned, but never ceased. In our day this struggle threatens more terribly than ever, for the mystic and mysterious East is now stirring to its utmost depth and its remotest range. In China, India, Persia, Syria, Arabia, the nearer and the farther East, the unnumbered multitudes of men are shaking themselves as from a mighty slumber, and preparing to face the West on its own terms and to its own ends. The gulf between these hemispheres of culture and civilization is one of the most terrifying phenomena in the world of our time. Deep down in its dark and unprobed depths lurk the hidden forces of war and revolution that may yet annihilate the race. What influence can bridge this gulf? How can these two divisions of mankind be brought together in a harmony of inquiry and understanding? Where can they learn to cooperate, and thus to avoid the rivalry and struggle in which both are doomed to perish.

George Eliot's Mordecai saw an answer to these questions in Zion—and so do Zionists to-day! Already in their schools and university, their playgrounds, settlements and hospitals, they are building the institutions and generating the forces which may develop this much desired "covenant of reconciliation."

"East is East, and West is West, and never the twain may meet," says Rudyard Kipling. But they *do* meet in Palestine. The peoples of the Orient and Occident have always met in Palestine. This land for ages has been the frontier between these severed worlds. As such, to be sure, it has been crossed and recrossed, fought over and died for, by an unceasing stream of contending armies—Egyptian and Babylonian, Greek and Persian, Roman and Parthian, Christian and Saracen, English and Turk. The wide valley of the Emek is sown with the bones of countless armies from both horizons. But a frontier not merely divides but joins. It is a place where peoples meet to clasp hands as well as to fight. For centuries Palestine has been known as the "bridge" between East and West. But over a bridge pass not only soldiers, but also travelers, traders, teachers. Where better than in Palestine, thus "poised between East and West," can the work of acquaintanceship and cooperation between these two worlds begin? And who better than the Jew is equipped to do this work?

For the Jew is himself an Oriental. His racial origin lies far east of Jordan, in the dim valleys of the Tigris and Euphrates. His mind flowers naturally into the poetry and parable of Eastern lore. His wisdom is the wisdom of the Orient, and his spiritual vision a product of the basic religious genius of this world. In body and blood, in temperament, in psychology, in inward range and depth of mystery, the Jew is a child of the East. But he lived his life for centuries on the frontier of the West. Then he crossed this frontier. Even before the destruction of his nation, the tribe had drifted by thousands and tens of thousands into the Graeco-Roman world. Greek thought and speech, and Roman citizenship, had become a part of Israel's experience. Finally with the fall of Jerusalem, came that far scattering through Europe, and ultimately to America, which has made the Jew a denizen of the West. Unchanged in nature, in his love of wisdom and his passion for religion, he has long been familiar with the languages, the modes of thought, the habits of life, the practical interests and activities of the peoples among whom he has dwelt, and now, in these days of wider enfranchisement, has become the master of their political insight, scientific knowledge, and technical equipment. Still the inward, he is become the outward man as well. Feeling the East and its dreams, he knows also the West and its ways. In him, as in no other man upon the earth, the Occident and Orient have met and mingled. The soul of the Jew represents a confluence of these two worlds. And now he comes again to the frontier in Palestine. What better work can he do, what work can he better do, than serve as an interpreter, a friend, a mediator between these worlds which are so truly both his own! In nothing is the Jew in Palestine so fully vindicating himself as in this work, already well begun, of bringing East and West together. Prejudices must long be bitter, and misunderstandings dark. Political intrusions from the one side will match religious fanaticisms on the other, and of both the Jew will be the victim. But he has but to endure, as he has endured from the beginning. In his dual genius is "the covenant of reconciliation." In Zion is the laboratory where will be found the formula of peace.

But Zion is a laboratory for other experiments as well. It is a universal laboratory for the study of social ills—and therein is the third and greatest aspect of its significance to the world.

The basic problem of men's lives upon this earth is that of learning to live together in peace and happiness. To ask why men should ever have allowed themselves to become divided into mutually hostile groups is a superficial way of probing into the fundamental and vastly intricate question of human rivalries and antagonisms which begins with outward facts of economic and political determinism, and ends with inward mysteries of psychological and spiritual reaction. Meanwhile, whatever the explanations, the hostile groups are here, and man's continued life upon this planet depends upon the discovery of methods of adjustment and reconciliation.

Now in Palestine would seem to be found all the occasions of diversity, all the issues of antagonism, which vex humanity. This little land appears as a kind of microcosm of all the hostilities which rend and tear the human organism. Is it racial differences?—here you have them in the intense race prejudice between the Arab and the Jew. Is it political differences?—here you find them in the clash between Arab nationalism, Jewish nationalism, and British imperialism. Is it religious differences?—here they are in the fierce fanaticisms of Christians and Moslems and the orthodox piety of Jews. Is it economic differences—here they flourish in the basic contention for the land upon which men must feed. Is it social and cultural differences?—here they abound in the *Fellaheen* shepherd, the Arab landlord and the Jewish *Chalutzim*.

It is because Palestine has always been the unhappy meeting place of differences of this kind, that the history of the land has been so tragic. And is so tragic still! But these same differences present opportunity, as well as prepare calamity. It is where diseases rage in pestilence that remedies are found. Palestine, in other words, may be made not merely a battleground but a laboratory. It needs but the presence of a determined mind, a courageous heart, an idealistic spirit, to make this country an experiment station for the healing of the ills of man. And it is just this which the Jew brings to Palestine in Zionism. Here in this adventure is the dream of a society of justice, righteousness and peace. Here on the scene of this adventure are all the diversive and divisive elements out of which this dream must fashion the substance of its reality. If the Jew succeeds in what he has so heroically undertaken, he will have discovered the solution of all social problems. It is in this sense that Zionism is far more than the hope of Israel. It is the hope, also, of the world.

Conclusion

Zion has thus a universal significance. This significance resides at bottom in Zion's vindication of man's insistence upon a spiritual interpretation of life—his belief in the triumph of right over wrong, of good over evil, of the spirit over the flesh. "The meek shall inherit the earth."

On my return from Palestine, I passed through Rome, and made a pilgrimage to the Arch of Titus. Proudly spanning the Appian Way on the high crest of the slope at the entrance of the Forum, this Arch was reared by the Emperor to celebrate through all future years his destruction of the Jews. Never had there been a greater military victory. Jerusalem, besieged and taken, was leveled to the dust, and all its people who were not butchered were strewn to the four winds of heaven. Here upon the Arch to-day are the sculptured pictures of the deed—the Jewish captives yoked to the Emperor's car, the table of shew bread and the seven-branched candlestick borne in triumph in his procession. When Titus died, so soon after his task was done, it must have been with complacent calm at the glory of his achievement.

The Arch still stands—and so does Jerusalem! And the Jews still live, though Titus is dead and his grave forgotten. And, wonder of wonders, these Jews are back in Jerusalem. The story of Rome and all its emperors ended more than fifteen hundred years ago, but the story of the Jews is beginning all anew. What irony is in these moldering stones and battered sculptures! An emperor's arch, which has now become the memorial of his slaves and victims? I smiled, as I gazed, at the littleness of kings and the feebleness of swords. And I thought of a story which had been told me by a certain Jew in Palestine.

This man had met Mussolini, and had been able to do him certain personal services. The Italian dictator was grateful, and at the moment of parting said that he would be glad to do anything in his power to show his appreciation.

"What can I do?" he said.

"There is one thing you can do," said this gallant son of Israel. "You can take down the Arch of Titus, stone by stone, and give it to the Jews, to be erected again upon Mt. Zion."

Mussolini did not grant this bold request. It is perhaps better so. Let the Arch stand in the Eternal City, to proclaim eternally, in its most appropriate setting, the truth which Napoleon discovered in the midst of his greatest triumphs, and phrased in immortal words:

"There are only two powers in the world, the spirit and the sword. In the long run the sword will always be conquered by the spirit."

26. A Pro-Arab View by a Biblical Scholar, 1938

Many biblical scholars in the twentieth century first made their acquaintance with the Holy Land in the Turkish or mandate periods when the Arab presence in the land was strong. They came to know and to appreciate the Arab perspective, and like many Arabs, were troubled by the advance of Zionism.

Elihu Grant (1873–1942), who earned three degrees at Boston University and was ordained a Methodist minister, served as superintendent of the American Friends School at Ramallah early in the century. Returning to the United States, he taught biblical literature, first at Smith College, then at Haverford. He was director of American excavations at Ain Shems, 1928–33, and served as president of the Society of Biblical Literature and of the American Friends of the Arabs. He wrote a number of books, notably The People of Palestine *(1907). In 1938 he prepared a small book asking that Palestine be left in the custody of its native Arab population; the book's first part, "Palestine Today," is reproduced here. Grant concluded the preface to his pamphlet by saying, "No matter how impatient some of these paragraphs may seem and that because of years of devotion and a sense of the logic and right of certain living facts, please be advised that the main note is irenic born of deep love for Palestine and a sincere respect for the best elements and the best intentions among the three outstanding factors of present day Palestine, the Arab, the Empire, the Jew."*

Source: Elihu Grant, *Palestine Today* (Baltimore: J. H. Furst Co., 1938), pp. 1–13.

No, I did not visit Palestine this year except for those few hours at Haifa necessary in order to take ship for home. Thus I made my quiet protest by keeping away from what to me has been very dear these many years. What do I protest? The meddling by outsiders with the peace of Palestine.

A great empire is paying a part of its war debt by forcing masses of poor immigrant refugees from Europe into a little helpless province. These refugees, the countries of Europe and America will not receive within their own borders. At Evian les Bains the powers paid lip-service to the expatriate sufferers but would they touch with a little finger the sufferers' need of refuge? No, they would not. But partly relying on certain ancient references in the Hebrew bible—God forgive the nonsense—and under terrible pressure of the most brazen of modern propaganda these nations through their delegates at Evian looked over the wide world and saw no place so convenient as a haven for the needy, as little Palestine, a land of farmers these thousands of years, citizens who are not consulted in any manner. May manners mend!

And what have we in this much wanted, much meddled-with Palestine? Holy Land to three great religions: Arab land for more than a thousand years. A country of farmers, gardeners, orchardists, and vine dressers: Not the least skillful either. More nearly European in their standard than most countries of farmers which have so recently been under oppressive alien regimes. Some farmers in this world have the fate to live on their patrimony even though it be near dangerous volcanoes or in earthquake zones. Palestine farmers must cultivate their gardens in the very focal centre of the world's desire for they live in holy land. It is certainly holy to them as the ground of their ancestors for many centuries, for they are Arab in the sense that they speak the Arabic language, and owe much to Arabian civilization, but actually they go back to ancestry very much more remote than the Arab in Palestine. Their most distinctive relation is with the Canaanites who were there long before Hebrews, Philistines, or Arabs.

When the Arab conquests threatened to sweep the world these farmers who were then Christians under the decadent Byzantine empire were subdued not only by armies but by a great missionary force. In time most of them were converted to Islam the faith of the Arab, Muhammad, but scores of thousands of them clung to their Christian profession and of those unconverted there are to this day a hundred thousand native Christians whom the world forgets. Surely it ought to appeal to Christian peoples that so sturdy and persisting a Christian population of farmers today should have more consideration in any plans for Palestine's future. True, these are out-numbered by their racial brethren who gave allegiance to Islam. All of these forming one of the most creditable farmer folk in the world should be consulted in any plans affecting their country.

But they are not consulted, their representations and pleas are flouted. Not only are they heavily taxed but they are oppressed with an immigration designed to help solve European problems, an experiment by the European powers enforced by the harshest measures. When the Palestine native quotes the revolt of the American Colonies in 1776 against taxation without representation he might well add this atrocity which we did not have to endure in those days, viz: that an alien population of immigrants from Europe which has increased from 80,000 to over 400,000 in twenty years and which loudly declares its intention to keep coming until the new ones reach a dominant majority which will take over the political control of the country of Palestine. When this threat, this boast, this determined planning continues in spite of every legal, every civilized protest by the native people of Palestine do you wonder that the situation spells WAR? Do you wonder that the deeply informed who wish for the well-being of all the parties to the dispute, see the failure of the whole mischievous "experiment" which will one day be labelled the crime it clearly is? And this experiment but little over twenty years old is already being spoken of as if it were on a parity with the thousand years of the native title to the country. If the western world cannot see the facts in their relations and tendency, then the Eastern world will. Perhaps its nearer blood relationship and certainly its religious sympathies will make the whole near East warm to the wrong that is being attempted. Do not all clearly see that whether it be one year, or ten, or a hundred, that the "experiment" is doomed? Along with the "experiment" will go much ruined prestige, faith and friendship. The "experiment" will fail but by the time that fact is clearly seen Palestine may be ruined. One of the loveliest and most loved of the old world gardens of naïve simplicity will have been seared with the ruthless iron of European "improvement." The flesh of Palestine will have been torn from the bones of its hills. The process is going on now. Still there are districts even now that have not felt the full blight of this meddlesome European experiment but even in those valleys lie the corpses of the resisters strafed from the air by British planes in mopping up the fleeing guerrilla warriors who bear two sets of names. To their kindred they are called brothers, husbands, sons, patriots, to the press of the world they are called terrorists, assassins, bandits!

Read such a book as Kenneth Roberts's *A Rabble in Arms* describing our experiences with the ancestors of the English who are perpetrating this scandal in Palestine. And, where are those English who are comparable with our friends who raised their voices for us in Parliament and elsewhere in England in the days of George III? Read for answer the article by Major E. T. Richmond in February, 1938 in *The Nineteenth Century and After,* pp. 186-192.

Besides the country people in Palestine there are the city folk, very mingled to be sure, but mainly dependent on the country stock for replenishing, of one blood, race, and language with the peasantry except for the peculiarity of the cities that there as nowhere else there is a strain from the days of the Conquerors of 632 A. D. For the conquest of Palestine by the Arabs antedates the Norman Conquest of England by hundreds of years. As for Jews in Palestine; there were very few when the Anglo-Saxons were coming to the British Isles; very few indeed since the conquests of Constantine the Great, or even since 135 A. D. when Hadrian, the Roman, changed the face of Jerusalem and its very name. If some European power or mandate sought to come to America to re-establish the Iroquois Indians in New York State we might have a more logical comparison though that would be a kind of bullying less likely to take place.

And who are the native people of Palestine? Way, way in the lead of

numbers, a devoted, patriotic Palestinian population, city or country, and
that is racially somewhat like the Syrian, a semitic peasantry, not nomads,
not wanderers, not tent dwellers, not wild men: Whoever put over that
nonsense on this believing world? A people who might most accurately be
called Canaanites, descendants of the thousands of years of settled stock
living on the land, many thousands in their stone houses and in spite of
wars and rumors of wars clinging, clinging to their beloved hills and
valleys, their garden plots, grape vineyards, olive orchards, flocks of sheep,
goats, their wheat and barley acres, their homes and wives and children
with a truly simple acceptance of a hard lot.

Across their little land, like a scourge of the dreaded locusts swept
European armies settling the dispute of continental Europe. Bled, blasted,
terrorized, victimized, these simple country folk saw every resource of
their impoverished country, moral and physical, sapped by the rapacity of
the politicians of the Central Powers and the Allies. Themselves, they
were technically the property of the Central Powers but threw their
sympathy and their puny but essential strength to the side of the Allies.
The victories of those Allies they hailed as from heaven—they even saw a
similarity between the name of the leading general of the Allied forces,
Allenby, with their word for a delivering prophet* AnNeby and, truth be
told, that man and his associates appreciated the humble folk in whose
territory they victoriously stalked.

But came the greedy politicians, the sappers and miners of European
quarrel, also those who sell into slavery, the book-keepers and the
financiers, and they passed sentence on the near-corpse of Palestine—
prostrate to its friends as it had not been even to its previous foes. "Came,"
I say, the politicians and with black magic of phrases, state papers and
judicious forgettings—"Came" and decided:

First: To call the people "Arabs," a name now fervently accepted by the
natives to point their struggle and their solidarity with Asia, since Europe
has so mistreated them.

Second: To declare the land empty though it has always had its fair quota
of people.

Third: To call it practically forfeit in the one-sided interpretation of
even so generous a document as the Balfour Declaration.

Fourth: To let it out to European "improvements" (God save the mark!)

Fifth: To allow it to become lawful (European law!) prey to heavily

---

*Spelled Al-neby, pronounced An-neby.

subsidized refugees from Europe whom Europeans would not receive within their own bounds.

Sixth: To call any opposition to themselves seditious, terroristic, the work of *effendiyeh*, white collar, absentees, etc. etc. though the much belabored *effendiyeh* could not possibly head off or stop the despairing defense of homeland by the peasants.

And these people of Palestine are defending their dearest right on earth. They have for years sought to do so by delegation, representation, pleading. Heavily taxed, unrepresented, with no wealth, no press-service, or publicity, they are at the mercy of the whim of those who want their land, who follow a policy destructive of their peace and prosperity, who bribe their poverty in land-purchase and take that land off from a free market, who intern, deport, exile every effective protester of the horrible "experiment."

The truth of the case of the Palestinian farmer, village dweller and citizen is only just now emerging in spite of powerful influences interested in keeping it back or misrepresenting it. So greatly do certain outsiders covet Palestine that they even think they clearly see the facts other than they are or have been these hundreds and thousands of years and even at the present moment. No where on earth is black more often called white than nowadays in and about Palestine.

Law, logic, right, every decent convention—history itself, gives the land to its own people. Let others be courteous guests, pilgrims, worshippers but let no queer canons of behavior make us think we can outrage the amenities over there.

How was it for the century before the Great World War? Let us go back to those years in order to see the normal conditions before the frenzy. How were travel, pilgrimage, business, ideals met then by the native population? Palestine's people would handle all those problems now much better with a decent measure of independence than they did before the war in their dependence. And we should have peace with honor, visit the shrines and have one place uncontaminated by western quarrels and chicanery. Christian, Moslem, and Jew would each fare better than in the proposed mess to which the Mandate has been heading.

Some one is sure to ask "What of the religions in Palestine" and almost as sure to forget a moment after being told. 100,000 native Christians in villages and cities, farmers, merchants, many of them highly cultivated. Will the world remember that? The native Christian of Palestine, descendant of original Christians of Jesus' own day in Jesus' own land and the country where He was put to death for truth, this native Christian of Palestine is the most often forgotten man in all the modern world. Many, most of his brethren, same blood and race and appearance, changed to the Muhammadan religion over 1300 years ago and still live there. Jews, you ask? Yes there were about 75,000 of them in the country before the World War and nowhere in the world were they more safe or decently treated. But at that time they followed their religion and had not reached out the hand for sovereign worldly power. And I firmly believe that the highest grade Jews today, the world around, believe that the status was better before the World War than since. I have many Jewish acquaintances of that persuasion.

Wouldn't it be better for the true Jew to go as a devout pilgrim to the shrines of his faith, to migrate to the land itself as a citizen if and when he wished, and be saved the awful incubus of materialism, the machine-made political Zionism, the brassy propaganda, the loud, stentorian demand for exclusive rights? Why should he ignore the title of devout Christians, devout Moslems, the comparative calm under the previous governmental and social set-up of hundreds of years which saw no such horrors as those now being enacted largely because he is there and the manner in which he has come there? He may have his University, his medical and humanitarian service, his decent business, his youth movement, his idealism, his religion, his soul which he is fast selling for Esau's mess of political pottage.

27. A Christian Call to Open the Holy Land
to Jewish Refugees

The desirability of opening Palestine to the growing hosts of Jewish refugees from Nazism during World War II enlisted the support of a number of influential Christian leaders of varying backgrounds. One expression was the organization in 1942 of the Christian Council on Palestine, of which Henry A. Atkinson (1877–1960) was a founder and chairman. A Congregational minister, he was general secretary of the Church Peace Union. Active in the council were such persons as archaeologist William F. Albright, Methodist Bishop Francis J. McConnell, editor Daniel A. Poling, theologians Reinhold Niebuhr and Paul Tillich, liberal minister John Haynes Holmes, and Congregational activist Carl Hermann Voss, who served as executive secretary. The council was committed to "the establishment of a Jewish commonwealth in Palestine in relation to an over-all settlement in the post-war era." The rationale for this position was succinctly stated in an article by the chairman in 1943.

Source: Henry A. Atkinson, "'The Jewish Problem' Is a Christian Problem," *Christianity and Crisis* 3 (June 28, 1943):3–4.

Christian ministers and laymen are painfully aware of the plight of the Jews and have decided to do something about it.

Not satisfied with pious resolutions of condolence, they realize that "being sorry" is not enough and a Day of Compassion does not suffice. Confessions of guilt and professions of contrition can be empty gestures; unless, and until, they are followed by concrete action.

The Christian conscience cannot rest content in expressions of goodwill and pious intentions but must be translated into a definite program of action. It is the conviction, therefore, of an increasing number of Christian leaders, that, in the present crisis, Palestine should be made accessible to Jewish refugees from lands of persecution. To this end we have formed the "Christian Council on Palestine" to which more than seven hundred ministers and laymen now belong.

As Dr. James G. McDonald, formerly League of Nations High Commissioner for Refugees, has pointed out, the time for discussion is past. The Jews of Europe, he notes, "live in an abyss of misery—human, economic and social—which only prompt international effort on the largest and most generously conceived scale would even partially alleviate."

The failure of the Bermuda Conference to develop a constructive program to help these millions of helpless Jews is a shocking scandal no less shameful than the ineptness and spiritual bankruptcy of the Evian Conference. The ghost of political expediency and appeasement hovered about Bermuda, and, while diplomats delayed, thousands more of hapless Jews were killed each day in Eastern and Central Europe! Torture and persecution and ultimate extermination are the result for this unhappy people.

If anyone doubts the truth of these tales of horror and incredibly savage slaughter, then let him turn to the scholarly study of "The Mass Murder of Jews in Europe" published in April by the *Information Service* of the Federal Council of Churches of Christ in America. Since war began in 1939, two to three million Jews have been relentlessly hounded to death. The remaining four to five million in Europe today are doomed as the victims of an avowed policy of extermination. These mass killings are not the "atrocity stories" of the hysterical propagandist. They are grim facts as horrible as they are true.

A minimal standard of justice would demand a place in this world where these gifted, but hunted people, may enjoy the privilege of living a normal, free, self-respecting life of its own.

We anticipate, of course, the triumph of United Nations' armies and of political democracy in Europe, as well as the ultimate establishment there of a social structure in consonance with a basic Christian ethic so that it will be possible for Jews, as well as for all others, to live in dignity and freedom. Nevertheless, we must be realistic enough to know that great difficulties stand in the way of rehabilitating Jews in Central and Western Europe. Anti-Semitism has been too long endemic in this part of the world to be routed out so quickly. The poison of Hitlerism will not be quickly purged from the body politic. Unfortunately, the noxious doctrines of the "Master Race" have done their work too well.

The usual answer which well-meaning people give to this question is: "Solve the minorities problem—and you solve the problem of the Jews." Quite true. But just when do we solve it? What of the meantime? Shall we condemn hundreds of thousands—eventually millions—to the murderous hands of Hitler's henchmen?

"Grant equal rights to everyone at the conclusion of the war" is another glib retort. That was done at the end of the first World War and of what avail? It did little for the Jews in such countries as Roumania and Poland. Unless much more is done, and at once, there will be little improvement in granting equal rights and achieving them when the war ends. The hunger and poverty, devastation and stress of present day Europe will contribute little to the eradication of anti-Semitism.

The democracies are able to handle this problem adequately in the future, but a thin trickle of immigrants to North and South America now is not the answer. Ideally, we wish that our own nation, Canada, Mexico and every European country would permit the settlement of Jews and grant them a chance to live in freedom from fear and want. Realistically, however, we know that this will not be done. Our immediate concern is what to do *in the meantime*, especially in the face of the Nazis' sworn policy to make the fate of the Jews nothing less than complete extermination.

Palestine—A Haven of Refuge

Suggestions that the Jewish refugees be sent to Madagascar, Guiana, Africa, the West Indies, and South America are well taken; but there is the great barrier of distance, climate, and political opposition. Palestine is the only feasible solution to offer an immediate haven of refuge in this desperate emergency. The only alternative is death.

Since no other country will throw open its doors, we must look to Palestine, and we believe this little country can be the haven of refuge for the millions of homeless Jews in Axis-occupied countries. It would not only be feasible to house them there but profitable as well. Britain is wrong in assuming that Palestine is simply her colonial problem. It is a world issue, and can be settled only by joint action of the United Nations.

The physical possibilities of Palestine are great, as pointed out by Dr. Walter Lowdermilk, Assistant Chief of Soil Reclamation for the United States Department of Agriculture, and former agricultural advisor to Generalissimo Chiang-Kai-Shek. Palestine can absorb four million Jews and, by programs of reclamation and irrigation, the inhabitants may thrive successfully upon the land.

We ask that the bars of immigration be lowered and that the homeless Jews of Europe be given a place of refuge. This is the greatest need of our tragic era. Palestine, as a homeland for the Jew, is our answer to a "Christian problem," for only in so-called Christian countries does anti-Semitism exist and create this tragic situation.

The Jews have an ancient moral claim to Palestine and have never relinquished it in all their history. This claim has been officially recognized and sanctioned by the Balfour Declaration, the Treaty of San Remo, and by statements of confirmation by various governments, including our own.

Rights of Arabs in Palestine

The rights of Arabs in Palestine must, of course, be fully recognized. Let that be completely and fully understood. The Arabs should be accorded every possible guarantee to participate freely in the political life of the land and should be granted full cultural and social autonomy. It is well to remember that the Arab has ample opportunity for self-determination in many lands, but that the Jewish people have no such hope except in Palestine.

Jewish immigration in Palestine, during the last quarter of a century, has granted unnumerable social, economic, cultural and hygienic benefits to the Arabs. The continuance of this immigration, especially through the influx of refugees from war-torn Europe, will not only increase the potential resources of the land but will benefit both Jew and Arab alike.

The willingness of Jewish leaders to meet the issue of the Jew and the Arab presents an opportunity for wise and sympathetic statesmanship. Competent authors have made it clear that Arabs and Jews can and do get along well, especially if legitimate points of friction are eased and fascist *agents provocateurs* are routed out. We believe in an international mandate for Palestine to administer the Commonwealth. We suggest that a capable and competent international Christian Commission be sent to Palestine to study and analyze the problems of Jew and Arab, and offer concrete solutions.

This is not a "Protestant Zionism." It is something far greater. It is an attempt to answer what is basically not a Jewish problem, but rather a Christian problem.

The Christian Council on Palestine is a specific project in the larger framework of our efforts to win the peace while we are winning the war, a part of the whole process of preserving and extending democracy. At the very least this is to fulfill the obligations laid upon us by the imperatives of our Christian faith.

28. Prevailing Opinion in the Missionary Movement

The attitude of many American Protestants to the Holy Land was strongly influenced by missionaries in the period covered by this book. As has often been noted, missionaries in the Middle East had developed educational and medical institutions whose primary clientele were among Arab populations, centering north and east of Palestine. Though not with unanimity, their sympathies were often on the Arab side in the tensions and conflicts which emerged. A summary statement of their views was written by Bayard Dodge (1888–1972) and published in Christianity and Crisis early in 1948, shortly before the proclamation of Israel's independence. Dodge, a graduate of Princeton University and Union Theological Seminary, was then completing a quarter century as president of the American University in Beirut. In a note following the article and reprinted with it, the editor, Reinhold Niebuhr, observes that Dodge's position accurately reflected the prevailing opinions in the missionary movement, but briefly criticizes such opinions.

Source: Bayard Dodge, "Peace or War in Palestine," *Christianity and Crisis* 8 (March 15, 1948):27–30.

Almost everybody in America is anxious to help the Jews, who have suffered so much during the past decade. We also desire peace. It is, therefore a great shock to follow the events in Palestine. It is becoming increasingly clear that, in order to introduce any large number of immigrants into the Holy Land, it will require a struggle, which may easily be on the scale of our own Civil War.

Not only well meaning Christian leaders, but even the highest executives in Washington, were so convinced that the Arabs would not raise serious objections to Partition, that they did not take seriously the warnings of missionaries, as well as of the experts of the Department of State and the Army Intelligence. Now everybody realizes that the Arabs really do object to the idea of Partition, as it has been recommended by the Assembly of the United Nations.

This objection on the part of the Arabs is likely to lead to a number of results, which Americans as a whole have not been able to foresee.

The attempt to aid the displaced persons in Europe, by sending them to Palestine, will place the Jews in the outlying districts of Palestine itself, as well as the quarter million Jews in the states of the Arab League, in great peril. By trying to help the Jews in Europe, we are likely to subject the Jews in the Near East to persecution and massacre.

The Jews in the Arab lands are aware of this danger. A recent letter from Beirut says that the Jewish merchants there are subscribing 200,000 Lebanese pounds to the Arab National Fund. A friend in the American

Consulate General in Jerusalem has told me that the Jews have been coming in large numbers for over a year to ask for visas, to enter the United States. The papers recently published that the representatives of the 125,000 Jews in Iraq informed the Arabs that they would be on their side. The Jewish members of both houses of the Egyptian Parliament announced that they would side with the Arabs, and the Grand Rabbi of the colony of 100,000 Jews in Egypt, went to the Palace, to assure the King that the Egyptian Jews would side with their fellow countrymen in Egypt, most of whom are Arabs.

If American Christians insist upon sending large numbers of Jewish immigrants to Palestine, it will wreck much of the work, which missionaries have carried on for a century, among Oriental Christians and Moslems of the Southern Near East.

At the same time that Christians are trying to overcome prejudice in America by upholding Partition, the American Council for Judaism, the President of the Hebrew University at Jerusalem, and numerous rabbis, are opposing the Zionist policy in Palestine. Many fear that it may produce the same sort of Anti-Semitism in America, which it has already caused in England. Perhaps the Jewish moderates are unduly cautious, but they feel that if explosives are shipped from American ports, if the blood of American boys is shed, if American stockholders incur losses, if Russia gains a foothold in the Middle East, and if the Hebrew people place their allegiance to an independent Jewish state ahead of their loyalty to the United States, it will increase Anti-Semitism in America.

The Secretary of Defense has told a Congressional Committee that the reconstruction and defense of Western Europe will depend largely upon making more of the Middle Eastern oil available on the Mediterranean coast. This means building new pipe lines and refineries. The construction of the largest of these pipe lines, which was due to begin in February, has been indefinitely postponed.

People in America supposed that it was an expression of moral idealism, for the United Nations to give the Jews a state of their own. It has, therefore, been upsetting to find that twenty members of the United Nations Assembly so seriously questioned the legality of Partition, that they wished to have the matter studied by the International Court of Justice, before taking final action. Only twenty-one members defeated this project, as many of the members did not feel sure enough about the question to vote.

When Russia and America voted in unison for Partition, there was a general feeling of satisfaction. Now the reasons for Russia's action are being explained by the experts. Russia desires anarchy, so as to tie up the petroleum industry and create an atmosphere favorable for Communist propaganda. Russia has already shown her desire to send immigrants to Palestine from the Black Sea ports and many suspect her motives. Russia is glad to have a precedent which will make it reasonable to split off the Armenian and Kurdish minorities from Turkey, Iran and Iraq, so as to establish them as autonomous soviets. Russia will be relieved to see the American prestige in the Southern Near East collapse and to feel that there may be a chance to send Communist units to Palestine, as part of an International Police Force.

If Russia, or some of her satellite states, do contribute troops to the International Police Force, and if this force is sent to Palestine, the much desired Jewish independence may not be any more satisfactory than the actual freedom of Korea and Austria.

Many believed that, even if the Arabs should make some objections, the Partition would remain a local Palestinian affair, which could be settled in a few months. Now they realize that it may continue indefinitely to be an international issue of major importance, involving the 38,000,000 people of seven Arab states, backed by Iran, Pakistan, and perhaps a number of the other great Asiatic countries.

I think that the reason why people have been so disillusioned by these unexpected events, is because they have not kept abreast of the rapid changes, which have taken place in the Middle East. They have supposed that the Arabs were ignorant nomads and peasants, too primitive to deserve political consideration.

In the states of the Arab League as a whole there are a large number of nomads and peasants, just as there are many Negro sharecroppers, "Poor Whites" and Indians in the United States. But there is also an increasingly important minority of wealthy, cultured people, who live in fine new residential districts, go about in the latest models of American cars, send their sons abroad for study, construct beautiful institutions, and develop modern forms of trade and professional life.

The Arab States have now become independent, with their own legations and representatives at the United Nations. Five of them have their own airplanes. Their combined armies number about 150,000, with considerable mechanization. The northern states have rapidly expanding school systems, good roads, new hospitals, radio stations, experimental farms, and other forms of progress.

Many people have thought that the quickest way to make the Arabs advance would be to bring in large numbers of Jews who could teach them modern methods. In theory the Jews ought to be able to bring great benefits to Palestine and its neighboring states.

The Jews have the most up-to-date hospital, the finest orchestra, the best agricultural laboratories, and the most modern factories in the Near East. Their beautiful farm colonies would do credit to California. Their chemical industries and citrus groves are models for all to admire.

But unfortunately the Arabs are too much afraid of Jewish expansion to be willing to learn from them. It is not boasting, but a statement of fact to say that Arab progress depends much more upon American industry and philanthropy, than it does on Jewish example.

American petroleum investments of over a billion dollars, added to those of the British and French, will provide the funds for most of the Arab states to carry out large scale irrigation projects, as well as to develop agriculture, health and education.

The Rockefeller Foundation and Near East Foundation can teach methods of developing peasant life, from the point of view of public health, and also of modern farming, home economics, child care, recreation, and rural education.

Our Protestant and Catholic missions and our non-sectarian colleges are developing leaders with the spiritual strength to demand integrity, toleration, and public service. Large numbers of them are in places of great influence in the different government departments, as well as in business and the professions.

The whole Arab world stands at a parting of the ways. On one side a very important minority of educated men and women is striving to follow the path of stability, toleration and progress. At the same time a majority of reactionary people is in danger of going the way of exploitation, violence and fanaticism.

If our American industry and philanthropy can carry on without interruption, I believe that the educated group will win and that the standards of living will be raised so much, that there will be little danger of reaction or social revolution. On the other hand, if the Arabs cut themselves off from the help, which we Americans are able to give them, I fear that there will be a return to low standards, with great danger of Communist penetration. Even though many of the educated chiefs may desire moderation, feeling is running so high, that I believe the Arabs will cripple or even close down our American activities, in case we back up the sending of large numbers of European immigrants to Palestine.

The petroleum companies expect to build five new pipe lines, as well as harbors and refineries. The Trans-Arabian Pipe Line alone will keep 15,000 laborers busy for a number of years, and the new refinery at Sidon will employ between five and ten thousand men permanently. Recent word from Lebanon says that, because pipe line construction has been interrupted, there is growing unemployment, poverty, and opportunity for Communist propaganda.

Let us now turn to the plan for Partition, which is causing so much excitement and giving so much concern to all who desire to see peace and progress in the Middle East.

The Arabs and Jews are to have separate governments, free to conduct foreign affairs, defense, education, land registry, immigration, and other activities, as though they were entirely independent states.

But there is to be an Economic Union, which is to administer many of the affairs of the two groups with close team work. Transportation, car licenses, railroads, telephones and telegraphs, pipe lines, mails, customs, currency, electric power, irrigation, control of diseases—human, animal and plant—supervision of narcotics, prostitution and crime, and last but not least care of pilgrims and tourists, must be managed with the closest kind of cooperation.

This Economic Union is needed, because the Holy Land is not to be divided into two well defined sections. It is rather to be broken up into a checkerboard pattern of zones:—three Jewish, three Arab, and one International, with Jaffa added as an isolated Arab city. A member of each race has the right to decide in which state he wishes to register his citizenship. At the start there will be nearly half a million Arabs in the Jewish zones.

The Arabs have refused to accept this arrangement from the start. I think that they made a mistake when they refused to cooperate with the United Nations Commission, which was sent to Palestine before the Assembly considered the plan. If they had made some constructive proposals at the very start, it might have prevented trouble later on. But it is significant that the Arabs did propose a compromise at the last minute; too late to be given the attention that it deserved.

The proposal was important, because it showed what the Arabs are willing to agree to and what they absolutely refuse to accept. The compromise was that the complex of Partition and Economic Union, voted by the Assembly, should be developed in a logical way, so as to become a federal state, with a canton system, similar to the federation of the French and Germans in Switzerland.

The Zionists opposed this plan, as they realized that the federal government would fix the immigration quotas and prevent the crowding of European immigrants into Palestine. It is this question of immigration which is the crux of the whole dispute.

I have been assured by competent Arab leaders that they are willing to accept some sort of a federal state, provided it can be conducted according to the regularly established principles of democratic government, with respect for human rights. Although they will insist upon limiting immigration, they will respect the rights of the Jewish cantons, so that they can form the sort of spiritual and cultural "National Home" which the non-Zionist Jews have asked for.

The Arabs feel that the development of the evidently unworkable Partition Plan, with its Economic Union, into a federal state, probably under United Nations trusteeship, will not be a step backwards, but rather a step forwards, for the United Nations to take.

Arabs are panic stricken over the prospect of immigration, because they believe that the Zionists wish to bring in so many young men of military age, with so many war supplies, that it will only be a matter of time before the Jews try to seize all of Palestine and lands east of Jordan as well.

Whether it is reasonable for the Arabs to feel this way is not the point. The trouble is they do feel this way, because the Zionists have spoken so freely and repeatedly about their rights to all of Palestine and Trans-Jordan. Thus the Arabs are willing to compromise about almost everything except immigration, while the Zionists stress large scale immigration as the important issue of their program.

On the other hand, the American Council for Judaism, the Jews living in Arab lands, and many independent persons feel that it would be better to have some sort of compromise, rather than to run the risk of bloodshed and of Anti-Semitic reaction.

Thus the American people are confronted by this question: Shall they encourage the United Nations Security Council to send troops to Palestine, so as to force the Arabs to accept unlimited immigration into a state the size of Vermont, although many of the Jews themselves oppose the plan, and although it is evident that the use of armed forces will result in war?

Would it be better for the Americans to use their influence in the

Security Council, to prevent the sending of troops to Palestine? If that alternative is chosen, the Council will probably order a "Cease fire" and try to persuade the moderates on both sides to settle the dispute by arbitration and compromise. If the two parties cannot agree, their fighting will be confined to Palestine, as a local matter, instead of being allowed to become a war of international proportions.

I do not pretend to be wise enough to serve as an oracle for Near Eastern affairs. But for what it is worth, my judgment is that if America encourages the Security Council to implement the Partition plan in its present form by force of arms, it will produce results of far reaching importance. Let me give three examples of the sort of things that I fear.

The United Nations will be unable to retain the Asiatic countries as loyal members. The friendship which exists between the Christians of the West and the quarter billion Moslems of the world will be partly or entirely destroyed. In the course of the next quarter century, the U.S.S.R. will become the dominant power in the Near East.

I should think that it would be better for the Arabs to show as much friendship as possible for the Jews, rather than to become involved in a war which may last for years. I should think that it would be better for the Jews to make sure of "The establishment in Palestine of a national home," to serve as a cultural and spiritual base for World Jewry, rather than to gamble on a war, in hopes of multiplying their population and setting up a sovereign state.

I should think that it would be better for America to solve the problem of displaced persons, by giving them refuge in the United States, rather than to try to force the refugees into Palestine, in a way that may render progress and stability in the Middle East impossible.

I should think that it would be better for the Security Council to base its prestige on its appeals to make peace by arbitration, rather than upon its power to implement by force of arms an issue which twenty of the members of the United Nations have challenged as illegal. A permanent solution can only be found, as during a number of years enough friendship and confidence can be produced, to quiet the Arab fears of Jewish expansion.

I am sure that it is the duty of Christian people to try to produce peace and progress in the Near East, by sending technical experts, doctors, missionaries and teachers, instead of by sending troops. Let us do honor to Mr. Gandhi, by learning a lesson from him. Let us not meet hate with more hate and force with more force.

Let us consistently entreat the extremists on both sides to refrain from violence. Let us encourage the moderates to find some middle ground. The Seers of old prophesied a return to Mt. Zion. But let us leave it to the Divine Providence to carry out his purposes, without human interference and bloodshed. For one greater than the Prophets has said: "Blessed are the peacemakers, for they shall be called the sons of God."

Editor's Note: President Dodge, who has spent a lifetime in the Middle East as President of Beirut University, was asked by the editorial board to give his impressions and convictions of the Palestinian situation. His position accurately reflects the prevailing opinion in the missionary movement of the Middle East.

The complexity of the issues in Palestine is attested by the fact that so many men of good will take completely contradictory views of the situation. President Dodge rightly points out that the Arab and the Jewish state, which would emerge from partition, could not become economically viable if the highest measure of economic cooperation were not achieved, an end which will not be easily attained within the present framework of animosity. On the other hand it must be pointed out that the bi-national state was found unacceptable by the United Nations, primarily because the Arabs were unwilling to grant the Jews any freedom in immigration in such a binational state.

It must also be observed that the proposal to resubmit the question to the United Nations is frought with the gravest perils. Responsible observers, close to the situation, express the fear that such a policy may completely destroy the United Nations because there is little prospect that an agreement could be reached on any alternative proposal, thus making confusion worse confounded.

29. The World Significance of a Jewish State

It has already been observed how certain Protestants of quite different theological positions had come to favor Zionism—from literalists who were informed by their prophetic interpretation of the Bible to liberals who cited historical, cultural, religious, and humanitarian reasons for their stance. Among the latter was Adolf A. Berle (1865–1960), a Congregational pastor and author who had served for three years as professor of applied Christianity at Tufts College. Though he had long been interested in Zionism, the Balfour Declaration stimulated his enthusiasm, and in a small book he discussed the political, sentimental, and religious significance for the world of a reborn Jewish state in the Holy Land. The informative foreword and section II of his essay are reproduced here. Looked at from the perspective of those who welcomed the emergence of the State of Israel in 1948, his work of 1918, though overly optimistic and somewhat utopian, seemed farsighted indeed.

Source: Adolf A. Berle, *The World Significance of a Jewish State* (New York: Mitchell Kennerley, 1918; reprinted in the Arno Press anthology, *Christian Protagonists for Jewish Restoration*, 1977), pp. 7–8, 31–41.

Foreword

It is many years since the author of this little essay became interested in the subject of which it treats. The Zionist movement, as such, has interest chiefly for Jews. But the history of the Jews is a human possession, priceless because of its influence upon the moral and religious conceptions of men. This essay does not treat of the Zionist movement, as such, but considers the proposed Jewish state for its significance to the Christian world.

The Jew himself is a social factor of such importance to the world that his racial and national interests are world-interests *per se;* and whatever tends to unify the Jews, especially religiously, and centre their thought and action in a solidarity, religious and social, in a concrete form representative of the highest and finest aspirations of the race, is a sublime subject for speculation. And when there appears on the horizon a possibility that this speculative centre of Jewish interests may become a practical reality, we may well take note of it for the sake of the whole world. That is what this essay attempts to do.

The present writer can think of no greater contribution to the world's life than the religious rehabilitation and unification of the Jews. And because a Jewish state looks like the best instrument to this end, the subject becomes commanding. I look to the Christian world to supplement, with generous enthusiasm, this national aspiration of devoted Jews, that

Americans may join with Englishmen, some of whose leading statesmen are already committed to the plan, in bringing their influence to bear upon our own government, toward the fulfilment of so worthy an international end.

A. A. B.

Boston, February, 1918.

II

Nor can there be any doubt that the establishment of a Jewish state will have great sentimental results, though this designation hardly expresses what we have in mind. Palestine is a land dear to the heart of the whole world. The events which have taken place there are of interest historically, socially, and linguistically, to the world of scholarship whether of history, romance, or literature. One needs to pause but a moment and remember simply the list of battles fought on the Plains of Esdraelon, to recall that the Assyrian, Babylonian, Persian, Egyptian, Greek and Roman Empires have all played a part on this historic soil. One needs but to recall the Eastern Empire, the Crusades, the Saracen, and follow all the way down to Napoleon and even the present moment to feel the immense historic sweep which is gathered in this little fragment of the earth's surface. There is probably no equal area anywhere in which so much has been enacted, which has a place in the thought and literature of the world. No place probably, upon which so much and such varied scholarship has been expended, and in which further results would arouse world-wide interest and enthusiasm! Hitherto, and especially in the modern world, Turkish control has stopped this development, and held up a stream of natural evolution, which once started to flowing again would have the greatest sentimental, scholastic, and ethical value to the world.

It is also entirely within the possibilities that, when the first economic struggles are over, and the first stages of organization and readjustment have been passed,—for the organization and making of such a state, with the diverse elements of which it necessarily will be composed at the outset, will itself be a work of great difficulty, and calling for the greatest possible skill in statecraft, social education, and leadership,—there will be a revival of the classical Hebrew language and literature since national development almost always follows the lines of language. The common denominator, linguistically, of the various kinds of Jewish elements which will be gathered, will be Hebrew, and a new blossoming of the Hebrew language will be a great thing for the world, not only for its own sake, and for the better interpretation of the Hebrew scriptures, but hardly less for the recovery of the lost elements of Semitic civilization. We are, as the case now stands, only on the brink of that vast lost world. But the revival of Hebrew culture and language, under the aegis of a Hebrew state, will unquestionably lead, not only to its wider and more sympathetic and skilful study, but contributions will unquestionably be made which cannot but be full of important results to scholarship everywhere. Here again Christian and Hebrew interests will coincide, and world interest will be spontaneous and enthusiastic. Moreover, such a revival will have in it elements, which will do more for the social unification of the world than almost any other single interest, except one still to be mentioned.

A Hebrew state must almost of necessity be governed by its ancient law. That law, only vaguely understood, and of only very limited application in world history, will have then a full exposition and a thorough working-out in terms of modern life. There have been many of us, who for many years have seen in the Hebrew laws the elements of the social regeneration of the world. Certainly many of the laws relating to the ordinary life and relations of mankind, as laid down in the ancient Mosaic law, if applied to a modern city block, would regenerate it, root and branch. It would have commanding interest to the entire world, to see a state, albeit a small one, work these problems through, and especially a state which could, and which would, call to its aid the finest body, collectively, of intellectual force and discrimination which the world knows. All this is but repeating what the Christian world has been saying about the culture of the Hebrews, as revealed in their own sacred writings for many centuries. A rationalized Hebrew state, founded on Hebrew fundamental laws, ethical, social, sanitary, dietary, and all the rest, would be a working laboratory of social regeneration which would excite breathless attention. And if, as may reasonably be expected, such a state should exhibit phenomena, in the conservation of human life, in the development of human genius and power, which we may also reasonably expect from the known history of the Jews, the effect upon civilization in general would be something sublime.

Here, again, we shall probably be confronted with the stale suggestion, that all this is mere conjecture and fanciful dreaming. But why should it be? We need only to sum up the achievements of the Jew, under the untoward conditions of his life, as an exotic in Christian civilization, persecuted for a thousand years, and not beyond the boundaries of anti-

Semitic hatred and pursuit even yet! Yet if his wonderful contributions to literature, to science, to philology, to music, to the arts, to diplomacy, be only casually tabulated, there is created a presumption, that even on the mere law of averages, there is a fund of genius among the Jews in the world, which has not been uncovered, which will enrich the social and spiritual life of the world immeasurably! And as stated already, one does not have to be a Jew, to feel all this! One does not have to be a Jew to realize and appreciate its value. One needs only to understand, and to give fair and just recognition to those who have written in these various branches of human endeavor such glorious pages in the world's story.

Take only the science of medicine. It takes no violent stretch of the imagination to see this modern Jewish state, the working model of the finest and highest physical development—far surpassing that of the Greeks in their prime, because that was based only upon selfish considerations while this will have to rest upon moral interests, which make the least of the brethren a member of the national family. Such a state would be a world teacher, par excellence, and one can imagine no finer or nobler hope, for the most gifted members of the race, than that they should cherish as a part of their life-work a contribution of some sort, personal or otherwise, to the realization of this great ideal. We have seen what superb results have been achieved socially by the great foreign missionary movement of the Christian church, starting as it did, with a mass of impossible narrow theological conceptions, and ending up as it is with an educational and social programme, which makes it one of the amazing accomplishments of humanity, much finer in temper and quality than the work of theological Christianity in the home lands.

But the Jews in a Palestinian state would not be missionaries to the world, but missionaries to each other; builders of an ancient national structure of ideas, laws, and precepts, which, made the basis of the national life, would create new moral types for the world's instruction and advancement. That it would result in the transformation of the Jewish life throughout the entire world, is almost certain, because the reaction from a state which was distinctly the working model of Jewish life and ideals upon the scattered elements of the nation throughout the world, would be both swift and decisive. This, again, would have an equally swift and decisive result in the nations wherein the Jews are in considerable numbers, which is to say, almost every population-centre in the world. We would thus see the entire scientific, artistic, and social aims of the Jewish race centred for exemplification in the new Jewish state, and the best of all there is in the world, instantly transferred and made available there. Here would be a state which, being at once a social unit, and a racial unit, and a religious unit, would be a field for laboratory work, such as has never before existed! All humanity would be perforce interested in the result, and whatever was thus achieved, would be made available for the enrichment of the world's life.

The Jew has shown himself so versatile in collaboration with the particular nation with which his lot has been thrown, that it is an interesting look forward to conjecture what his art will be, what his education will be, what his science will be, when it is transferred to a field where he has every part of it, filled with the sense of national coöperation and national glory. That the contribution will be something distinctive, and possibly something greater than the world has yet seen is not unreasonable. The arrested movement of Semitic civilization and culture may then proceed possibly to its full development, only it will be the more glorious for its deferred ripening, and will bring to it elements of cosmopolitanism which were not possible hitherto. What would we not give to have undisturbed the glories of Greece! But here we shall see one of the oldest races of history literally born again. The Gentile world cannot be indifferent to such a chance to see a work, which will bring glory to humanity and a possible release from bondages which have hitherto kept us in the eternal fear which even now drenches the world with blood, and fills the hearts of men with terror. The Greece of Pericles restored on the Acropolis does not begin to furnish the inspiration that is aroused by the thought of Jerusalem restored and glorious again, under the rule of her own sons and resounding once more with the songs of David, and the minstrels of the noblest religious poetry that ever filled the heart of man.

Intimately connected with this vision are certain facts which are peculiarly favorable for such a development as we have here described. The purpose to build up a Jewish state, on a model hitherto unknown, finds special impetus, in the consideration that it will have a fair, if not indeed a flying, start toward a "social commonwealth," quite unlike anything yet attempted. Palestine has, as yet, escaped that grasp of corporate and exploiting interest, which makes social development difficult and often impossible. There are no vast corporations, no immense "vested interests" to be placated or bought off; there is the virgin undeveloped territory, with railways yet to build, and connections yet to establish with neighboring states and lands, all of which form an unexampled opportunity for experiments *de novo* in state building. Concessions to intending builders could be made on the national plan, and automatically agreeing with the national interest and the public welfare. The industrial expansion, therefore, could be without those weary steps toward freedom which all other industrial civilizations have had to undergo. Almost from the beginning, land and industries, public resources, mineral and otherwise, could be nationally administered, and all this would make a most novel and striking page in statecraft. Once more, as a working model for vast lands as yet undeveloped, in Africa and Asia, the influence of such a state would be very great. Moreover, working thus in contrast to the land-grabbing policies of hitherto unrestrained imperialism, this would be a great service to the nations of the East, as yet unborn.

Epilog

The documents selected for this volume came from a wide range of materials. Those seeking to go further in studying relationships between the Holy Land and American Protestantism (and related topics) for the period 1800 to 1948 will find a valuable resource in the 1977 Arno Press collection of seventy-two volumes, "America and the Holy Land," and in several bibliographies which point to other materials.[1] Because the present documentary is primarily concerned with the public attitudes of various types of American Protestants toward the Holy Land, it has focused on published materials that for the most part were widely disseminated and were influential in molding public opinion. It has sought to provide a panoramic view. But to understand in greater depth matters mentioned here—and many others not included—it will be necessary to delve into the riches of archival and manuscript materials relevant to the theme in such places as the United States National Archives, the American Jewish Archives, the Zionist Archives, the Library of Congress, and libraries of the American Jewish Historical Society, Harvard University, Jewish Theological Seminary, Union Theological Seminary, and Yale University—to mention only a few.[2]

There are many reasons for probing deeper into this important literature. It casts much light on the long, often tragic history of the relations between Christians and Jews, and can bring students of various religious and national backgrounds into fruitful partnerships in scholarly quests for fuller and more informed understandings of pasts that influence present and future.[3] This volume has focused on Protestantism; important materials relating to American Roman Catholic and Eastern Orthodox attitudes toward the Holy Land need investigation, publication, and interpretation. The Holy Land, however, is precious to three faiths; the ways Americans have perceived and related to Islam have been influenced by its long presence in the land of the Bible—another topic that needs more scholarly attention. But not only those interested in religion can profit from involvement in this field of study: students of political and diplomatic history can reach deeper understandings of the roots of many historic and present difficulties through acquaintance with the materials of America-Holy Land interrelationships. Also, those drawn to the study of cultural history can find illumination in considering the long and continuing influence of the Bible, the imagery of Zion, and the varied concepts of the Holy Land in American life.[4]

The story reflected in this volume is important for an appreciation of the long fascination of American Christians with the Holy Land and of their concern, often intense, with the well-being of that small but important part of the globe. In focusing on the period 1800-1948, the present work has traced foundations of complex Protestant attitudes toward the land itself and toward the Zionist movement and the emergence of the State of Israel. Though it has not gone into the exciting story of the controversial decades since 1948, the more recent years cannot be fully understood apart from serious consideration of the century and a half that preceded them.

1. See David H. Finnie, *Pioneers East: The Early American Experience in the Middle East* (Cambridge: Harvard University Press, 1967), pp. 287-94; the bibliography compiled by Yohai Goell and Martha B. Katz-Hyman, "Americans in the Holy Land, 1850-1900: A Select Bibliography," in Moshe Davis, ed., *With Eyes Toward Zion: Scholars Colloquium on America-Holy Land Studies* (New York: Arno Press, 1977), pp. 100-125; and Nathan M. Kaganoff, *Guide to America-Holy Land Studies, vol. 1, American Presence* (New York: Arno Press, 1980).

2. Moshe Davis, ed., *Guide for America-Holy Land Studies: Section on American Individual and Institutional Presence, 1620-1948* (Jerusalem: Institute of Contemporary Jewry, 1973).

3. See my article, "Studies in the Interrelationships between America and the Holy Land: A Fruitful Field for Interdisciplinary and Interfaith Cooperation," *Journal of Church and State* 13 (1971): 283-301, reprinted in James E. Wood, Jr., ed., *Jewish-Christian Relations in Today's World* (Waco, TX: Markham Press Fund of Baylor University Press, 1971), pp. 105-23.

4. See the seminal article by Carlos Baker, "The Place of the Bible in American Fiction," in James Ward Smith and A. Leland Jamison, eds., *Religious Perspectives in American Culture* (Princeton, NJ: Princeton University Press, 1961), pp. 243-72.

Index

Abraham, 39–40, 50, 57, 68, 69, 70, 71, 76, 78, 113–14, 115, 116
Achad Ha-Am, 214, 215
Acra, 153
Acre, 11
Acre, Bay of, 41, 128
Adams, J. McKee, 98–103
Adamson, A.Q., 177
Ai, 59
Ain Anoub, 95
Ain Shems, 220
Akabah, 8, 13
'Akabah, Gulf of, 28–29
Albright, Dr. William F., 49–50, 52–60, 66, 226
    "The Discovery of Ancient Palestine," 55
Alford, Dean, 188
Allegheny Theological Seminary, 65
Allenby, General, 175, 223
Alt, Professor, 57
Amarna Tablets, 59
"America and the Holy Land," 245
American Board of Commissioners for Foreign Missions, 75, 87, 88, 169

American Council for Judaism, 231, 235
American Friends' Mission, 159
American Friends of the Arabs, 220
American Friends School (Ramallah), 220
American Fundamentalism and Israel: The Relation of Fundamentalist Churches to Zionism and the State of Israel, 198
American Palestine Exploration Society, 147
American Protestant residents:
    the American Colony, 164–72
    "The War of the Graveyard," 167, 168–71
    Merrill, archaeologist and consul, 147–53
    Wallace, consul and interpreter of Holy City, 154–63
    Y.M.C.A. in Jerusalem, 173–78
American School of Oriental Research in Bagdad, 48, 54
American School of Oriental Research in Jerusalem, 48–51, 52, 53, 54, 65, 66, 68, 96
    teaching scholars, 49, 65

American Society of Church
History, 112
Ancient Jerusalem, 147–53
Andover Theological Seminary, 8,
37, 75, 147
Anti-Lebanon, 16, 43
Antioch, 12
Anti-Semitism, 139–41, 142,
189–91, 203, 206, 227, 228,
240–41
fear of, in America, 231
Appleton's Magazine, "Our
American Colony at
Jerusalem," 164–72
Arab League, 230, 232
Arab National Fund, 230
Arabs:
anti-Semitism of, 140–41,
208–209
claim to Palestine by, 139,
220–224
definitions of, 58
inability to compete with Jews,
208–209
inertia of, 211
material and cultural progress
of, 232
opposition to Palestine
Partition, 230, 232, 233–34,
235
Arba' în, el-, 27, 28, 29
*Archaeology of Palestine and the Bible,
The*, 52–60
Arimathaea, 143
Armenian Monastery of St. James,
91–93
monks studying at, 92–93
Armenian Theological School, 90,
93

Armstrong, 18
Arnon River, 44, 69
Ascalon, 11
Ashdod, 11
Atkinson, Henry A., 226–29
Auburn, Frederick, 178
Authority, making of an, 147–53
Merrill's position, 150–53

Baalbec, 5, 11
Bab-ed-Dra'a, 67, 68
Balfour Declaration, 139, 203,
209, 223, 228, 238
Banias, 11
Barclay, Dr. James T., 83–89
Beersheba, 8, 11, 18, 41, 43, 59,
112, 114, 131
Beit Jibrîn, 12
Berkeley Divinity School, 96
Berle, Adolf A., 238–43
Bermuda Conference, 226
Bethany, 45, 95, 109, 117
Bethel (Beitin), 40, 59, 117, 131
Bethhoron, 117
Bethlehem, 42, 43, 94, 117, 120,
131, 132, 158, 161, 177
Bethsaida, 134, 135, 136
Beth-shan, 60
Bethshemesh (Beckshemesh), 54,
143
Beto Gabra, 12
Beyrout (Beirut), 10, 11, 120
Bible:
clarification of, through
archaeological research,
55–60
geographical accuracy of, 38–40
as guide-book for travel,
108–11, 116

verification of Sodom
   holocaust, 67–71
Biblical Repository, 8
Biblical Researches in Palestine, Mount
   Sinai and Arabia
   Petraea . . . by E. Robinson
   and E. Smith . . ., 6, 7, 9n,
   9–11, 12–23, 25–36
Blackstone, William E., 181,
   187–93, 194–97
   Memorial to President
   Harrison, 194–97
Blaine, James G., 195
Bliss, Frederick Jones, 3
Böhl, Professor, 57
Bottoms, Mr. and Mrs. George
   W., 100
Boudinot, Elias, 181–87
Breasted, Prof. J.H., 53–54
Bridgeman, Rev. Charles T., 90,
   95, 96
Bronze Age civilization, 58–60, 68
Bulletin of the American Schools of
   Oriental Research, "The
   'New York Times'
   Correspondent Describes
   the School in Jerusalem,"
   48–51
Bunce, James, 177
Burckhardt, 6, 9, 13, 27, 29n, 35
Burnet, D.S., 83

Caesarea, 11
Caesarea Philippi, 118
Camels, 127
Campbell, Alexander, 83
Canaan, 118, 143
Canaan, Dr. T., 173
Canaan, Rev. B., 173

Canaanites, 221, 222–23
Capernaum, 16, 43, 134–35, 136
Carmel, 11, 17
Carmel, Mt., 100, 102, 159
Carroll, William, 66
Catherwood, 15
Chicago, University of, Oriental
   Institute, 54
Christian Churches (Disciples of
   Christ), 83
Christian Council on Palestine,
   226, 229
Christian Herald, 122
Christian Protagonists for Jewish
   Restoration, 194, 238
Christianity and Crisis:
   " 'The Jewish Problem' Is a
   Christian Problem,"
   226–29
   "Peace or War in Palestine,"
   230–37
Church Peace Union, 226
City of the Great King, The: or,
   Jerusalem as it was, as it is,
   and as it is to be, 83
City of the Moon, 50
Clay, Professor, 49
Clor, Elsie, 101
Conder, 15
Conference of Christians and
   Jews, 195, 196
Congregational Foreign Mission
   Board, 96
Constantine, Emperor, 19, 20–22,
   31, 152, 222
Cross, Mount of the, 28, 29

Damascus, 11, 16, 38, 114, 128,
   160, 196

Damascus Mission, 11

Dan, 41, 112

Daniel Deronda, 215

Darby, John Nelson, 181

David, 114, 118, 130
    Castle of, 153

Davison, George W., 177

Day, Prof. Albert, 66

Dead Sea, 6n, 39–40, 41, 42–43, 44,
    50, 93, 109, 117, 161, 208

Deburieh (Daberath), 38

*Dereliction and Restoration of the Jews,
    The: A Sermon Preached in
    Park-Street Church Boston,
    Sabbath, Oct. 31, 1819, just
    before the Departure of the
    Palestine Mission*, 75–82

*Development of Palestine Exploration,
    The: Being the Ely Lectures
    for 1903*, 3

Dhoheriyeh, 23

Dickinson, Consul General, 170

Dilb (Kiryat Anavim), 203–205

Dinsmore, Mr., 66

Dodge, Bayard, 230–37

Donnithorne, Stuart, 174

Dorcas, 125–26

Dothan, 59

Eder, Dr., 209

Eddleman, Rev. H. Leo, 101, 102

Eddy, Rev. William K., 170

Egypt, 116

Ekron, 43, 143

Eldridge, Fred I., 176

Eleutheropolis, 12, 17

Eliot, George, 215, 216

Elusa, 9

Engeddi, 109

Ephraim, 44, 126

Ephron the Hittite, 114, 115, 116

Esdraelon, plain of, 44, 58, 100,
    118, 119, 211, 239

Eshcol, Valley (brook) of, 113, 114

Euphrates valley, 196

Eusebius, 4, 19–22, 34

Evian Conference, 226

Exploration East of the Jordan, 147

*Explorations at Sodom: The Story of
    Ancient Sodom in the Light of
    Modern Research*, 65–71

Federal Council of Churches of
    Christ in America,
    Information Service, 227

Fellowship of Reconciliation, 213

Fenderson, Eunice, 101

Fisk, Pliny, 75

Fondè, Dr. and Mrs. George
    Heustis, 177

Ford, Alexander Hume, 164–72

Fosdick, Harry Emerson, 41–47,
    203–12

Francis, Bishop, 95

Frederick William, King, 87

"From Manger to Throne, + 123

Galilee, 10, 11, 15, 44, 176

Galilee, Sea of, 41, 42, 50, 107,
    109–11, 122, 134–37, 160
    fly-fishing in, 136

Galilee in the Time of Christ, 147

Gandhi, [Mohandas K.], 236

Garland, Bishop, 95

Garstang, Prof. John, 53

Gath, 43

Gaza, 11, 16, 113

General Theological Seminary, 90

Gennesaret, Lake of, 110, 111, 118

Gennesaret, Plain of, 119, 134
Geographical accuracy of Bible,
    38-40
George III, 222
Gerar, 59
Gerasa, 54
Gerizim, Mount, 117
German Reformed Church,
    seminary of, 112
Gethsemane, 107, 108, 110, 113,
    117, 129
Gezer, 68
Ghôr, southern, 60, 67
Gibeah, 59
Gibeon, 117
Gideon, Fountain of, 118
Gilboa, Mount, 118
Gilead, 161
Glunker, Herman, 177-78
Golgotha, 129
Gomorrah, 39, 50, 67, 70, 114
Gott der Väter, Der, 57
Grant, Elihu, 220-25

Hackett, Horatio B., 37-40
Hadrian, 222
Haifa, 95, 98, 100, 119, 138, 139,
    159, 160, 208
    Baptist missionaries in, 102-103
Hanauer, Rev. Canon J.E., 173
Hannah, Rev. and Mrs. L.V., 100
Harmon, Arthur Loomis, 177
Harrison, President Benjamin,
    194, 195
Harte, Dr. A.C., 173, 175-76, 177,
    178
    Scholarship Fund, 177
Harvard Divinity School, 213
Hasbêya, 11

Haupt, Paul, 49
Haurân, 12, 119, 160
*Heart of the Levant, Palestine-Syria,
    The: A Survey of Ancient
    Countries in the Interest of
    Modern Missions*, 98-103
Hebron, 23, 39-40, 59, 70, 71, 96,
    112, 113, 114, 131
    Great Mosque in, 115
    Machpelah, 115-16
Heinrichs, Waldo H., 178
Helena, 21, 22, 31, 34
Hermon, Little, 210-11
Hermon, Mount, 11, 16, 42, 43, 44,
    100, 118
Herzl, Dr. Theodore, 190, 192,
    201
Higgins, Dr. C.C., 172
Himmon (Hinnom), Valley of, 132
"Historical Geography of the
    Holy Land," 24
"History of the Jerusalem Young
    Men's Christian
    Association," 173-78
Hitchcock, Roswell D., 3, 6, 7n, 8,
    9, 14, 24
Hitler, [Adolf], 227
Holmes, John Haynes, 213-19, 226
Holy cities of Islam and Judaism,
    114
"Holy City," 88-89
Holy Land:
    agricultural resurgence
        feasible, 119, 158-59
    archaeological research in,
        52-60
    clarification of Bible
        through, 55-60, 67-71
    Christian proselytism in, 85-89

diversity of, 43–47
early information and historians
  of, 3–6
missionaries in, 75–82, 83–89,
  90–97, 98–103
native Christians, 93–95, 156–57
natural resources for
  exploitation, 161
need for further study of,
  245–46
physical improvements in, 160
pilgrimages in: black pastor,
  138–43
  church historian, 112–21
  evangelical layman, 107–11
  preacher, 122–30
  professor, 131–37
restoration to the Jews, 78–80,
  122, 128, 159–61, 163,
  181–93, 194–97, 220–25,
  226–29, 230–37, 238–43
Robinson's explorations, 8–23,
  25–36
small size of, 41–43, 112
Turkish backwardness and
  opposition, 119, 120,
  124–25, 155, 160
Holy Land Missions and Missionaries,
  75
Holy Orthodox Patriarchate of
  Jerusalem, 176
Holy Sepulchre, Church of the,
  18–22, 23, 107, 108, 109,
  129, 151
Hommel, 57
Hopper, Margaret, 176
Hor, Mt., 23
Horeb, 27, 28, 29

House-top:
  dwelling on the, 38
  praying on the, 37
Huleh, 17
Hums, 12
Hussani, Ismail El, 170
Idumea, 40
*Illustrations of Scripture: Suggested by
  a Tour through the Holy
  Land*, 37
Innocents Abroad, The, 107
Institute for Jewish Studies, 49–50
International Court of Justice, 231
Ishbosheth, 114
Jacob's Well, 117
Jaffa (Joppa), 37, 42, 117, 119, 138,
  139, 154, 159, 160, 211, 234.
  See also Joppa
James, Dr., 96
James, Prof. Fleming, 96
Jarvie, Amelia F.G., 176
Jarvie, James Newbegin, 176, 177
Jebel Mûsa, 27, 29
Jebel Usdum, 69, 70
Jenkins, Isaac C., 177
Jericho, 45, 46, 53, 67, 68, 117
Jerome, 4, 14, 34
Jerusalem, 10, 11, 15, 16, 18–19, 23,
  31–34, 37, 42, 44, 45, 59, 94,
  98, 107, 114, 117, 119, 128,
  129–33, 138, 196, 219, 222
  biblical prophecies concerning
    future, 162–63
  modern activities toward,
    163
  destruction of, 76–77
  lack of modernization, 154–55
  Levels of, 152

missionaries in, 86–89, 90–97
  evangelical Baptist, 100–102
  institutions of, 95, 96, 119–20
  occupation during World War
    I, 175
  poor site of, 157–58
  population, numbers and
    diversification, 155–57
  Second Wall, 153
  space for growth, 161
  natural resources, 161
  water, problem of, 161–62
  Y.M.C.A. in, 173–78
Jerusalem and the East Mission, 95
  Good Friday Offering, 95
*Jerusalem Mission, The: Under the
  Direction of the American
  Christian Missionary Society,*
  83

*Jerusalem the Holy: A Brief History of
  Ancient Jerusalem, with an
  Account of the Modern City
  and its Conditions, Political
  Religious and Social,* 154–63
Jesus is Coming, 181, 187–93
Jewish Mass Meeting Invitation
  Committee, 198
Jewish state, world significance
  of, 238–43
  flowering of genius, 240–42
  revival of Hebrew culture,
    239–40

Jews:
  captivity of, 77
  Christian proselytism among,
    80–82, 83, 85, 101–102
  claims of, upon Gentile Church,
    80–82

Gadites, return of, 168
immigration into Palestine, 120,
  127–28, 139–40, 229, 235,
  237
opposition to Zionist policy by
  American, 231
population of Jerusalem, 156,
  157
pro-Arab sympathies of Near
  Eastern, 230–31
restoration of, 78–80, 122, 128,
  159–61, 163, 181–93,
  194–97, 220–25, 226–29,
  230–37, 238–43
Zionism, *see* Zion Movement
Jezreel, 17, 160
Joppa, 124–26, 128, 196. *See also*
  Jaffa
Jordan River, 11–12, 42, 107, 117,
  132, 208
Jordan Valley, 6n, 50, 58, 131, 159,
  161
Josephus, 77, 113, 116, 151
Joy, Mount of, 42
Judah, 16–17, 114, 126
Judea, 11, 42, 44, 45, 47, 85, 93, 98,
  131
Juilliard Musical Foundation of
  New York, 176

Kadesh-Barnea, 113
Kedron (Kidron), valley of, 109,
  132
Kent, Homer B., 66
Khabiru, the, 59
Kipling, Rudyard, 216
Kirkland, Eliza, 7
Kuenen, 57
Kyle, Dr. Melvin Grove, 60, 65–71

Laidlaw, Sir Robert, 174
Later Biblical Researches in Palestine,
    and in the Adjacent Regions,
    by E. Robinson, E. Smith, and
    Others, 25
Lattof, Nicholas M., 178
Lebanon, 11, 42, 161, 197, 234
Levy, Joseph M., 48
Life, Writings and Character of
    Edward Robinson, The, 3, 7
Lisan, El, 67
London Jews' Society, 87, 156
Lot, 68, 69, 70, 77
Lowdermilk, Dr. Walter, 228
Luise, Therese Albertine, 8
Lydda, 142-43

Macarius, Bishop, 20, 21, 22
McConnell, Bishop Francis J., 226
McCown, C.C., 50
McDonald, Dr. James G., 226
Machpelah, Cave of, 59, 114,
    115-16, 117
MacInnes, Right Rev. Rennie, 95
MacLean, Mrs. Charles F., 176
Magdala, 134
Makhouli, Na'im, 66
Malachy, Yona, 198
Mallon, Père, 60, 66
Mamre, plains (oaks) of, 39, 113,
    117
Mar Saba, 46
"Mass Murder of Jews in Europe,
    The," 227
Mecca, 114
Medeba, 45
Medinah, 114
Megiddo, 17
    excavation of, 53, 54, 68

Merom, Waters of, 42
Merrill, Rev. Selah, 147-53, 164,
    166-67, 168-69, 170-71, 172
Messada, 69
Metallurgy, dawn of, 68
Meyer, Eduard, 60
Millenial Harbinger, The, 83
Missionaries, 75-82, 83-89, 90-97
    evangelical Baptist, 98-103
    institutions of, 95, 96
Mizpah, 42, 59
Moab, 40, 42, 43, 46, 65, 93, 117,
    161
Monasteries, 134-35
    in Jerusalem, 91
        Armenian Monastery of St.
            James, 91-93
Montfort, 17
Montgomery, Prof. J.A., 48
Montefiore, Sir Moses, 120, 127
Moriah, Mount, 108-109, 129
Moslems, mission to, 85-87, 95
Mosul (Nineveh), 90, 96
Mott, Dr. John R., 174, 176
Musa, Rev. and Mrs. M.S., 100
Mussolini, [Benito], 219

Nain, 118
"Names and Places," 18
Napoleon, 219, 239
National Council of the Episcopal
    Church, 90
Nazareth, 43, 94, 98, 118, 120
    Baptist missionaries in, 99-100
Near East Foundation, 233
Near East Relief, 97
Nebo, Mount, 42
Neby Samwil, 42, 117
Neby Yûnis, 10

Negeb, 58
Negroes, improving position of, 141–42
New Brunswick Theological Seminary, 122
New York Journal of Commerce, 107
New York Times, 48
Newton Theological Institute, 37
Niebuhr, Reinhold, 226, 230, 237
Nies, Dr. James B., and Jane Dows Nies, 50
Nineteenth Century and After, The, 222
Nordau, Dr. Max, 190, 201

Oak (or Terebinth) of Abraham, 113
Old Syrian (Jacobite) Church, 93
Olives (Olivet), Mount of, 34, 45, 93, 108, 109, 117, 129
Olshausen, 15
Omar, mosque of, 167–68
Onomasticon, 4, 12, 34
Oriental Institute, University of Chicago, 54
Orthodox Church, 94–95
Our Church's Work in the Levant, 90
Our Jerusalem: an American Family in the Holy City, 164
Out-of-Doors in the Holy Land: Impressions of Travel in Body and Spirit, 131–37
Owens, Rev. and Mrs. Roswell E., 103

Palestine, British mandate in, 52, 53, 139
    anti-Jewish policies in, 139–40
    Antiquities Ordinance, 53

Department of Antiquities, 53, 66
Archaeological Advisory Board, 53
Palestine and Saints in Caesar's Household, 138–43
Palestine Exploration Fund, 15
Palestine Exploration Society, 66
Palestine for the Jews: A Copy of the Memorial Presented to President Harrison, March 5, 1891, 194–97
Palestine Museum of Archaeology (Jerusalem), 53, 54
Palestine Oriental Society, 49
    Journal of, 49
Palestine Today, 220–25
Palestine To-Day and To-Morrow: A Gentile's Survey of Zionism, "The Promise," 213–19
Palestine Weekly, 209
Panfil, Mr., 96
Parsons, Levi, 75
Partition of Palestine, 230–37
    American dilemma over, 235–36
    plan for, 234
Pastor Russell's Sermons: A Choice Collection of his most Important Discourses on all Phases of Christian Doctrine and Practice, "Zionism in Prophecy," 198–202
Patriarchs, Age of the, 56, 57–60
Pella, 11, 60
People of Palestine, The, 220
Petra, 5, 15, 23
Philistia, 11, 42, 43, 44, 45, 119, 131
Phythian-Adams, 66

Pilgrimage to Palestine, A, 41–47
  "Palestine Tomorrow," 203–12
Pius XII, Pope, 141
Place names, 16–17, 34–35
Plumer, Lord, 176
Pococke, 5, 27n, 38
Poling, Daniel A., 226
Powell, Adam Clayton, Sr.,
  138–43
Presbyterian Foreign Mission
  Board, 96, 169
Prime, William C., 107–111
Princeton Theological Seminary,
  131, 154
Protestant Episcopal Church in
  the U.S.A., 90, 96–97

Rabble in Arms, A, 222
Râhah, er-, 27, 28, 29, 30
Ramah, 43
Ramallah, 94, 143, 159
  American Friends School at,
  220
Râs es-Sûfsâfeh, 28, 30
Rehoboth, 18
Rephaim, Plain of, 161
Restoration of Jews into Palestine,
  78–80, 122, 128, 159–61,
  163, 181–93
  Blackstone Memorial to Pres.
  Harrison, 194–97
  escape outlet for refugees from
  Nazis, 226–29
  a Christian problem, 228, 229
  safeguarding Arab rights,
  228–29
  Jewish state, significance of,
  238–43
  prevailing missionary opinion,

  statement on (1948),
  230–37
  pro-Arab view on, 220–25
  prophetic traditions, 78, 160–61,
  181–88, 192–93
  Zionism, *see* Zion Movement
Richmond, Major E.T., 53, 222
Ritter, 14–15
"Robbers' Gorge," 134
Roberts, Kenneth, 222
Robinson, Edward, 3, 6–36, 37,
  114n
  Biblical Researches, 6, 7, 9n,
  9–11, 12–23, 25–36
  explorations of Holy Land,
  8–23, 25–36
  love of Palestine, 7–8, 25
  Physical and Historical
  Geography of the Holy
  Land, 23–24
  "The Physical Geography of
  Syria Proper," 24
Robinson's Arch, 15
Robson, Dr., 11, 13
Rockefeller, John D., Jr., 53, 54
Rockefeller Foundation, 54, 233
Rothschild, Baron Edmund, 120,
  127
Royal Geographic Society of
  London, 14
Rüppell, 27–28, 29n
Rüssegger, 5, 6n, 28n, 29n
Russell, Charles Taze, 198–202
Russian motives for favoring
  Partition, 231–32

Safed, 114
St. Catherine, peak of, 28, 29

St. George's Cathedral
(Jerusalem), 90, 95
Saladin, 115, 129
Salisbury, Lord, 159
Samaria, 11, 47, 98, 117
Samuel, Sir Herbert, Viscount,
140, 210
San Remo, Treaty of, 228
Sandys, 14
Sayce, 57
Schaff, Philip, 112-21
Schick, Mr., 153
Schubert, 9, 26, 28n
Seetzen, 5-6, 16, 35
Serbâl, 29
Sharon, Plain of, 45, 117, 119, 142
Shaw, 14
Shechem, 10, 59, 115, 131
Shephelah hills, 42, 44, 203
Shiloh, 43, 117, 131
Shu'eib, valley of, 29
Shŭrm, 29
Sidon, 11, 161, 234
Siloam, Fountain of, 107, 109
Siloam, Pool of, 15, 162
Siloam Tunnel, 15, 19

Sinai, Mount, 8, 26, 27, 29, 116-17
Smith Dr. Eli, 8, 9-11, 13, 16, 23,
25, 26
Smith, George Adam, 24
Smith, Henry B., 3, 7n
Smith, Wm. Hind, 173-74
Society of Biblical Literature, 220
Sodom, 39, 40, 50, 65, 114
verification of holocaust at,
67-71
Sorek, Vale of, 143
Southern Baptist Convention, 98
evangelical missionaries of,

98-103
in Haifa, 102-103
in Jerusalem, 100-102
in Nazareth, 99-100
Women's Missionary Union,
101
Southern Baptist Theological
Seminary, 98
Spafford, Anna, 164, 166, 172
Spafford, Horatio, 164, 166, 167,
168, 172
Spencer, Mr., 88
*Star in the West, A: A Humble
Attempt to Discover the Long
Lost Ten Tribes of Israel,
Preparatory to their Return to
their Beloved City, Jerusalem,*
181-87
Sternberg, David, 138
Stone, Barton, 83
"Story of Our Work, The," 90
Stuart, Prof. Moses, 8
Suez, Gulf of, 29
Sukenik, E.L., 66
Syria, 8, 11, 12, 158, 197

Tabor, Mount, 38, 118
Tadmore, 196
Talmage, T. De Witt, 122-30
*Talmage on Palestine: A Series of
Sermons,* 122-30
Tattooing, 127
Tay, Herbert H., 66
Tel-Aviv, 102, 138, 211
Tell Beit Mirsim, 54
Tell el-Hesi (Lachish), 68
Tell en-Nasbeh, 54
Tell es-Sultan (Jericho), 68
Tell Hûm, 15, 118, 134

Tent Life in the Holy Land, 107–111
Thompson, Mr., 86
Thomson, Dr., 11, 17, 115
Through Bible Lands: Notes of Travel in Egypt, the Desert, and Palestine, 112–21
Tiberias, 38, 109, 111, 114, 115
Tillich, Paul, 226
Tînia, [Mt.], 29
Tîrân, 29
Tischendorf, Dr., 89
Titus, 151, 152, 218–19
   Arch of, 218–19
Tourian, His Beatitude Elisse, 92, 93
Trans-Arabian Pipe Line, 234
Trans-Jordan, 94, 235
"Travels in the East," 89
Tristram, Canon, 12, 17, 115
Turner, James, 176
Twain, Mark, 107
Tyre, 11

Um Shaumer, 29
Union Theological Seminary, 8, 23, 49, 112, 230, 245
United Nations, 227, 228, 235, 237
   Assembly, 230, 231, 234
   Commission, 234
   Security Council, 235–36
Universal Israelitish Alliance, 127, 190

Van Dyke, Henry, 131–37
Vester, Bertha Spafford, 164
Victoria, Queen, 87, 195
Vincent, Père, 66
Virgin's Fountain, 15, 162
Voris, John R., 90, 96–97
Voss, Carl Hermann, 226

Wady el-Leja, 27, 29
Wady esh-Sheikh, 28, 30
Wady es-Sabâ'îyeh, 28
Wady Nŭsb, 28
Wallace, Rev. Edwin Sherman, 154–63, 164, 169
Wa'rah, el-, 28
Warburton, Bishop, 184
Warren, Sir Charles, 15
Watch Tower Bible and Tract Society (Jehovah's Witnesses), 198
Waters of Merom, 17
Weizmann, Dr. [Chaim], 207
Wellhausen, Julius, 57, 58, 59
Williams, George, 174
Williams, Mr., 88–89
Winckler, 57
Wishard, Luther D., 174
World Significance of a Jewish State, The, 238–43
World's Sunday School Association, 94, 97

Xenia (Pittsburgh) Theological Seminary, 65–66, 68

Yale Divinity School, 66, 138
Yedhna (Idhna), 12
Y.M.C.A., 97
   facilities of, 176–77
   International Committee of, of North America, 173, 175, 176, 177
   in Jerusalem, 173–78
   in Near East in World War I, 175
Young Men's Christian Association. *See* Y.M.C.A.